FORMS AT WAR

FC2 1999–2009

FORMS AT WAR
FC2 1999–2009

EDITED BY R.M. BERRY

FC2

TUSCALOOSA

The University of Alabama Press
Tuscaloosa, Alabama 35487-0380

First Edition

Published by FC2, an imprint of the University of Alabama Press, with support provided by Florida State University, the Publications Unit of the Department of English at Illinois State University, and the School of Arts and Sciences, University of Houston–Victoria

Address all editorial inquiries to: Fiction Collective Two, University of Houston–Victoria, School of Arts and Sciences, Victoria, TX 77901-5731

⊗

The paper on which this book is printed meets the minimum requirements of American National Standard for Information Sciences—Permanence of Paper for Printed Library Materials, ANSI Z39.48–1984

Library of Congress Cataloging-in-Publication Data
Forms at war : FC2, 1999-2009 / edited by R. M. Berry. — 1st ed.
p. cm.
Includes bibliographical references.
ISBN-13: 978-1-57366-806-4 (pbk. : alk. paper)
ISBN-10: 1-57366-806-0 (pbk. : alk. paper)
1. American literature—21st century. 2. American fiction—21st century. 3. War and literature—United States—History—21st century—Literary collections. I. Berry, R. M. II. Fiction Collective Two (U.S.)
PS509.W3F67 2009
810.8'03581—dc22

2008047152

Book Design: Tara Reeser
Production Assistant: Stephen Shoup
Cover Design: Lou Robinson
Typeface: Garamond
Produced and printed in the United States of America

FOR RONALD SUKENICK (1932–2004)

CONTENTS

INTRODUCTION:
WRITING IN THE PRESENT

Shortly after ten p.m. eastern time on the night of March 19, 2003, George W. Bush appeared on national television to tell America that we'd started to bomb Iraq. His brief address was marked by a sense of presentness, of self-conscious contemporaneity, notably missing from his pre-war polemics. His first words stressed the moment of speaking: "My fellow citizens, at this hour...." Of the thirty-three sentences that followed, nearly two-thirds were in the present tense. The adverb "now" appeared repeatedly, as did phrases suggesting a threshold or incipience: "early stages," "opening stages," "enters," "we come." Although he was anxious to connect this present to a particular future—the auxiliary verb "will" occurred sixteen times—exactly *what* we were entering remained abstract. Bush spoke of a campaign, a commitment, a conflict, a passage, a time. His most concrete description referred to a military operation "to disarm Iraq, to free its people and to defend the world from grave danger." If no one now believes such words describe what we were entering into, then that's not just because Bush was lying. Or if we speak of lies, then we should imagine a vaster conspiracy, one encompassing our news media, blogs, midnight bar quarrels, and universities. As I write these words the 2008 presidential hopefuls scramble to retract their pre-war votes, lamenting that if only they'd known in October of 2002 what they know now..., as if we still believed bombing Iraq was the result of inaccurate information. Literary forms don't cause actions; literary forms *are* actions, but for that reason they can function as inescapably as fate. No information our leaders lacked in 2002 would've saved Baghdad. Of the remainder of the thirty-three sentences in Bush's short speech, a third were in the future tense—"We *will* pass through this time of peril... We *will* defend our freedom. We *will* bring freedom to others"—and none were in the past. Only one sentence, positioned squarely in the middle of his remarks, was in the conditional. It alone suggested that the limits of what we'd entered into were nothing we could foresee: "A campaign on the harsh terrain of a nation as large as California could be longer and more difficult than some predict." Was there anyone in America who didn't know this? Then why, as the bombs started to fall, was Bush saying it?

Forms at War excerpts twenty-three of the sixty-five prose works published by Fiction Collective Two (FC2) between 1999 and 2009, the period spanning the Florida Bush's inauguration and appointment of his brother president to the Texas Bush's departure from Washington. All twenty-three can be variously described as experimental, innovative, heterodox, conceptual, or alternative, and all are by writers previously unaffiliated with FC2. As FC2's publisher during this period, I have gathered them here as a counter history, a documentary account contesting the false present of Bush's March 19, 2003, address. However, my counter history may be hard to follow. Few of these works mention the 2000 election, the World Trade Center attack, the invasion of Afghanistan, the Iraq War, Hurricane Katrina, or any of America's other recent catastrophes. Nevertheless, as the prefatory notes try to bring out, these works were formed under intense pressure, a pressure felt by all Americans, but by writers in particular ways. Set against the backdrop of our nation's increasing xenophobia and moral defensiveness, these twenty-three inventions—in many cases occurring independently of each other and in no deliberate way comprising a school—continue a development, one that stretches into the past, grounding present expectations and making their departures meaningful. As such, my counter history forms an episode in a longer story, one that in different contexts has been called modernism, postmodernism, feminism, postfeminism, the avant-garde, the novel, literature, America, or the Fiction Collective. Although no author here feels identified by all of these terms and many wish to be identified with none, the importance of their writing remains inseparable from a narrative in which these terms, with their attendant controversies and bad faith, form events.

The political inconsequence of these events is what the twenty-three works here contest. In a 1991 article Judith Butler described how the news broadcasts of our first Middle East war realized a modern fantasy, one in which the partiality of all past knowledge would be overcome. When our television screens became the camera on a smart-bomb's nose, we were able for the first time to witness at an absolute remove what we simultaneously witnessed at absolute proximity. No distance separated us from the violence we saw. To observe it more closely, we would've had to traverse, not space, but time, to return to the bomb site before it vaporized. It was as though we were living in our past and present simultaneously, undergoing every new occurrence with a fullness of comprehension afforded normally by retrospection alone. As a result, the war itself felt like a representation, a making present of events already over. This hindsight accompanied the very moment of seeing, enabling us to follow our own history from a vantage simultaneously within and beyond it. Heidegger's characterization of our age as the first to which viewing its own worldview seems natural, captures this dream of transcendence. It's a dream apart from which the decision to destabilize a nation whose people we understood hardly at all would've seemed mad. How could anyone have been *surprised* by Iraq's disintegration? The widespread criticism of Bush's post-invasion plans misses the point. Our presidential candidates find it no more preposterous in 2008 than in 2002 to imagine that, with sufficient planning, advanced technology, and accurate intelligence, we could invade another country without endangering our own. For what transcendence means is precisely this sort of knowledge without risk, the practical foresight born of painful experience but with none of the accompanying exposure, bewilderment, disillusion. It's as though we *ought to know* what other people will do, shouldn't have to first find out. The freedom we purportedly brought the Iraqis, by imagining they lacked it, we'd already taken away.

One way to characterize experimental writing from modernism to the present is that it dispels transcendence, means to resume proximity's risks, to be right where its words are happening. William Carlos Williams in 1923 described it as leaving readers naked, deprived of their protective barrier or covering. "The reader knows himself as he was twenty years ago and he has also in mind a vision of what he would be, some day. Oh, some day! But the thing he never knows and never dares to know is what he is at the exact moment that he is." The idea is that, even in the greatest achievements of lyric and narrative, an alienation has already occurred, a distancing of readers from the reality they inhabit. This may not sound new, but Williams's innovation—like that of modernism generally—was in giving this alienation a temporal accent. That is, what readers are protected from is not so much horrific facts as an action or event, a reality that's ongoing. Like other experimentalists, Williams when pressed would call this ongoing reality the words themselves, as though in previous writing readers had overlooked the letters or printing, and yet treating words as objects was precisely what Williams determined not to do. Instead, he sought to make words unapproachable, not because his writing was esoteric or off-putting, but because the distance necessary for interpreting it had collapsed. Gerald Bruns has suggested that, when writing brings us down to earth in this way, we hear rather than understand it. The idea is that our words exist closer to us than representations, as "close" as our skin. To hear them is to attend before their meaning occurs to anyone, to take responsibility for exactly what we can't say. At such moments our meaning ceases to be ours, not because it has been foisted off by powers and institutions—although that's true enough—but because *we* become what's happening, the ongoing reality, a meaning we've grasped too late. Imagine the bomb's target growing larger on your TV screen and then recognizing your own house.

What seemed to strike no one as odd about Bush's March 19, 2003, address was its form. We can easily tell, at least in retrospect, that when Bush said "we come to Iraq with respect for its citizens" he was uttering a preposterous falsehood, but we still have difficulty telling, even in retrospect, that he was already telling in retrospect. That is, it seems both to us and to Bush that he must've known from the start how he felt about the Iraqis, that his profession of respect was either yahoo sincerity or cynicism. It's not my worry here whether there really is a difference between bombing with respect for citizens or without—maybe that's what distinguishes warfare from terrorism—but, if there is a difference, it won't be how the bomber felt about it. In addressing us while the bombs fell, Bush wasn't expressing his feelings about the war; he was conducting it. His words attempted to form solidarity, mobilize fears and resentments, prepare for scenes of devastation, and he was in no better position to tell what he'd done—the significance of having said *these* words in *these* circumstances—than Oedipus. It's as though, in professing his respect, he imagined he could just rerun the video later and prove it, but what distinguished Bush's words that night from the words of every other being on the planet wasn't that they were insincere, but that they weren't subject to what was happening. That is, Bush spoke as history's creator—"On my orders, coalition forces have begun striking selected targets"—and simultaneously as its historian, as though only hours into the fighting he were already in a position to recount it: "The people you liberate will witness...." If asked to plot this position, we might not know how, since it appears to be nowhere and everywhere, narrating and creating the same instant, but no one then or now found it unfamiliar. It is, after all, the customary position of the novelist.

In his 1953 book, *Writing Degree Zero*, Roland Barthes maintained that the political significance of a writer's work was not located in anything new it had to tell us. For him, the history of modern literature was the history of efforts to achieve a genuinely democratic form of expression, to articulate interests that were broadly human, not the interests of a particular class or group. The developing suspicion during the latter half of the 19th century that broadly human interests were just class interests by another name turned this effort against itself. According to Barthes, subsequent writers felt compelled either to identify with the political left, expressing interests already known prior to their literary formation, or to remove from their work the form of literariness altogether, to purify writing of its covertly imperialist ambitions.

This latter project, Barthes's notorious zero-degree *écriture*, seems remote from the fiction promoted by the largest American publishers today, but for Barthes, as for his predecessor Theodor Adorno, it embodied writing's commitment. By refusing the bad-faith compromises of literary conventions, canons of taste, and mass marketing, a writer could establish solidarity with all those whom literature's institutions had ignored, making her work's barrenness a sign of hope. J. F. Lyotard would later describe such work, not in terms of its stylistic features, but in terms of its time sense. Its characteristic appearance would be an enigmatic thereness, an event prior to any meaning, as though art were appearing before our knowledge of it. Call this the zero-degree of history. The avant-garde, for Lyotard, didn't want to surpass the present. It merely wanted to be there. This was, in his view, what the established order couldn't tolerate.

Although the writing included in this anthology may not look continuous with Barthes's political program, I believe these writers' discomfort with Bush's March 19, 2003, address arises from a similar perception. If reading Noy Holland's prose we become so arrested by its rhythm and syntax that we momentarily lose track of her story, or if the arrangement of Susan Steinberg's sentences feels to us more palpable than her protagonist, or if Michael Martone's proliferating contributor's notes strike us as monstrosities of extraneousness, we'll be experiencing their discomfort very directly. In each of these twenty-three fictions something stable and negligible in other writing has been dynamized, put either to work or into play, and the result is that it has started competing for our attention. This ongoing action, occurring closer to us than any represented action, is what readers of mainstream fiction are likely to find distracting. It's as though these writers want us to know, not what Bush was saying, but what he was doing, something he didn't acknowledge at the time and that, for untold reasons, they won't tell us either. Instead, they seem preoccupied with matters presupposed by telling, qualities of medium and practice and genre without which representation never occurs at all. Their suggestion is that something happens *here*, in this prior positioning toward what happens, but their way of acknowledging it is precisely not by narrating. On the contrary, their position is more that of its discoverer than its creator or historian. That is, they can't tell what their experiments mean, may not foresee their beginning or end, and are far from sure of their own activity's purpose. If asked why, during a time of war, such writing still matters, they might answer, "That's what we're trying to find out." This is how presentness speaks.

What Bush misrepresented March 19, 2003, about our undertaking in Iraq—not because his representations were only partial but because they were representations—is what our war shares with every present undertaking: its boundless immediacy. His pre-war insistence that the Iraqis were like us, that they wanted security and opportunity and freedom as much as we do, wasn't just a lie, but it downplayed the risks of discovering such things. It was as though others could be known without being encountered, without confounding us, without deciding whether to reveal themselves: like casual sex with a whole country. However, once the bombs started to fall, this stabilizing worldview—call it our conviction in our common humanity—came itself under attack. How could our common humanity abide those spectacles of burning neighborhoods, those faces? The novelist's voice on March 19, 2003, was meant to restore perspective, re-establish distance, recall the long view, but in the midst of battle, it's precisely the long view that starts to look absurd. Nobody can tell how close danger lies, what's happening one instant to the next. If there's a political implication to the scarcity of explicit protest in the twenty-three fictions collected here, it's that Bush led America into war, not by telling lies, but by telling per se, by positioning us toward our most immediate experience as toward a history, something about which it seemed meaningful to ask, true or false? For what happens in the moment of narrating, however, true and false are already alienations. What if our effort to tell what we're doing in Iraq is itself what we're doing in Iraq? It has been the major lesson of modernist narrative, from Stein and Joyce through Beckett and Barthelme, that to be in the present is never to be in the most recent stage of the past, nor in a period of transition, nor upon the threshold of the future. To be in the present is to be *in*. Period. And what one is in is always *this*, a condition that's both now here and nowhere at one time. When it's love, it's ecstasy, and when it's war, it's just hell.

Because this anthology wants to recount what passed uncounted before, its counter history is a narrative, not of narratives, but of forms. It seeks to document a development as invisible to commentators of the left as to Rush Limbaugh, a challenge to the specific conditions of historical representation that were already assumed on March 19, 2003, by both Bush and his audience. Its events comprise twenty-three answers to the question: How is writing written, not to tell the truth, but to discover what writing it here and now means? Gertrude Stein's answer, also referencing a war, was that such writing differs in "being made by being made." That is, it comes into being as continuous responsiveness, through attention to what materializes only with its writing, as the event of making happens. No one hoping to expose Bush's lies will feel it has much to tell us, but dismissing the fiction of Magdalena Zurawski or Kim Addonizio or Kate Bernheimer as so much navel-gazing ironically recognizes their achievement. For the aim of such experiments is to make writing and reading, the making and the made, simultaneous. Stein never tired of saying that war and presentness happen to people. Even when provoked by a fool, they aren't willed, aren't decisions: "Naturally one does not know how it happened until it is well over beginning happening." What feels like lying each time Bush opens his mouth is not misinformation, but our being told what no one could be in a better position to know than ourselves. Our punishment for listening to our leaders make war in this way, that is, in the form of narrating it, is that we have now become the people accustomed to such things, who habitually undergo events in retrospect, for whom almost nothing counts unless it's over. If only we'd known in 2003 what we know now, if only we could've told at the start what we can tell so plainly today, then we would've acted differently. That's the lie.

My recounting of the last decade is merely a preparation for the work to follow, for every history ends at the present of writing. Therefore, the twenty-three fictions I've included here function only secondarily as documents. Before all, they function as forays, trials, as experimental treatments of an alienation we've all come to regard as second nature. What happens in their making is that something dead and forgotten returns to life. That is, some feature of ordinary communication unfixes itself, dislodges from its seemingly inert proximity, and becomes the acknowledged maker of significance: the alphabet, in Alexandra Chasin's work; the computer screen, in Debra Di Blasi's; the personal pronoun, in Lidia Yuknavitch's. The aim of these reanimations is to arouse our interest, but not in a story or its writer, for what seems forgotten is much nearer, a reality happening to and through us every time we write or read. So attention gets redirected to seemingly obvious facts: i.e., that one thing follows another, that "I" is singular, that anyone can say "anyone can say," that meanings occur to us all. These commonplaces now become exactly what we can no longer determine. Although they are countless, the ones resuscitated here comprise a group, representing the features of any speech act that identify it as literary. As a result, if we don't understand the writing of Diane Williams or Michael Joyce or Leslie Scalapino, we won't normally wonder what their words mean. We'll wonder what their words make: a puzzle, a pastiche, a collage, a plot, a spoof, an essay, a mess. This question of form matters, not because form matters, but because it's a question of our comportment. That is, our bewilderment feels less like encountering a new vocabulary than like entering a foreign country, a place where our expectations can lead us astray, where continuity with our past life is at every moment staked. We will never venture deeply into the foreigness of another culture until we venture more deeply into this foreigness within our own.

So, why did both Bush and his audience on March 19, 2003, find the novelist's customary stance toward events a form of address appropriate to democracy? The answer to this question, which would be a history of modernity and of its betrayal, isn't provided by the works in this anthology, but it is demanded—perhaps with a vengeance—by their achievement. To participate in it, that is, to engage in the forms of responsiveness that will enact their work, is to begin to experience Bush's war address as an unnatural act. How could anyone be in a position to inform us what our intentions are? What information could foretell what here and now we're in the early stages of? And the warning that "a campaign on the harsh terrain of a nation as large as California could be longer and more difficult than some predict"—who voiced it but the seer who'd earlier proclaimed that "the human heart desires the same good things everywhere on earth," that "freedom and democracy will always and everywhere have greater appeal than...terror," and who as the bombs fell reassured us, "We will prevail"? All this novelistic prescience, its externality to the actions described, its ventriloquism of others' desires, to an ear attuned to writing's present, sounds like extoling chastity to teenagers. And yet sitting before our televisions on March 19, 2003, did any of us feel that its falsity was a matter of misinformation? And once history had intervened, as we looked back on this nightmare of our creation, was it really what we *didn't* know in 2003 that upset us? Before determining if war should be fought, every citizen knows what the word "war" means, and it is on this unplumbed depth of cultural expertise that both literature and democracy depend. To be attuned to the present occurrence of words is to hear the obsessive presentness of Bush's March 19, 2003, address as our national repressed recurring, reasserting those common conditions that, had they been acknowledged at the time, would've silenced all talk of preemption. Having disregarded what was nearest then, we find ourselves now in the midst of exactly what we can't say. It's a position the writers in this anthology have long been struggling to occupy. It's being made as it's being made. There are no boundaries. The form of writing now is presentness or bad faith.

R.M. Berry
Tallahassee, March 2008

FROM IN THE BOX CALLED PLEASURE

BY KIM ADDONIZIO (1999)

EDITOR'S NOTE: Many of those attracted to Kim Addonizio's writing are drawn by its matter-of-fact sexuality and insinuation of boundless desire. While I wouldn't minimize those qualities, my initial attraction to *In the Box Called Pleasure* was different. Kim's fiction, for all its untamed candor, struck me as conceptual. Many of her prose works developed from a premise that staked the writing itself, generating tension by uncompromising fidelity to it. Although "A Brief History of Condoms" is in some ways not typical of Kim's work, I consider it a pure example of the quality I have in mind. Its force seems to result from a repression produced by its form, its concept of itself. That is, the scientifically chaste prose ("A condom is a simple one-celled organism…") and ordered categories of a natural history article, instead of shaping expression, marginalize it, haunting the prose with vestigial narratives ("One Condom's Story"), missing histories ("The Big O Theory"), and various openings into which a story might go ("I won't fuck you if I have to wear that thing on my dick"). In truth, the whole implies an absent narrator, a woman, whose voice is never heard until the eloquent outburst in note 4: "Go fuck yourself." Because I already suspected in 1999 that form was the most consequential dimension of any writing—a dimension I had begun to call "presentness"—Kim's success at putting form to work exemplified for me FC2's mission.

—RMB

"My writing is really about exploring my own head, my questions and fears. Whether it has any political significance depends on factors outside of me, like who is reading it, what they are getting from it, and what they might use it for. I hope my writing can result in some kind of empowerment of the spirit for the reader."

—Kim Addonizio

A BRIEF HISTORY OF CONDOMS

1. *Origins of the American Condom*

The so-called American Condom (*Prophylacticus Americanus*) began behind the counters of druggists, springing to life in the dust and dark among prescription bottles.[1] In the diaspora which followed, some migrated into the air-conditioned light of Walgreens and Thriftys, others to the flickering fluorescent haze of convenience stores. Still others settled behind glass cabinets in large grocery chains. The most colorful varieties live crowded in

[1] The largely discredited "Big O Theory," first developed by Holstein, posits a divine origin, to wit: that the universe was originally the size and shape of a gigantic, cosmically conscious condom, which masturbated itself and exploded into particles which ripped it apart and sent particles streaming outward into space. There are still some elements of the scientific community who claim

baskets on the counters of medical clinics. Condoms thrive in great numbers throughout the continent of North America, and tend to be concentrated in large cities. Fundamentalist Christians and the occasional zealous Catholic have decreased their numbers slightly, but the overall impact of such predation has been insignificant on the population as a whole.

2. *Life Cycle of the Condom*

A condom is a simple one-celled organism which appears, at first look, to be round and flat. When released from its foil "nest" and massaged, it changes its shape into a sock-like, membraneous creature which clings to human flesh—specifically, the male sexual organ. Condoms have a symbiotic relationship with humans; sperm released during human sexual activity is caught and eaten by the condom, allowing the condom to reproduce itself. Having fulfilled its evolutionary purpose, the condom then shrivels and dies. The fetus, or "conda," microscopic in size at this point, becomes airborne until it finds a suitable "nest," slips inside it and gestates in the warmth and protection the foil offers. A condom may lie dormant in its nest for years, but life outside the nest last from only a few minutes to half an hour or so.[2] It is fair to say that these brief moments, however, are by far the most gratifying;

that there is an inner condom in each of us, remnant of the Great Rubber, and that we are reabsorbed into it at the end of earthly life. It's interesting to note that numerous mythologies of so-called primitive peoples offer variants of this proposition.

[2] The briefest known lifespan is .078 seconds; the longest, evidenced by a videotape of pornographic artist Jackoff Holmes, was well over an hour. Research has indicated that short-lived condoms tend to exhibit a high level of anxiety, whereas the longest-living emit alpha waves—an indication that, in human terms, these latter condoms tend to "stop and smell the roses," i.e. the odors of anal or vaginal secretions.

condoms have been observed to burst from sheer pleasure, and occasionally to squirm off of the male penis and travel excitedly upwards into the interior regions of the partner's body.[3]

3. *Common Uses of the Condom*

There are many valuable uses of the condom beyond the aforementioned use in sexual activity. Condoms may be filled with water and dropped from high windows to terrify old people, or loaded with jello and thrown at parties. They may be blown up like balloons. The flavored variety, once the lubricant is wiped away, is favored for eating by adolescent girls. Condoms may be used in delaying sexual activity, as in, "I won't fuck you if I have to wear that thing on my dick."[4] Such a statement may have unfortunate results if the condom is then discarded, as it will simply dry up and die without reproducing itself. Condoms are dependent on human males, some of whom have an ambivalent relationship with them, and see them at best as a necessary evil.

4. *Inner Life of the Condom*

It is hard to ascertain whether a condom is capable of the emotions you and I regard as a part of sentient life. Does a condom experience depression, or fear death? Does it have a soul? If so, then we must examine carefully our treatment of this useful creature. Should it, for example, be so quickly relegated to the floor beside the bed, or the trash in the bathroom, or the

[3] Emergency Room records indicate that a small percentage of patients seek treatment, but the incidence is undoubtedly more frequent, according to anecdotal sources.

[4] In the late twentieth century, this statement is an indication of gross stupidity on the part of the speaker. The best response to such an attitude is probably, "Go fuck yourself."

weeds of the vacant lot? Perhaps our responsibility should extend to a decent burial, a few words said to mark the passing of our pleasure-seeking, short-lived friend. Perhaps it loves the woman whose vaginal walls drench it for a few minutes, or the man whose anus contracts around it. Perhaps it realizes that such bliss must soon, too soon, turn into pain and diminishment, into the awful isolation of the separate self. If the condom could speak, what truths might it tell us, privy as it is to some of our most intimate moments?

5. *One Condom's Story*

She carries me in her purse. She intends to be faithful, but just in case, she wants to be prepared. She is on a long trip, away from her lover. She meets a man who delights her, who is clever and interesting. He puts his hand on her hip as they are walking. They find a bar and drink until they can hardly stand up, then stagger to a hotel room. I hear them laughing and giggling, hear the rustle of clothes and good intentions being rapidly discarded. There is a blinding light as I am freed, feeling the cool air wash deliciously over me, and then I am lost in sensation, nothing matters but this, it is glorious, I am stretched taut, headed for that beautiful deadly opening; I go in and in. My head floods with sperm and I gorge myself, losing consciousness, and when I wake I find myself flushed down the pipes, along the sewers and out into the great river of the unborn, riding the currents down to the mothering sea.[5]

[5]The account is fictional; see Christopher Peckerwood's *I Am A Condom.* There are no authenticated stories of condoms speaking or writing their views, though apocryphal ones abound. Various people have claimed to be kidnapped by condoms from outer space, or to hear the voices of dead condoms speaking to them.

6. *Social Organization of Condom Communities*

There are many classes—one might even say castes—in the condom community. Brightly colored and flavored condoms are usually ostracized by those with a more uniform look and packaging. These second-class citizens are more likely to attempt to form what we can only call personal attachments with other condoms. Through a process known as "nest-ripping," two separate condoms may leak their lubricants and form a sort of gluey mass which causes the nests to bind to each other. They then become unfit for human use and hence unable to reproduce, so why this occurs remains an evolutionary mystery.[6]

7. *In Conclusion: A Personal Note*

There is much still to learn about this deceptively simple creature. I have here attempted the briefest outline of serious study and research. My own fascination began, perhaps, when as I boy I unrolled my first condom and jerked off into it, finding it a much neater method than rutting into the sheets my mother would have to wash. I have, frankly, never encountered a human body which gave me as much pleasure as the simple, unassuming condom, always eager to please, ready to take my jism and lap it up deliriously, then lie peacefully hanging from my penis while I relaxed with a cigarette. Several times during these jottings I have stopped to "denest" and massage one of the little creatures, to slip it over me and caress it, to squeeze and pull until we were both deliciously sated.[7] I confess to you now that I love them, that I think of

[6] For further readings see "Nest-ripping: Nature or Nurture?" in *Scientific American*; "Nest-Rippers, Menace to Society," ibid.; and the San Francisco journal *Honey, Let It Rip*.

[7] I can't get enough. Desire is endless. Sometimes I want to fuck everything in sight. I want to fuck the sheets, the trees outside my window, the men and

nothing but their moist dripping bodies, that at night they come to me in my dreams, they hover over me and smile, and at last begin to speak.

women passing on the streets below; I want that ecstasy that only sex provides, the loss of self and finding of it, the *petit-morte* that tells me there is no true death, there is only connection and ceaseless change, there is only love against the darkness surrounding us, we are all ripped from the nest, helpless and exposed together; oh friends and colleagues, it all comes down to this: So many condoms. So little time.

FROM THE FAST RED ROAD: A PLAINSONG

BY STEPHEN GRAHAM JONES (2000)

EDITOR'S NOTE: I met Stephen Jones in 1996 in a graduate course I taught on Gertrude Stein, a lanky Native American who sat immobile in his desk, listened attentively, and never spoke. However, his critical writing was brilliant, and we developed an acquaintance based on our love of experimental literature and our lack of others to talk to. A year later Stephen asked me to replace a vacationing member of his doctoral committee, and it was then, while reading what FC2 would eventually publish as *The Fast Red Road: A Plainsong*, that I realized two things: first, that Stephen was an immensely gifted novelist, and, second, that he was unlikely to publish his work with a trade press. Like Beckett, billboards, *Finnegans Wake*, and slips of the tongue, Stephen's writing acquires its interest through literalized figures, metaphors made palpable, but in *The Fast Red Road* these figures can become dizzying. When Pidgin and Charlie Ward in their stolen Trans-Am approach a Hopi reservation at triple digit speed, they confront "a mile-long line of wooden Indians, pilfered from the cigar-smelling conscience of america." Although sounding like a metaphor, the "mile-long line of wooden Indians" literally describes a barrier across the interstate, while "pilfered from the cigar-smelling conscience of america" is merely metaphorical, although true. Like Jackson Pollock's all-over line, which achieved delineation without the illusion of depth, Jones's plastic syntax creates figuration without a contrasting experience of stable ground, of literal meaning. It's as though the obvious has gone missing.

—RMB

"With me, anyway, and I'm all I really have to generalize from, the politics, the politics that *I know* are there, what it informs more than anything, I think, is what's going to seem funny to me."

—Stephen Graham Jones

Pidgin dusted himself off, climbed down the ladder and into the widow's weeds, which turned out to be a silk pirate shirt and lowslung leather pants with silver conchos up the side. Pidgin looked down the length of both arms and told Charlie Ward three things: that he was neither a widow, nor a ninja—and he sure wasn't Jim Morrison; he just needed something black for the interment, that was all. Charlie Ward said what they needed now was a fast car for the procession, and then they were off again, to Juanita's for breakfast and a ride. Charlie Ward said there the cars were painless, sometimes he could just lead them away. Pidgin didn't tell him there would be no procession. Instead he held him up by the arm as they went the long way around the trailer, picking tenderly through a prairie dog town taken over by yellow-eyed owls who made them feel like trespassers. Charlie Ward said it reminded him of a story about a man hung like a moose, peeing one day, but then he couldn't remember it all.

Juanita's rippled in the distance for a solid two miles and then in the next step they were there, at a table, Juanita herself making them pay before eating. Charlie Ward laid the money down slap slap slap. They ate breakfast burritos and made them last, waited for the oilmen to roost. Charlie Ward watched for which ones stepped into the bathroom. After the first one had been gone awhile, Pidgin asked, *now*? but Charlie Ward waved a finger close to the table, *no*. Through the plate glass they could see the trucks and cars lined up outside. Over teatwarm goatmilk they kept tabs on who drove what. Finally, Charlie Ward motioned at the one in the laminated straw hat, a single black braid trailing down his spine, silver at the toes and heels of his boots. A turquoise bolo. He even had oldstyle cuffs on, with fringe. Pidgin could tell they had been Wild Bill gloves not long ago. He'd had a pair once; they came with a cap gun.

Together they tried to will the Indian's bowels to move.

After thirty minutes, it worked. He rose suddenly, already untucking his shirt, and stumbled towards the bathroom. In his wake Pidgin and Charlie Ward walked calmly out to his bandit-black Trans-Am. Charlie Ward ran his hand along the hood, over the cowl induction and the firebird beak, and then they were stepping over the doors, standing up through the T-tops, and reclined in the bucket seats. It was theirs. 'Black for the funeral, grandson,' Charlie Ward said, and in the time it took for the dashboard to quit blinding Pidgin it was hotwired and they were gone, easing out in reverse, undetected, smooth.

Once clear of Juanita's, Pidgin said no, please, but Charlie Ward said he just wanted to see what it would do on the highway. It wouldn't take long. They stopped at the liquor store for ice, and Charlie Ward reached into the past and left a yellow handprint on the flank that almost matched the gold pinstriping. It was close enough. He packed the turbo with the ice then, and when it was cooled down and they had a half-gallon of wine, they were the next best thing to airborne, the engine screaming, the wind whipping in and even dragging the headliner loose, so it billowed for a split second then let go, taking the rear window with it in a cascade of glass Pidgin never heard. Charlie Ward had his head out the T-top, being force fed his own war whoops, the tendons in his neck standing out. The speedometer wouldn't do what they were doing, and Pidgin's math was too bad to try and calculate it out. It was wrapped though, the peg broken long ago. When they finally leveled off to a cool one-fifty-something and the gravity acceleration let go of Pidgin, he reached an arm across to Charlie Ward and begged him to stop. But the mile markers merged into an unbroken green line of denial. They were headed west, with the train tracks again, overcorrecting for Texas, missing Clovis altogether.

And there was nothing they couldn't outrun.

Pidgin could feel it for a moment, passing a moving train like it was standing still. In front of them the cars were lining up on the shoulder, to get out of the way. To let them pass. All except the black and white cruiser. Pidgin just made out the trooper's profile for the nanosecond they were alongside him, and his mouth was already held hard to the state radio. And then they were running. And the trooper was running after them, his blue lights in the mirror shifting red, the signs on the road reading Vaughn and then getting sucked up. Pidgin felt Clovis slipping away at a steady hundred and fifty miles per hour. And there was the gearshift just past his left hand, within reach. He pushed the button in and the click went unnoticed. He breathed twice and did it then, pushed the stick up into neutral, the engine winding up to an unhealthy pitch and flattening out there, the aluminum block white hot with anger. Charlie Ward's hand became bodiless and reacted, turned the key back, pulled the machine from the throes. They coasted for a clean and sober two miles, and hung one side of the car in the ditch when there was nothing left.

Charlie Ward looked at Pidgin and Pidgin looked at Charlie Ward. Pidgin said he was sorry and Charlie Ward said back that cars remember people the same as people remember cars. Nothing else. Just the trooper spending hours in his cruiser, preparing, talking himself out of the scattergun maybe. Hopefully. When he finally approached he was all smiles.

'You know that's bad for the turbo,' he said, fatherlike. 'You should let it idle down there, Chief. Go ahead, start it. It's not too late.'

The car came to life between Charlie Ward's thumb and forefinger, loping in place. The trooper slid the stiff leather catch off the back of his gun. It was one of those go-ahead-and-run-boy things. Ten little Indians, fifteen bullets in the clip; the odds were against them. Pidgin had played all their games before; he returned his hand to the leather handle of the parked shifter, to keep it in place, to keep them alive for the interment.

Charlie Ward smiled and said *officer*, and that was all. No cars passed stocked with witnesses. It was only them and a sound, a lone Peano whistle, from across miles, but close, too close. Pidgin felt like they were in the opening credits of a western. The engine climbed to two grand in response to the whistle, and Charlie Ward's eyes went with it. And the sharp corners of his mouth. The three of them watched the tach bounce up and up like a secondhand. Charlie Ward drew his accelerator leg knee to chest, to prove it wasn't him, but still, the trooper already had his gun drawn, hammer thumbed back and not yet clicked in place.

He was laughing, too, in his way. He asked what a couple of blanket Indians like themselves had to do with a *man's* car, like this.

Charlie Ward said without emotion that he *was* a man, and then the whistle came again, no train, no anything.

The trooper leveled his gun on Charlie Ward's ear, at an angle where the exit wound would be low down on the other side of the neck, in Pidgin's lap. He told them they were in no position to be pulling schoolboy Indian pranks. It was no joke, though: Pidgin could feel the engine, humming up the metal shifter through the stitched leather handle and into his waiting palm. It was anxious. Over the lakepipes the trooper finally called to Charlie Ward to shut the damn thing off, screw the fucking turbo, but the key would no longer turn, and the trooper wouldn't reach in to see for himself. Not a chance. Instead he just started twitching and talking low, his chin shiny with saliva, his mirrored glasses askew, khaki armpits dark brown and dripping. He was saying to Charlie Ward that he was a *trooper*, not a damn *officer*, and was trying to get Charlie Ward to say it with him when it came without warning—the bullet, the slug, the greased shooter—ripping directly above the T-tops at an easy thirty-two hundred feet per second, whining over their heads and away, the sudden clap from the barrel nudging the three of them out of the ditch and onto a stage where their roles were predefined. Another day at the blood theater. The trooper played his part with precision, with stock movements, looking at his gun as if it was a new thing, watching the smoke rise, and then easing into the initial motions of the solemn shoulder shrug that comes right before finishing a thing already started, out of duty. Everything would come clean in the paperwork. From the corner of his seat Pidgin could read this, and all they had to protect them was the Trans-Am. He breathed out and pulled it deep into first, and for an impossible second the car didn't move, just spun in place, but then it was standing up half in the ditch, traction bars keeping it stuck and in line, fist-sized chunks of asphalt assaulting the trooper's cruiser

Charlie Ward held onto the steering wheel as best he could, whooping and stomping and shifting into second, the tires scratching at forty-five, the bandit-black car leaping forward into history. Pidgin imagined a sharp-edged 2 carved into the ground behind them, or Jay Silverheels grunting something inarticulate into the trooper's CB, to confuse the cavalry, or Marshall Dillon calling in Chuck Connors, to fan the lever of his rifle and take down everything in sight, telegraph poles and all.

They were running, hard.

Soon a helicopter shadow blotted out the sun. A wide chevron of cruisers fell in behind them too, their blackbird running point. Charlie Ward wiped his eyes with one hand, and looked to Pidgin. The old horse thief was unsure. It was there in his eyes. Pidgin pointed his chin in front of them. There was nothing else to do now. So they did it. And there were no roadblocks, because everyone was behind them and nobody ever thought two longhairs could outrun New Mexico's finest.

But then a thing happened in Vaughn: Charlie Ward eased into the brake and the steering wheel at the same time, trying to make the turn south, towards the fugitive myth of Old Mexico, but the car only swerved back north, and then kept on in a westerly direction. Charlie Ward looked around for a second, then lifted his right knee again. Nothing. They didn't slow at all. He visibly relaxed his hands on the wheel, and it stayed true without him. This went deeper than computer alignment and unbent tie rods. Pidgin put on his seatbelt, and Charlie Ward started laughing, his eyebrows stitched together tight with nerves. Pidgin said his mother's name to himself over and over; half the DPS of New Mexico was behind them, and they couldn't give themselves up if they wanted to. And the gas gauge wasn't falling. And the temperature wasn't rising. Pidgin saw himself a week later wearing a Wild Bill get-up like the original owner at Juanita's. God.

There was still the bottle in the backseat. They fell into it. New Mexico slipped by in a rage of sirens.

When they finally hit a last minute roadblock at dusk on some backroad just outside Albuquerque, the Trans-Am took to the ditch, unplanting fence poles Dukestyle, and then screamed back onto the blacktop. It was unstoppable, a sleek Indian juggernaut. When Pidgin was done with the bottle he held it out the window and it was sucked away. Behind them a cruiser fell. They huddled with their arms in the bucket seats, because night was coming and it was cold in the wind. Above them the helicopter stood on its beam of light, everything in the front seat empty and bright, the dash shining off at crazy angles, Charlie Ward holding onto the wheel because they didn't know when the car would let go.

They were hundreds of miles away from Clovis. Even if Birdfinger had grandstood again, the interment had to be long over, the ground even filled in and tamped down. Pidgin asked Charlie Ward where this car was taking them, and Charlie Ward just shrugged and said it was looking like Navajo land to him, at least what used to be Navajo land. 'But then again,' he said, the end too obvious for him to voice. Pidgin got it, didn't smile, kept to himself, watched Charlie Ward's hands on the wheel to see if there was anything that needed to be said. He couldn't tell, but wanted to say it anyway. He turned the radio on loud to keep from it, but still they had to put their ears to the speakers to hear the news about themselves, how they had become Joaquin Murieta reborn and one of his aged stand-ins, carving up the twentieth century with a single car. They were said to be carrying a payload of feather headdresses, peace pipes and old bones, all museum property, all movie memorabilia, all restolen.

Pidgin said he wanted it to be over.

In another hour, he was answered: they heard about it on the radio before they saw it, but when they saw it they were already there. It was a mile-long line of wooden Indians, pilfered from the cigar-smelling conscience of america. The Hopi had lined them up shoulder to shoulder, strung barbwire through the knees and armpits, and each one was cradling an armful of dynamite the old time miners had left behind, beaded now with nitroglycerin like tears. It was Kawliga crying, Tecumseh there beside him for consolation purposes, staid and stoic and grave in the face, frowning hard into the camera. The radio DJ was reading in a monotone, whispering between words *nine-eleven, nine eleven.* A hammer clicked audibly then, and the DJ went on, delivering the message over and over in his coliseum-sized voice: *this far and no farther, this far and no farther.* There was urgent laughing in the background, and fire crackling like static, cleansing the airwaves.

When Pidgin and Charlie Ward approached the fence at one-hundred-plus, dragging interstate cops like tin cans, a gate swung back on skateboard wheels, making an opening maybe six and a half feet wide. The Trans-Am shot through like threading a needle, the passenger-mirror dinging hello, and then the hole closed itself, had never been. The cruisers stood on their noses coming to a stop, but they didn't cross the line, couldn't. And there were no shots, just one warning flare from behind the wooden Indians, at the helicopter, which kissed the blades and made the sky a huge catherine wheel for a brief moment. The smell of radiator water filled the air. There were already vendors set up, for the hungry troopers. From the Hopi side of the line, people were chanting *red rover red rover.* A stray com chip tossed in fatigue at the wooden Indians could get things started once and for all.

Pidgin rubbed warmth into his face and looked straight ahead. Beside him Charlie Ward said he was sorry. Pidgin shrugged it off. They were on Hopi land, Hopi backroads, and now they were in front of a Hopi prefab that still had a tractor truck hitched to it, stripped, rusting into the ground, the house tilting at a bad angle. The road made an awkward U around the place, banked bermstyle on the far side, but the car didn't take it. It coasted to the other side instead, near a horse trough, and finally rested, the turbo sighing.

The man who came out to greet them was barechested and wearing Jim Morrison pants too, with a brass zipper down the buttcrack. He didn't take his sunglasses off. He just approached the car and ran his hand along the hood, winced at the fence post impressions, inspected the tires and then spit on the sidepipes, making them hiss, stink filling the air; he never looked at Pidgin or at Charlie Ward. Soon enough he was laughing and whooping and doing some cheap stomp dance in the dirt beside his car, knees going high. A group of children joined him reluctantly and together they covered the Trans-Am in a camo tarp. Pidgin and Charlie Ward scrambled out at the last instant, and the children screamed and either scattered or became dogs.

'Hello there,' the man said, then started to say something else but his mouth filled with emotion, and he had to just wave an upturned palm in the direction of the Trans-Am, wait it out. He said it when he could: 'Thank you for bringing her back.'

FROM THE COMPLETE TALES OF KETZIA GOLD

BY KATE BERNHEIMER (2001)

EDITOR'S NOTE: When I became publisher of FC2 in summer of 1999, I received along with files and press records a foot-high stack of MSS. Among these was an early version of Kate Bernheimer's novel *The Complete Tales of Ketzia Gold.* What impressed me about it was its dreamy illogic, the quality Cris Mazza in her reader's report called its "episodic, non-linear, and surreal structure." At a glance *The Complete Tales of Ketzia Gold* resembles a formal anarchy, comprising its text from non-sequiturs, incongruities, and silences, as though some unseen pattern were organizing its surface disparities: "This is all in the country by the sea where a lobster chased me to a field of windflowers enclosed by a wall." In "The Star Pennies" the distraught Ketzia re-enacts Grimms' tale, "The Star Talers," about a young girl who gives away all she owns and is reimbursed by the sky. What seems odd about Ketzia's mimickry is that her reading of the folktale can't explain her ecstatic charity, since the pious girl's act in the Ur-story is as much in need of explanation as Ketzia's. It's as though both heroines were responding to something unseen, a fate encrypted in old men's jokes and childhood fears. "Outside, coyotes sang. At first, I thought I was hearing a gang of weeping children come to cover the earth. Soon their howls sent words and I knew what they meant." It seems uncanny that this novel of omens and portents was published September, 2001.

—RMB

"For all my novels and stories, fairy tales provide the form and language, the feeling and syntax. This kind of work hinges on reversals—weakness to strength, sadness to rapture, ashes to air or air to ashes and back again. In that I cannot, as a writer, imagine abandoning fairy tales, I cannot imagine abandoning the weak, the lost. This is deeply political for me."

—Kate Bernheimer

THE SALTMARSH TALE OF LIES

I want to tell you something, so listen. I saw two bathers flying. They flew with their breasts turned heavenward and their backs faced hellward. The first wore a striped bikini, the second a plain pair of trunks. Once I saw a bird in a shake at the boardwalk's fancy ice-cream stand, and then an anchor and some dune grass swam across the bay just as gracefully as you please. The anchor was surprising but dune grass is more lovely. Four girls in eyeglasses tried to catch a rabbit that lived in the mansion lawn. The first girl was sad, the second girl was afraid, the third girl was insecure and the fourth girl was just plain mean. Do you want to know what happened? The first saw the animal and tearfully told the second, who ran away to tell the third, who tried in vain to catch the rabbit. Shut up if you don't believe me. This is all in the country by the sea where a lobster chased me to a field of windflowers enclosed by a wall. Inside I saw a cow, who had gotten there by leaping. There are greenflies and blackflies and dragonflies there. So open the window and let the lies out, I say.

THE STAR PENNIES

I'm going to tell you something. For a long time I was so poor that I only had one room to live in with a small cot to sleep on. This room was on the road of oracles. You could hear the cars go by through the thin motel door. I did have some real things in storage at my parents' house—a brass bed, an automatic drip coffee maker, a woolen pea coat—but I was too old to go home. And my husband and I were no longer together.

I was tired a lot of the time. I was in a warm place that on the map was always orange, sometimes lined in red. This is on the television, and in the paper. I spent my days walking the desert under the hot sun in a cowboy hat Adam had bought me downtown in another state. We saw the swans that day, and a pigeon ate peanuts off Adam's shoulder while I screeched with fake terror, nearby.

I managed to keep myself fed. I was too proud to ask Adam for money. Money should not pass hands that way, though one must give it to strangers. My parents had lent me so much over the years I was finally too embarrassed to ask them for more. I had learned my lesson well.

I walked down a hot, six-laned speedway every blazing morning to a shop where two teenage boys gave me a plastic bag full of bagels. They did not sell all the bagels every day, they said. "We have yesterday's bagels for you," they said. The boys wore shirts of many colors with bursts of white naked fabric throughout the colors.

Pumpernickel, garlic, sesame, raisin, a wondrous kind called everything.

I'd walk west on the speedway, past the road of oracles to a red-rocked hilly place called the monument. Then I wandered up and down dried-out riverbeds. Thorny plants were all about and when the sun set and snakes came out onto the thin-shaded sand, I'd walk east to the road of oracles and leave the desert behind.

Back at the motel I would pass by the office and lower my chin in a kind of greeting. I entered my small motel room through a door that was never locked and felt as though made of cardboard. The manager had given me a cheap monthly rate. He knew I got my money selling plasma. He mostly let rooms by the hour and had a place for me.

As part payment the manager could see me through a glass window that was shady and grey, though I could only see myself. Inside, everything was dark and seemed like a photograph negative.

Each evening I would strip and wash my body head to foot with soap the manager, with his biker's t-shirt and beautiful hair, left on the sink for me daily. This soap was wrapped in white paper and you could smell the soap through the paper when you entered the room from the road. I would hang my brown dress—so delicately flecked with tiny pink roses—in the bathroom, so the steam could straighten all the small wrinkles. I'd pull my hair back into a tight, wet ponytail and face the mirror, dimming my expression and shrinking into my body. Then, I would lie on the bed in my pale slip and let hot tears burn lines on my cheeks. But only for a moment.

Taking a deep breath, I would try to imagine an erotic scene that might save me. I'd stretch my body out so my hands brushed the pressboard wall and my feet dangled in the hot desert air. Lying flat, I would wait for someone to come. I barely slept that entire year, there was so much to hear inside my head, and out. Inside was the waiting game. Outside, coyotes sang. At first I thought I was hearing a gang of weeping children come to cover the earth. Soon their howls sent words and I knew what they meant.

I started to call Adam from the motel desk every morning to tell him. I knew we would not be together, which made me ashamed, so I'd hang up as soon as I heard his voice. Every day I did this, but by winter's end, that first season of no food or money and only me to walk and weep, I was so weak the telephone seemed too heavy for my hand. Yet still I would call. I'd go into the office where the manager would hand me the phone without a word, his head tilted back, mid-dream. I would dial the number and let the receiver thud down to the counter, then leave for my walk. I guess the manager hung it up later, upon waking.

In spring I called for the very last time. I was so hopeless I had decided the whole world had forsaken me and it was only a matter of time until the real end. An owl with a snake in its mouth had flown by my face one dawn, darkening my skin. Telling Adam of my troubles was beside the point, now the true end was on its way.

I continued to walk the desert floor daily. With my stale bagels and in my floral dress and western hat, which I kept quite clean despite my despair, I made a pretty picture for many gaping tourists. "A native," I would occasionally hear one whisper. This struck me as hysterical, for it's all a terrible mistake. Still, I knew much about the desert and I tried to communicate all I knew with my eyes. The end is coming, my eyebrows warned them, heed the prickly pear. If the prickly pear has bloomed, find cover!

One pale day I walked farther than ever. It was the hottest time I had ever known in the desert. Even my bones felt the sun. Everything was dead, dried up in the vast oven of sky and earth. I came upon a man poorer than even myself. "I'm so hungry," he said. His skin looked made of wood. I let the plastic bag fall from my hand and watched as it landed and melted onto a rock. My head burned so, the burning felt cold, and I felt a solitary ice cube melt through my skull. I walked from the man and my bagels.

Soon I found a child resting near a spiny ocotillo. "My head is so cold," the child said. "Mine too," I answered. "My head is so hot, it's cold." She just stared. I took the leather hat Adam had given me and placed it on the child's head. She reached her hands up and felt along its band, patterned with colors and made of bird's feathers. The child leaned against the ocotillo. "No!" I cried, because the ocotillo is like nails. She fell asleep, apparently unharmed. I bid farewell to the hat and the girl.

Farther along, I saw another child. He had no shirt and small circles under his eyes. "Take my dress," I told him. "It's made of rayon, a fabric they say is fine as silk. You can wash it when the monsoons come just by standing beneath a cloud." The dress swept the desert floor as the boy walked away, the dress covered his hands with its long flowing sleeves.

At last I came to the deep saguaro forest, with its angular cacti, tired and old. The sun no longer slapped my head. It was so dark that when the last child asked me for my underslip I thought, what does it matter, no one will see me in this dark. Stepping out of the pink slip, I remembered how I used to vacuum in my underwear while Adam slept. I said, "This slip is from a special shop. There they sell only lingerie. My husband bought it for me, he picked it out for me." This was a lie, since I'd bought it myself at Val-U-Village, which was across from the motel. It cost one dollar.

As I stood there naked with nothing left, I looked toward the flickering lights of the desert city's limits. And I thought of the people who inhabited the place, in their kitchens and bathrooms and garages and yards. I didn't know what they were trying to tell me with the lights that turned on and turned off. They made a pattern I could not yet discern. Why were so many people flickering lights for me to read? All I could tell was that the end was surely imminent. As I lowered my body to sit on the ground and receive it, all the trailers and houses went dim. Then the dimmed lights became stars, and those dull amber stars rose to the sky and then fell. I crouched on the ground, trying to gather the stars, which glittered darkly like jewels, or like pennies. I held some in my hands and found my way through the night.

Back at the motel, on the narrow but clean cot, I lay down for my first good sleep since winter. I put the star pennies under my pillow for luck.

When I woke what I believe now to have been many days and nights later, I did not understand where my dress was, and why my cheek was pressed into what seemed to be gravel. The manager stood above me, lifted my cageling arms into one of his grey-black t-shirts with an eagle on the back. He gave me some leather pants to wear. The pants were so heavy on my legs that I understood how we are all animals.

I let myself be sheparded into the motel office, where I took the phone and called Adam. When I heard Adam's voice rise toward me, I wavered and almost fell down. The manager spoke into the phone for me then, eyeballing me kindly for the very last time.

In my room I changed into a new pink dress, which the manager bought me at Val-U-Village. It had an elastic waist and sleeves like wings and it opened between my legs when I walked. I peered into the one-way mirror.

Back in the office I sat on the counter and slung my legs toward the manager, who stroked them. I turned myself toward the door. I fingered the money Adam had wired, and the dress, soft as light, and watched for the sunflower cab.

A RIDDLING TALE

For a short but rather confusing time when I was younger, my sisters and I turned into flowers. We were left to grow in a window box all day, and only my sister was allowed inside at night. She had strong leaves and many blooms, like us all then, but hers were stronger, and more many. My mother kept her by the bedside to sleep, and returned her to our box for day.

One morning, as my older sister fixed the crystals for my mother's coffee before going back to the box, she said, "If you come pick me this morning, and let me inside for the day, I'll never leave home for some man."

And so later my mother went to the window box and pulled her from the roots. After that, my sister wasn't a portulaca.

Here is a riddle for you. How did my mother know which one was my older sister, if we were three identical ground roses among the wandering jew? That riddle is easy to answer. My older sister had been indoors all night and had no dew upon her. She stood out in matte-red dullness.

An other riddle is harder to answer. My older sister married just one year later, leaving me and my little sister with my mother and her moods. Why?

"The Beginning of a Long and Unpleasant Relationship"

FROM WAKENIGHT EMPORIUM

BY A. B. WEST (2002)

EDITOR'S NOTE: A. B. West's remarkable *Wakenight Emporium* came to FC2 through the intervention of the French Americanist Marc Chenetier who'd heard Anne read it in Paris. Brenda Mills, the FC2 managing editor, found the MS in a pile and, unaware of who Marc was, urged it on me. It was Brenda's excitement that initially got everyone's attention. In a real sense *Wakenight Emporium* is about what it creates: alien being. The youth who in "Three" witnesses a jet plane crash in a Nebraska cornfield and "is no longer one of his species" represents the experience of those in the book—lost in a conversation crossing the city or standing in a parking lot after a crummy meal or falling into a time fault in Gencives—and those reading it. That matters should be *thus*, not otherwise, seems a preposterous accident, while the idea of nothing following from anything seems quite natural. In *Wakenight Emporium* the inevitable forms a thin veneer, and because Anne is a prose artist, she calls everything under this veneer time. Alien beings live there. They aren't better than we are, and becoming alien isn't a choice or invention, but aliens will find our conversation arousing, regard marriage with curiosity, and know catastrophic violence as a change of velocity, the normal acceleration and reversal of clocks. Death isn't disruption, and the present, the plunge into *this*, is a kind of friction, what we call a plot. Freedom amounts to plot reversal. We experience it as alien.

—RMB

"I believe it's generally held that an artistic discourse, or any cultural artifact, has political significance whether or not it so intends.... This said, I don't feel inclined to politically nutshell my work. Even if I thought it lent itself to that treatment, it would entail reverting to a form of discourse that I write to avoid. It's depressing how long it took me to summon up these truisms."

—A. B. West

THE THING ABOUT THE FUTURE

The thing about the future and about changing is…

For much of the period between the moment of our transition from non-existence to existence, and that moment of our dying and mouldering from existence back to non-existence, we are aware of ourselves as solitary entities in an uncomprehending multitude, our allotted time rushing noisily past our ears.

We stand aghast on the window ledge overlooking the next instant… our little interior voices shouting *Jump! Jump!* or *Don't Jump! Don't Jump!*

And the building whose umpteenth floor we are teetering on spirals through nothingness, a speck on the back of a speck-like planet…

And we hear a person next to us… or is it some disembodied voice… or is it a person inside us, saying…

may he turn the light of his countenance upon us and make his face to shine upon us.

We feel indeed that such a *he* as may be is ahead of us, not behind us.

For *we* are the past, the just past at least. We are, by the manner in which we are perched on time, the very stuff of the past. For, before it passed, the past was the future, and it loomed before us, and it wasn't us… and then we became it, and then it became the past.

For us, therefore, the past is safe; we are already past it; are sure we have definitely survived it… It's the thing we know, and that we know we have borne, if only by some insult of coincidence. And we can't die retroactively. We can only die in some future instance…

And so, to keep our senses of self warm as we forge unavoidably ahead, we wrap ourselves in the past—in the flag of whatever scrap of soil we happen to be standing on, in the lore of anything that waves or hollers… countries, peoples, brave men… cars, gadgets, fashionable trousers… And, with this infernal buzz heating our behinds like some almighty blow torch, we look forward with scant faith to the future that starts, as it has always started, the following instant, as if from scratch. The future…

…from which direction the light of his countenance will reach us we pray… from that point where he is, and where what he is is… who some say is the eternal burning of all instants, where all moments burn for eternity… one of these instants being the one in which we came into existence, one of them being the one in which we shall exist no longer… and which has already happened, as have all instants, forever… because that's what eternity means… although admittedly some days we can know this better than others.

Bless our hearts.

I can't recall what I was going to say about the future… One leaves one's self a reminder, one doesn't necessarily remember *re* what…

Or perhaps I simply can't remember it yet… inasmuch as I have yet to say it.

Oh yes. This was it: a fragment of prose.

> …and yet each day tenders us one chance anew… just as each lays the same snares that we should squander it. The chance resides in the day, where our gods and devils have put it. The squander protocol is ours; we call it our freedom. And so our days whiz by like a traffic of wasps along a gutter.

No… I'm afraid that isn't what I was going to say yet. I happened to have it to hand and thought… But, now I see…

This is quarrel two. Life is nailed about with meaningless quarrels.

TWO YOUNG MEN

Two young men in great coats cross Brussels in the dark dank Brussels night, talking about art, one accompanying the other to his doorstep. The conversation has its own momentum, so that, without even interrupting themselves, they do as they do so many nights: they about-face upon reaching their target residence and start back across town towards the doorstep of the other. Where, still rapt in conversation, they arrive, face about, and charge out through the night mists towards their previous destination… and thuswise until dawn.

There are 4 or 5 phone booths on their path as they cross the city, according to which route they take, and this seems to depend as little on the exercise of choice as if someone were switching the points on their rails. Every time they come to a phone booth, if some night caller has left the door ajar, the slighter of the two men rushes over without pausing, shuts the door, and returns to his friend's side… slipping into his own discourse as soon as there is a gasp for breath or rhetorical pause—sometimes blocks later—the brief comment "a draft."

In later years, when the two men, their shared convictions still lying fallow, have quit each other's nights, they recall at various moments of desperate social tedium in their now separate lives how rich and free they seemed to themselves then, wielding their ideas like flashing broadswords on the dim deserted battlements.

Each whispers gratefully to the absent other, "you made me listen to me, friend. I was good."

And the taller of the men marvels at how his companion never interrupted him with his chronic closing of the doors and cursory explanations, even if it meant an hour of forbearance across the street from a yawning phone box until the end of a filibuster. And he regrets never having quizzed him about the door ajar… was it an ingress of air into the phone booth or an egress of air into the world that disconcerted him?

As it happens, a phone call to resolve such enigmas and renew ties, although often contemplated with amusement, does not take place. Indeed no contact is ever made between the two again.

Years later, in some home or other, one of these still celibate and reflective men will read the unassuming necrology of his Horatio, who will die in a similar establishment across the city of natural causes related to neglected health and complications resulting in pneumonia. Later still, marked by an unassuming necrology, he will leave the world and his sword in exactly identical fashion—as so many of us will—thinking "how does what happens mean?"… his favourite thought.

THREE

And I heard myself think, *I may be about to have the last lovely moment of my life… the first lovely moment of my life.*

I had heard someone use this expression on the radio.

Start here.

Yes, we were all fiddling with these little packets, transparent packets of fiddley things. And then suddenly the whole shebang of us were in the parking lot.
The surprised attendant of a conveniently located parking lot found a peanut inside an entire fiddley packet of peanuts.
Of course it wasn't in a parking lot.
But it was.

We had all been thinking variously—*what a crummy meal, what a crummy bread roll, what a crummy plastic spoon, what a crummy dessert.* And then we all thought something else almost simultaneously. Unbelievably. Irremediably.

And all the crummy food threw itself up all over us.

All over us. And we didn't even care.

The man next to me was a famous radio announcer

a relatively well-known radio…

had a popular radio show

had a popular local morning radio show

had said two hours ago, "well, we'll be back tomorrow. Be sure to join us then."

and had once taken a course in after-dinner speaking

wasn't next to me

was three rows up

was in first class

wakenight emporium

was on the same flight three months earlier… figuratively speaking the same flight, only two months later… still it could have been me… him…

We were falling, or screaming.

And then it was over. It was happening again.

It wasn't happening.

I might as well start here.

Another hypothesis asserts that quick time is possible because the planet is not flat. It is curved and time curves above it. When an accelerating bird goes from point A to point B, cutting across in a straight line (instead of following the curve), it arrives at point B slightly "ahead of Time." See illustration III.

Man has neither the "quickening" skills nor the freedom from the earth's curve, so the theory says. His gravity is so to speak soldered to the orbicular surface of the globe. Some say this thesis creates more problems than it resolves. Others make do.

Be that as it may, jets also adhere to such principles:

by skimming the surface of the present and going just a bit faster than time, jets zoom us from one continent to another. Everybody has experienced that troubling of one's sense of time that follows air travel. We blame dehydration and "biological clocks."

However, the few people who know that time is actually elastic keep it to themselves. Because to share it would mean world chaos. Fortunately, when it does squeak out, the idea seems so improbable; it's like saying you can walk up a wall… which of course you can, but more of that later.

A despairing adolescent, sent by his European parent to visit his American parent, wanders alone under a full moon in a solitary Nebraskan corn field, when, unexpectedly, unbelievably, irremediably, an airliner plummets from the sky and crashes before his eyes, throwing huge slabs of blazing debris and baggage and bodies and trays around the very field whose bleakness he had just been contemplating. It is a scene of unfathomable horror… for him alone… during the hour it takes the emergency services to find the place. He stumbles helplessly from body to body through the smouldering shards. Thinks he sees a twitch of life, detects a murmur, a stifled cry. But he can't clear his eyes of tears, nor hear above the din of blood pounding in his head. Except someone howling… he is not infrequently aware that he is howling. The people and parts of people flung about are no longer of his species—he himself is no longer of his species—living and dead thrown together, each locked in a blind and terminal self.

And his affliction is not less absolute than theirs.
He never recovers.

He still strides a moonlit night wishing he had never been worlded… sobbing and quaking, the sound man in the wreckage.

Upon a card were writ these words:
The last four things will happen
The end of all things will happen
And it will be the end.
We don't know the precise nature of the first two things.
We know they happen almost simultaneously.
Three's a cloud.
Little can be surmised regarding the fourth of the last four things…
to wit, the last of them.

And I heard myself think, *I may be about to have the last lovely moment of my life… the first lovely moment of my life.*

Start here.

FRICTION

Time may be in truth a piece of psycho-scenery— a vast Coney Island we use to keep appointments with ourselves... something only we experience to keep us from thinking everything at once... which is presumably what god does... he thinks everything at once.

(According to which soi disant theory there is no music in eternity because all the notes would have to be played and not played at once and forever... the kind of thing like when you drop a drowned spaniel on a piano keyboard and don't drop a drowned spaniel on a piano keyboard at the same time, for all time, till the skies spill down their grief.)

Because we are not everything—as god is—or everywhere (which is the same thing) we live in relationships of contiguity. We can only know or experience one thing "at a time"... (or a few things "at a time," which is the same thing). If we were everywhere in all dimensions at once, we would be the biggest and the smallest everything and all things would be actual always, and...

...and there would be no time. For Time is...

Our "now" is the friction of events against our fixed position... warped like a tiny smear around us each—ever changing, no two the same. "Now" is the rub.

If Time were a river—a cheery old-timey notion—we stand as crayfish on the riverbed, beckoning to no one in particular, filtering out of the wide waters washing over us the mere several ingredients of our "now," in a seemingly meaningless... or at least, not particularly successful metaphor... which is the same thing.

FROM THE END OF FREE LOVE

BY SUSAN STEINBERG (2003)

EDITOR'S NOTE: Susan Steinberg's MS, which FC2 subsequently published under the title *The End of Free Love*, was one of two dozen selected from our "slush pile" by screeners at Illinois State University and then read by Jeffrey DeShell, who recommended it to our editorial board. In his report Jeffrey noted Susan's virtuoso handling of repetition, her skill at creating tension by reiterating phrases, words, or lines, and her extraordinary ability to estrange and absorb readers simultaneously. Susan went on to have many FC2 admirers, including Brian Evenson who appreciated, among other qualities, the tightness of her constructions and Matt Roberson who praised Susan's attention to narrative rhythm and language. However, what initially attracted me was the way each fiction in *The End of Free Love* imagined a distinct form for itself, as though Susan's inventions were as much new concepts of story as new stories. I suspect that this foregrounding of form had something to do with the estrangement that Jeffrey had first noted, since Susan's lyricism can feel paradoxically impersonal, almost distant. For me, "Isla" seems a perfect example of these complex qualities. The absence of the daughter's voice, combined with the numbering of the father's remarks—so many of which are instructions—creates a smothering atmosphere of incest. By repressing its explicit subject in this way, Susan's form ceases to function as a container merely and becomes itself expressive. I experience this shift as an increase in fiction's immediacy, its presentness.

—RMB

"…I mean, here I am, seriously suited up and ready to go to battle…, but when I march up to the front line and stare my enemy in the eyes, I'm not convinced I'm looking at the right enemy. Is it too late to rework the battle plan?"

—Susan Steinberg

ISLA

1. Never tuck the napkin.
2. Four stars means tops. One two three four. Meaning the top. Número uno.
3. Spread the napkin like this. A flick and drop. Do it. These are real cloth. A flick. Drop in the lap.
4. Tell the waitress your drink. Tea please por favor and bread.
5. Always ask for by the window. For the sunset.
6. Sugar is the enemy. It gets in the blood and spreads. We all get it from the sugar. Our one enemy number one is sweets.
7. Trust me. They aren't Jews. There by the kitchen. Don't look.
8. White sand is all you need. Setting sun. What more could you need?
9. Salt slows the blood. It poisons. Take a glass of water.

Pour in a shaker of salt. Now two. The blood from salt.

10. Never buy German made.
11. Seabirds are dirty and beggars.
12. An apéritif. Rouge. A twist.
13. They work the native girls hard. These girls are close to your age. They make a nickel an hour. Just nickels in a four star. How would you survive? This is why we tip. We're known for good tipping.
14. Hard liquor is the enemy. It poisons the bloodstream. Hard liquor is for the crass. The whiskies and gins. They can have it.
15. There are things your old pop knows.
16. Never gamble.
17. Never smoke.
18. Sometimes we cheat.
19. Red sunsets are all you need. See the sailboats? A picture postcard. When have you seen a red sunset? Think. Never. I like the blue boat there but sailboats tip. One tilt and splash.
20. New Yorkers are crass. Look at that fellow eating.
21. By the kitchen. What a piece of meat. Look. Showy. An animal from New York you know it. 22. That slob. Napkin tucked. He's hard from the city living don't I know it.
21. Apéritifs come rouge and blonde. Some ice and a twist of lemon and you sip. Apéritifs come first before dinner. With a twist. Sip slow. After dinner drinks come after.
22. When you want more tea. Cuando quieres más tea. Say, more tea. Dices, más tea por favor.
23. The waitress thinks you're my girlfriend.
24. Blonde. Ice and a twist.
25. They make nickels an hour. They have children at home. They live in shanties in ghettoes. How would you survive?

They start when they're thirteen. No car no trips. No Sunday school. Some start at twelve.

26. Never bring home a New Yorker. You'll kill me. Never bring home a non-Jew.
27. A trip for my girl and we deserve it don't we Sweetie?
28. Never feed the seabirds. They carry sickness. They eat garbage from the ghettoes. Let the slobs bring them bread.
29. You can tell non-Jews. Even dark-haired ones. The small handbags. Plastic beads. Fake stones.
30. I can still get a young girl.
31. Four stars means tops. Not three but four. Straighten. Look proud. Four stars Sweetie. Wait until your mother hears. Her head will go through the roof.
32. Never sit by the kitchen. You don't want to hear it. The clatter. Or see it.
33. Never go to the ghetto.
34. We'll start with this. Soup. Then this. Ensalada. How old are you? I guess seventeen. Am I right? Seventeen. Sweetie what do you think? How old is she? Wipe your face. She must be seventeen. This here's my girlfriend. You laugh. This is my lucky lady. Say hello Sweetie. Say hola to the waitress. Hola Sweetie. I want this here and my lucky girl friend will have this and done well-done. And bring me a clean knife.
35. First blow on the spoon.
36. If it's too hot add ice.
37. New Yorkers are showy. They drive German cars. You know this.
38. Playing slots is not gambling. Five dollars big deal. Nickels.
39. Place the knife on the plate. All the way top and bottom against the rim. Not like this but like this. It shouldn't

touch the table.

40. Never ride a sailboat. One tip then splash and you drown. Would you like to drown? Would you? You don't want to find out. Trust me.
41. Leave a bite on your plate.
42. We can fool the waitress. She's staring. Look. I'll put my arm around you. Sit still. Don't look she's looking. We're so bad.
43. Jews don't drink beer with dinner. They don't drink milk. They don't drink hard liquor. We don't have the stomachs. Besides.
44. No one drinks the native coffee. It will put you under the table. You could stand a knife up in their coffee.
45. Taste before salting. Always. Why presume? Your mother the way she shakes the salt. She salts meat. Soup. Foods salted. Am I right? She would salt a cake if you didn't take the shaker. Her blood will screech to a halt. I always told her. Watch it.
46. You're the tops.
47. Jews don't call dinner supper.
48. If you laugh then laugh quiet.
49. New Yorkers are slobs. Look tugging on his meat. Crass. A zoo animal.
50. Cut three squares of meat. Then eat them one two three. Then cut three more. Then eat one two three.
51. Your eyes are bigger than your stomach.
52. You need fat on the skeleton. Why don't you eat up? You would never survive a roundup. Do you know what a roundup is? What do they teach in that slob Sunday school? You need some fat.
53. If it turned cold send it back.
54. Blondes are lookers. The New Yorker's date. Mean looking

but a blonde. That my Sweetie is a looker. By the kitchen. Your mother was a looker a long way back.

55. You don't eat the garnish.
56. Cut smaller pieces. Do you want to choke?
57. We can't go into the ghetto. We can drive around the edge. I can show you how the other half survives. Would you like that Sweetie? They carry pistols and knives. They sell their trinkets. We don't need that garbage. And the poor children. We'll keep our doors locked.
58. Un vaso de vino. For my young lady. White or red? Wait don't tell me. Blanca o rojo? Am I right? Blanco or rojo Sweetie? How about it? She's shy and always has been. She can sip some blanco. Her mother's head will shoot to the stars. Her first glass.
59. Solamente cuando su madre no está aquí. Comprendes?
60. Your pop takes care. This ring will be yours. Solid fourteen. This is fashion. Not a trinket. Your mother chose the stone and one day my sweets. All for you. But what's the hurry am I right?
61. The world is unfair. A looker and a slob. Turn slowly and tell me. The blonde with the. Tell me is she a looker? Mean looking with the cigarette. The lipstick. Now look. Am I right? Don't look.
62. If you can't pay you wash dishes.
63. The middle of the island is a zoo. Pistol shooting. Stray goats. They shoot dogs and live in shanties. They live in ghettoes. Such litter. They race cars.
64. I'll never let you starve.
65. There are things we do when no one's looking. Everyone does. Your old pop isn't so bad. There are just things that happen. You understand this Sweetie. Things. Comprendes for me por favor.

66. We all used to struggle. We ate soup from cans. Before you Sweetie. Before we left the zoo. But we danced. We went dancing. But soups from cans imagine can you?
67. Let's be extravagant.
68. Tap the water glass for attention. Ting ting. Or raise one finger like this.
69. American coffee por favor black no sugar. Más tea for my lady.
70. Eat up. You're a skeleton. Skin on a skeleton. Don't you like dinner? This isn't a joke. Eat up. Let's see you eat. Is it any good? Chew first then swallow. Slow. This isn't a race.
71. German cars are the enemy. Do you know this? Do you know why? What do they teach you on Sundays? Peace and love? The happy world? To hell. Ask me about the car seats. Come on Sweetie. Ask me about the ghettoes.
72. There are things your old pop knows.
73. Dessert is for slobs. The sugar is what kills. The sugar got all your grandparents. All your aunts and uncles. That and the smoking. The drinking. All of them. Ask your mother and still she eats desserts. She pours the salt. She smokes and drinks. Did you know this? She keeps it quiet. You didn't know.
74. The waitress thinks I'm twenty years younger.
75. The waitress never went to school. Imagine no school Sweetie.
76. There is always someone better smarter funnier. Always someone richer happier better. Always someone nipping at your seat. Shoving you out. Tell your poor mother. She never listened. You have to watch it or you'll fall. I warned her. She was in fashion. I got a fat wallet. They colored her hair. Fatter and they painted her nails. Magic. How she looked on our honeymoon. But now? Shape up I told her. Someone will push you out. Did she listen? Eat Sweetie. Watch it I told

her. Does she listen?

77. The waitress is no older than seventeen. She's closer to your age. You're close to seventeen hard to believe. You're fourteen hard to believe.
78. Your pop's a strong man. Look at the size of this fist. Let's see your little hand Sweetie. Make a fist. I could crush that little thing.
79. I'll never let you get hurt.
80. They grow up quick here. They know how to make a man happy. They cook can they ever. Rice and beans and meat from their farms. Imagine a farm of stupid skinny goats Sweetie. Would you eat goat? They eat the meat and boy can they clean a house. They treat men as men. The boss of the house. They work as maids. Waitresses. They know when enough's enough. They know how to give. How to listen. How to milk a goat. And they keep quiet.
81. Chew then swallow. There's no race.
82. You can always send it back.
83. Watch your old pop in action. Come here honey. Ting. Ting. An after dinner por favor. Surprise me.
84. I'm the boss. Do you hear me? I can always disown you.
85. You never can win.
86. Sometimes we lie.
87. Obesity is a crime that poor slob. He should be dragged out and shot. I'll hold a pistol. You grab the steak knife. Cut off his fingers. He'll still eat poor slob. We can take his date and drive and drive until they find us.
88. Never drive German made.
89. I was an expert dancer way back. Ask your mother.
90. Breathe the air. It's the real thing. Salt air. Sun. You can taste it in the air.
91. You're my lucky lady. My Sweetie. Say hola to the waitress.

My girl here's a good girl. She goes to school. Not a brain though. You know what a brain is? She's not the brainy type. Cómo se dice? Who knows right? But she'll make me proud. I have plans for this one. I have a business. I'm el presidente. She'll learn the ropes. Just a joke. She's not good with business. Easy. Where's your humor? A joke Sweetie. Joking.

92. You're number one.
93. Say, dónde está el cuarto de baño?
94. No dessert. I'm watching it. How about you Sweetie? Do you dare? Some cake? Pie? Look at those eyes. Her eyes are bigger than her stomach. Look at her looking but I think she knows better.
95. I love you Sweetie.
96. Picture the ghettoes. Shanties. Little shack houses. Hardly a window. Goats chewing the dried up grass. Thin dirt roads. Cars racing past. They race into children. We're so lucky. Guess what else. They toss children from roofs. The accidents.
97. The only good German is a what Sweetie? The only good German is a what German? Come on Sweetie.
98. You're a lucky thing.
99. You're Jewish first. American second. German last.
100. The slots age is eighteen. I'll give you five dollars. All those nickels. Your mother's head will hit the ceiling. We won't tell her. She used to be different way back. She was some looker. You don't remember. This was in New York. She could dance. We danced like a couple of kids.
101. American coffee. You can always tell American.
102. The salt air clears the head. Don't worry about your mother. She'll snap back. I did nothing wrong. We'll send a postcard. I did nothing at all. She can't say I did. What has she said? She can't say anything. I warned her. You can't listen to her.
103. You wave away musicians like this. A flick of the wrist.

They're a pain in the seat. They play for tips. Beggars.

104. Never bring home a musician.

105. We can make you eighteen. Some lipstick. Magic. Four years older. You'll be my girlfriend. We'll dance.

106. I should never have married your mother.

107. The sky's the limit. How about that Sweetie? How about we get you in fashion? New shoes Sweetie. The ones they wear now. The ones they wear here. Tops. Lipsticks. You'll come back a new you. Your mother will die from shock. We'll get you a hairdo. New nails. The sun's the limit.

108. The Germans are the enemy. They got your great grandparents.

109. You die you rot.

110. I always told her no children. She was too young.

111. And why did I need children? She should have never. She wasn't ready. Accidents happen. But did she listen? Does she ever?

111. It's good to get away. You leave everything behind. But it catches you Sweetie. I hate to say it. But it nips you in the seat.

112. Never ask me why.

113. You pour a dot of cream. Wait. Another dot. Wait. See how it lightens? If you pour too much you mess the whole cup. I mean do you want coffee or a glass of milk? Ask yourself.

114. I deserve the best don't I? She couldn't give the best. She gave half that. A. quarter that. This fat wallet and she gave nothing. Don't I deserve the most?

115. Guess the check. Hurry Sweetie. Guess it. A hint. Think high. Higher. Higher. You'll never guess. Never.

116. Don't stare. Look at them stumbling out. Poor slobs.

117. A nice Jew is all you need. A nice home. I'll fill your wallet. You don't need your mother. You don't need school. Finish junior high if you like. Find a nice Jew. A nice house. Take an

island honeymoon.

118. Don't listen to your mother.
119. You're Jewish first. American second. German last.
120. Your mother never loved her child.
121. You're my número uno.
122. Wipe your face.
123. Take the check. You're paying. You're my lucky girlfriend right? Dinner's on you. Come on Sweetie. Where's your wallet? Show the waitress your fat wallet. Who's going to pay if not you? There are dishes waiting. Come on Sweetie. We're waiting for you. Come on. Waiting.
124. A joke. Just a joke. Where's your humor? Both of you.
125. Put the napkin on your plate.
126. You are your own worst enemy.
127. A five-dollar tip can buy a new goat.
128. A trip just you and me. It's been fun hasn't it? We'll get you in fashion. Then we can see some of that white sand and look for shells. We can lie around the sand like a couple of kids. How about it Sweetie? We'll race past the ghetto. I have friends in there. Would you eat goat? We can race through the ghetto and see what's what.
129. How about it Sweetie? Let's do this again sometime. While we still can.
130. I love you Sweetie. How about that?
131. Wipe here Sweetie. Wipe your eyes.
132. Give me the napkin. Let me help.
133. How can I help?
134. How can I help Sweetie?

FROM REAL TO REEL

BY LIDIA YUKNAVITCH (2003)

EDITOR'S NOTE: Lidia Yuknavitch is one of the remarkable writers whom in the late 90s and early 21st century Cris Mazza brought to FC2. No account of FC2's transformation from an almost exclusively male collective in the '70s to a non-profit press led predominantly by women today will make sense without Cris's forward-looking leadership. Through her efforts Kim Addonizio, Kit Reed, Lucy Corin, Jessica Treat, Lou Robinson, Karen Brennan, and Lidia—to mention only those we published—all came to FC2, and it has been their innovative books that have helped shape our present identity. Partly because it links sexual experimentation with literary experimentation and partly because it locates the problem of freedom within writing itself, Lidia's work seems to me exemplary. Her fiction "Scripted" presents competing versions of the writer's practice, versions in which stories are more real than being, stories are identical with being, and beings are more real than stories. These three correspond to the personal pronouns, and taken together they suggest that both desire and its repression originate in our dividedness, our capacity for being simultaneously narrator, narrated, narratee. As in so much fiction published by FC2, language in Lidia's work is a place where politics and imagination collide. The problem is never just out *there*, never limited to the President's or some CEO's spectacular presumption. Because the enemy already occupies her medium, because her struggle is both far-reaching and close to home, Lidia's writing is forced to go deeper, and it is this radical ambition that, for me, accounts for its extraordinary power.

—RMB

"I have zero interest in shock value...I'm looking for articulations which get underneath cultural cover stories. Here's an example: when Bush says he believes in and promotes a culture of life, I think that's about the most violent thing I've ever heard. It's obscene. It's pornographic."

—Lidia Yuknavitch

SCRIPTED

I am not myself. It seems some slippage has occurred. I am not exactly sure when, but I suspect it began just under a year ago, perhaps closer to two. In some ways the slipping might be attributed to the normal flow of events. Changes in one's life, for example, function rather simplistically in this way, and I have never been one to be thrown or alarmed by what appear to be movements completely in line with ordinary or even cosmic patterns. Aging, seasons and tides, the way consciousness or wisdom

She is not herself. It feels as if someone has sliced open her belly and is reaching inside. She closes her eyes. She places her hands—one under each lower rib—and pulls. Like a surgeon's tool. This is what it feels like to be her. And yet she does not count this as damaging or traumatic or depressing or terrifying; somehow this seems the natural order of things, like an animal shedding its skin or something dying giving way to new life. Bees swarming out of the carcass of a cow—isn't that how Virgil made

You are not yourself, and what's worse, you know it. It's been clear to you for some time, though you seem to have hoodwinked friends, colleagues, ordinary people such as grocery store clerks, gas station attendants, and waitresses. You exchange money and goods and services in the usual way, you arrive and depart as always, but secretly you know that these are acts of extreme stealth. At first you had some concern that someone would notice, as if you were carrying around a wound, but as time passed it became changes the structure of things. The way thought rescues us from action time and again.

After all. I am old enough now to have a vantage point from which to view the story, so to speak, of a life. I can see plots, turns, echoes, the recurrence of main and subordinate characters, tensions, conflicts, resolutions, and epiphanies all in perfect little rows. Some no doubt would identify this as a kind of wisdom. However, something nags at me in the back of my head like a small worm burrowing through my skull. It says: this is not so. In other words I am struck with the feeling that I am entirely deluded at the very point at which this mythological wisdom is presenting itself. The tunnel that the little worm has dug reveals a vacant tube of ignorance. The vantage point moves. It is a blur of pure motion, thus, invisible.

Spinning in this way, I try to track what's what. As near as I can determine, this slippage of self may have a cause and effect relationship, or a kind of fated fall motif (you know, the adage that there are no accidents…) or even an Eastern metaphysical shape, but it seems equally possible that the entire falling is

spring happen from all that death? Poetry saves us. Words give us the ability to move.

After all, she has been moved by a single line, a page, she has been literally moved. Once at a bar drinking scotch she seized-up mid-sip, the scotch dribbling down her lip and chin; the words, a poet's; her mind, convulsing; her body, a plethora of blood and channels of veinlike worm colonies mapping out whole new geographies. The line had so overtaken her that she had walked directly out into the street into the rain and the night and stood there until she had been entirely soaked, looking out into space, into the street itself, the black and white schemata of night, knowing with perfect certainty that she had to leave that city and go to another, without cause or effect, without reason, syntax, or insight. It was simply the line moving her.

Spinning in this way she enters a new city again or for the first time. Her clothes change, her hair, her creature comforts, what moves her, everything reinvented. She takes up philosophy not as hobby but as obsession. Finds herself inside books palm side up, Kant and Hegel, Wittgenstein. The

obvious that no one at all noticed, and wouldn't. Ever. In fact, you could be anyone.

After all, you don't give a flying crap about any of the people that people your life, now do you? Their inane and idle chatter and petty microscopic concerns. Their crawling through their own lives like blind earthworms in a clod of dirt no bigger than a baseball diamond. Their overwrought pathos and their absurd, tiny victories. They are cartoons of themselves. Their needs don't just bore the shit out of you, they actually repulse you. The way they proclaim insight from bogus interpretations of little events in their lives. Or how they are moved by great works of art and questions of being. A pile of steaming shit is what you really think even as you move through lively dinner conversations, attend concerts, go to funerals. You immovable fuck.

Spinning in this cesspool called a melting pot you wonder what's the use of this idiotic farce called democracy, and your place in it as an individual, the whole social organization of human culture into capitalist segments. Like chocolates in a box, prison cells, office cubicles. Lines at restaurants accidental, without cause, effect, or meaning. It's not as if building a self over the course of one's life is tantamount to designing and constructing a building, now is it? In that architecture such systems and equations drive the movement that one cannot at any point step back and extract oneself from the matrix of its meaning. Conversely, a life, though we see it as designed (through our own consciousness or larger than ourselves), is.

Take Wittgenstein: "The flashing of an aspect of being seems half visual experience, half thought." Unlike artistic forms, being, to put it simply, wavers. Where art is open to interpretation, being is open to dissolution. The two cross paths however at the interstices of making and of signification; each thrusts its meaning forward toward an other and in that relationship we come to "know" or experience. And history, personal as well as cultural, derives from just these relationships. So in the case of Wittgenstein then we are speaking about being not as transcendent of meaning (as in god), but rather tethered, forever grounded, to the process of sight and insight. So my own slippage of self in this regard might be said to represent this fluctuation.

words so moving at times her head rocks back. Secretly she reads Simone Weil, *Lives of the Saints*; their ecstasies keep moving her to ask, where are the bodies? She reads phenomenology thinking it will track the corporeal but finds that she is wrong. Sometimes it helps her to read direct medical descriptions of death, so the ideas that lift her in that transcendent way are always tethered to the ground of a human corpse.

Take Joan of Arc. She can see the image of her death. The details move her. The written account by Vita Sackville-West: "The sulfur was lit and the top layers of skin burned away; a faint honey smell was recorded." And Falconetti. In the silent black and white film. Her face is the word for it. Artaud's mad longing, his desire mixing with sacrament like blood and dirt from wounds in battle. These speak to her. Inside these words and images a body comes alive, faith made corporeal in wounding and even death. Love. She can make herself dizzy simply by thinking of it. She could probably faint right now if she let herself. Certainly she has been moved to tears publicly and endlessly simply by the named thing.

and museums, like cattle, like food in jars and cans and boxes. Like knowledge alphabetized and stacked, burned onto computer disks, kept safe from expansion by ever wily forms of containment feigning systemization. Even the sky is charted, the human body. Ranges of emotions and psychologies. Money. God. What a punk, you think. How a whole culture can be tricked by clever stories, movies, and mappings.

Take technology. Do you know what happens if you type "being" into a search engine? Try it. Try Yahoo or Google. (First take a moment to think about the words "search engine," "yahoo," and "google." These are our knowledge bases. No shit.) Since nearly every person you know is a lazy ass, you withdraw the projection of the question. In your own mind you answer it: "crockofshit" comes up. The total tonnage of perfect shit—but accurate about us, nonetheless—that this represents to you is enough to fill a stadium. Being. Now that's a good one. Breathing, eating, shitting, eating, fucking. You would not even include thinking in the list. Descartes. What kind of asshole thinks that piece of crap up?

Making meaning, however, has its tricks. Part of how we most acutely make meaning of the events in our lives is theological in nature. I do not mean to say that we are yet bound to old notions of god and heaven. But we are still bound to their forms. For instance, when we hit any kind of difficulty or crisis, the first impulse of course is to narrativize, to make a story out of the event, a story complete with sin and redemption, moral trial and condemnation, transcendence, forgiveness, and resurrection. We take our emotions and make story from biblical form, from The Story, as it were. Thus all our smaller stories carry with them the plot elements of The Story: suffering, anguish, punishment, transcendence.... Do you see?

I will give you an example. A small and familiar human drama. Let's say a man cheats on his wife with a younger woman. Let's say the man and the wife's relationship, over time and with ordinary inevitability, has become rote. Not necessarily cold or sterile, not without love, not even without compassion. But habitual. The ease with which the man leans into the younger woman is based on

The meaning of things makes her. What moves her, makes her. In this way she becomes exactly what she is reading, she becomes Wittgenstein's line, she becomes Falconetti's face, she becomes a description of burning flesh. In slow walks down city streets into bars she is pale and lonesome, so pale and lonesome someone is always moved to ask her why she is so sad, exactly as in a movie or novel, exactly like the constellation of a philosophy answering the question, what is a woman, she becomes the embodiment of the knowledge to the point of near iconography. Seated at a table drinking she places a hand to her cheek and the other at her collarbone, she closes her eyes, she is seeing lines and lines.... Can you see her?

She is an example of the thing itself. She has been betrayed, scorned, shamed. A lover takes her, she falls. Then, inevitable, disgusted with her mind, with its complications and little weavings, with her constant weeping and overdramatic scenes, her cerebral contortions, turns her out either verbally or physically or emotionally. He either returns to his wife or former lover, or he gains self-worth

Why not make it up? Make up a version of things since no one will notice anyway. The colossal stupidity of your fellow man will make it simple. Someone asks you your name, make one up. See what changes. Someone asks you what you do for a living, if you are married, have children, what your age is, your income, what kind of car you drive, where you are from—fictionalize it all. You think it will make a difference but it won't make the kind of difference you are hoping that it will. Instead of stunning or changing or warping anything in your life, it will simply make people more interested in the person you are describing than they were in you. There is absolutely no distance between blindness and insight.

Look at these lame idiots, you think. Are they not repeating the same goddamn piece of shit story that all of pukey humanity has Xeroxed since the dawn of time, you think. Some middle-aged fuck needing to fuck some empty need-machine of youth who didn't get proper daddy or who is just generally let down by this culture's available roles for being—women, who can blame them for being pissed and insane—

another old story; she is attracted by his wisdom, or what she perceives to be his wisdom. He doesn't even have to do anything but look her way, pay attention to her. He need only be older and wiser than the young woman. Who is, of course, beautiful. Already the setting, characters, conflict, and resolution are clear, yes?

You don't have to have read any canon to comprehend the idea here. You need only to have lived a life, subjected yourself to a culture's discourses. You need only to have been alive. These stories have supersaturated being, so to speak, and so they are no longer jettisoned away from us, they are in us, as in us as DNA, as close to us as skin. It does not matter what one chooses or doesn't choose in a life. Certain stories override any will you may or may not have. Certain stories write us. If you doubt what I am speaking of, make a list of the last five movies or books or songs or news stories which moved you. I suggest to you that each will have one thing in common. Each will draw from a very short list of pre-existing scripts.

So the man and the woman fall to desire, or the story of a desire which entirely always and insight from their encounter; what it revealed to him about himself, his vulnerabilities, his being and purpose in life. First she is broken. And then she is simply a self again, but without ownership of any sort, she is simply a self set sailing across a sea of signifiers as if lifted from the pages of a story.

Books are not people. She knows that. And yet don't all of the people who people her life behave exactly as she has read? She has a private thought which is "all being is textual." She knows now not to tell anyone this thought. She keeps lines such as this inside of a dialogue never uttered. Her lines thus correspond with lines she has read in a complex discussion without beginning, middle, or end. Without primary characters or directed action. Just lines in the mind of one woman. She knows now that if someone speaks to her she ought to respond not with any of these lines, but with pre-coded body-specific phrases, like sound-bites or authorized advertisements. Someone says are you from here. Animal instinct-like she knows to say yes.

Yes she says to a man. To men. Any men. Yes like a serial. Yes to a desire her mouth endlessly open, her tears neverending, his moronic lunging even though his nut-sack is sagging and his life's worth is wrinkled and gray and about the only thing he can point to and say this exists is his wife at home with her own deflated blown-out balloons for tits…stop me when this story sounds FAMILIAR.

Fuck literature. I mean let's be real. We don't need it anymore. I say get rid of all the books since no one, anywhere, has the patience or time to read them anymore. Yeah, I know some of you out there will CLAIM that you are a reader of texts, that you read every word from beginning to end, but I say you are full of shit. You know how many academics I know that get away with reading the back jacket of a book instead of its contents? Let's just say a lot. Because what matters is that they can talk the talk, not that they have read something in its entirety. What matters is that they can tell a story of experience. The experience itself, of a book, of a life, it doesn't matter—everybody has already done and heard everything enough to puke.

Open your mouth and eat shit. What I'm saying is every single time someone already contains them. So too they exit that story with experiences which will no doubt shape their futures. Perhaps the man goes back to his wife, or divorces his wife and marries the younger woman, only to have another affair five years later. Perhaps the woman moves to the city in which the man lives, takes up a life with him, takes on his life as her narration. However, there are two interpretations here. Either the experience of desire changes them and influences their future actions or decisions, or the experience of desire neither changes nor influences them at all and is itself merely a nexus within which we dip in and out as individuals. Like a universe.

And so the end of this point. I did not mean to imply that I had an answer, either for myself, or in the form of advice for a reader. I meant merely to raise the question. In my individual case the question came to be about being, an old question, I admit, perhaps a dull one to some. I am not so much interested in whether or not I am, but rather, how I am. And certainly phenomenology, epistemology, ontology all rake through the chaos of that. But my "how" is without origin, without specific bodies, and yet located in her flesh perpetually. Yes to a future, as long as each future posits and then erases itself forever. Yes to a husband, a new city, yes to being, as long as being always posits itself and then erases itself forever. Yes to all of language, to all cities, all names, to open mouths and legs. Yes to life in Paris, in Seattle, in Los Angeles, New York, Berlin, Texas. Yes to metamorphosis, catharsis, epiphany, transcendence. Yes to the order inside of chaos, the moving particles underneath what appears to be immovable skin, yes to the entire nebula, to the entire night sky, to the endless cosmos.

Her telos has become beloved to her. She thinks this sentence as a man is coming inside of her. She does not speak it. She moans in the voice of a woman in ecstasy. He is pleased. Her telos, secret, private, entirely an ecstatic state, will be that which is closest to death. The last page. The last sentence. The last image. The last word, letter. The silence which comes then. Alive and unflinching and nearly unbearable, the space wherein one is compelled to find the next book, film, speaks their mind you are, in effect, eating shit. Their shit. What's more, every time you open your own mouth you are spewing shit. The entire human race is idle chatter. North America, chatter. Europe, chatter with an accent. Africa and other third world victimized poor little boobies scrounging around for food or governments, nations, blah blah blah blah blah blah shit. Men and women, worse than excrement. Ask yourself this: are we better than we used to be together? Men and women? Have things improved in ways that you can point to and feel good about? How? What do you do in your little cosmology with race class gender? You punk.

I don't have anything else to say. You'll reject all this crap anyway, right? You fucking "reader" of other people's ideas. You can simply say, this asshole is full of shit, wrongheaded, uneducated, biased, crass, mistaken, misguided, full of themselves, confused, high, nuts, immoral, damaged, imbecilic, delusional, without a grasp of basic humanity or language or being or community or social processes or human history or knowledge or order or science or law or cultural embedded with perhaps a more subtle and urgent question…a question I would leave with you, reader, as Keats leaving his hand, open and extended: this living, isn't it simply to be storied?

lover, event, life, self. Hurry, they all think. She thinks, die die die die die die in a loop. She smiles. He smiles back. Two lovers fucking. It is the way of the world. It is every story ever told, and she inhabits them all.

production or awareness or love…the stupidest of all…love…what the fuck do we know about love? Love doesn't know from Adam. Don't bother thinking or being. Don't bother moving. Get real.

FROM DAHLIA'S IRIS: SECRET AUTOBIOGRAPHY AND FICTION

BY LESLIE SCALAPINO (2003)

EDITOR'S NOTE: Leslie Scalapino's remarkable work, *Dahlia's Iris: Secret Autobiography and Fiction*, came to us through Adalaide Morris, who recommended it to me at the 2001 Modernist Studies Association Convention. What caught my attention was the way the work's politics, instead of being exclusively thematic, were embodied in the work's struggle with itself, with its existence as narrative. Initially, I saw this struggle in the way the detective plot (Cloe, Grace, Andrew, et al) metamorphosed into versions of the plots of popular movies, *The Terminator*, *Invasion of the Body Snatchers*, etc, as though no story were itself alone, but instead were an allegory or interpretation of all stories. The frustration that lovers of detective plots will feel reading Leslie's work seemed to me indicative of a deeper frustration, one arising from the historical situatedness of history itself, of our narrative knowledge of the world. But I was also impressed by the way the non-genre of the "secret autobiography" emerged as a topic and a teleology in the form of *Dahlia's Iris*. That is, I came to appreciate as a positive achievement the fact that I could not say what a "secret autobiography" was, could only acknowledge its existence after every attempt to identify it was voided. The result for me was that Leslie's fiction ceased to represent an action and became an ongoing action itself. Its struggle to bring itself into being became a struggle to bring *ourselves*—readers? writers? Americans? humans?—into being.

—RMB

"The U.S. is occupied by 'itself.'"

—Leslie Scalapino

INDIGO AT NIGHT

The visual space is authoritarian space, controlled from the air.

The collapsing vast tiered polluted ruin that is (future) San Francisco as (as if even one vast building is abandoned cities, people having moved off-world to the colonies) illuminated vertical landscape of vast tiered building-pyramid-slabs (like space platforms) are already ruins, merely the reflection of images the viewer can't see (in the 'future' retina then of the boy running, a part of the indentured labor force, without papers) of that which *he* has seen off-world before.

The off-world—the colonies are the vast unseen, of which there are no flashbacks or forward—is the enslaved present then.

One boy has been 'retired' (listed as suicide or accidental death) found apparently fallen from one of the skyscrapers on an alley. Unidentified, Hispanic, perhaps fourteen years old or twelve.

Another repetition:

The reindeer come off the ship, a herd, then another herd of them come off. The seals having been exterminated by white trappers brought famine. In black night on a desert of ice the starved Eskimo set out to hunt in the herds of transplanted reindeer now.

Detective Grace Abe wakes—opening within her lids first—having slept in her office, intercepted in sleep by Cloe (Officer Cloe O'Brien) entering speaking to her.

In Grace the thought of a day is ahead, as is a sight (though a sight is only memory instantly of something one'd seen).

You've been here all night, Cloe states. Below their police precinct tenth-story office, there's a bus stalled outside in the San Francisco street.

All the passengers are bursting threaded wet-bulb-flowers. The horn of the bus blasting endlessly. Detective Grace Abe, her lids almost closed as she's glancing downward at the bus, closes the tenth-story window.

The lips and eyes of a brown-haired fleshy woman are distorted meshed when she whines.

Seated in a café with another woman, flesh whines that she also feels grief for her friends and a loved-one who have died of AIDS but she does not have the right to feel this.

I have no right to grief (sing-song repetition is here the only language in public). The AIDS epidemic still rages, but the drug treatment now confining the symptoms prolonging the embattled life of the ill—the number of ill still proliferate—the public is lulled, not perceiving this proliferation. It's doubling: ten years ago 40,000 new cases, now 80,000 new. The first germ-line transmissions.

The news mentions only the subject of the masses from other nations being ill. Their masses not having access to the drug treatment is touched on in the news, so that the presence of AIDS spreading here may be hidden from the public view, Officer Andrew Chen thinks.

The regimen of trembling lips which suffocate feeling infantilize them, the public. Sentiment.

The friend, with whom the flesh speaks, murmurs to her astonished You can feel grief, regardless of the 'right' to it. Immediately the brown-haired flesh snaps I *can not!* I *don't* have a right to feel grief.

Their conversation brushes against Officer Andrew Chen who considers it pleasantly, a moth flying on the light: on a bulb in day, the amber moth is becoming another amber moth. Andrew lifts his eyes as Grace and Cloe enter the café.

They are followed by Captain Jasper Frank, a man slumped vibrant with grey thatch of hair floating on dove's lids, lids which spill sagging on the collapsing stubbled jowls. An aging elephant, Captain Jasper Frank moves to join them at a table.

Brown-haired flesh continues her whining next to them, punctuated by the surprised friend murmuring Janice, in the background of their conversation—which is about another accidental death, possible suicide, also an unidentified, Hispanic boy found in the business district skyscrapers. He's apparently fallen, his corpse crushed by flight.

The future is seen akin to the physiological process of the amber moth.

Bifurcating, it does not progress. They flit ahead and behind, in the midst one walking appearing. One appears to be resting walking in the crowd, which flits backward at times and hanging then at the instant jets forward still as if flitting in bleached lit space that opens—they are not there. Then fills with them (people flitting into the space ahead fill it, appear even to be running).

Change is rarely seen in people walking. They don't appear to change there. One time, someone saw a man change as his character while walking quickly with the others blank, blank crowd on their way somewhere who are buoyant.

Illegal aliens are landed in small boats on the California coast at night. They are already indentured servants who are bound to work off their fare. Sometimes the traders, fearing apprehension, drowned their illegal cargo or locked them in the hold starving and thirsty. Others curled in the hold wake on the pitching sea. One has split away from the self felt in that one's skin. Before that night which is passed, a self had been felt in one person's skin.

Grace bathing lying in the bath submerged is a bead holding the soft skin under which pink pulsing capillaries hold darting. There's a cough in the hall. Someone passes. Her lids closed. And ran her hand down her side under water. Under water the side is velvet from the frame interiorly and from the hand.

1. DAHLIA

Crushing a rose. The corpse of the boy is a crushed rose on the cement in the alley below.

A boy flown at night is a kite in the black from the tenth story suite of a skyscraper wall of glass. Whirling in the sky, he lands on his back.

Dahlias are yellow in a bouquet. Detective Grace Abe submerged in it, an owl gliding in a silver day sky also submerges and is visible there (an owl somewhere else). (Don't veer, stay in one place.)

Indigo at Night is not based on realism but on repetition. It is a detective novel, a form which depends on realism only—but maybe repetition of that convention and of events will make a crack, will crack realism.

One boy has been 'retired' (listed as suicide or accidental death), found apparently fallen from one of the skyscrapers on an alley.

Another boy, two weeks before, was also found in an alley, the corpse also crushed, consistent with having fallen from a height. He'd been found several blocks from the spot of the present one, the boy who'd jumped. They're not necessarily related.

TOR dot.com is a pornography internet company, which borders the alley, the initials standing for TORRID.

Two weeks before, Officer Cloe O'Brien kneeling in the nearby alley amidst overturned garbage cans by the busted-screen of the back door of a restaurant. Hearing clattering inside in the kitchen, Cloe'd squatted on the crumpled small corpse.

About eleven or twelve years old, she estimated the corpse. Hispanic. Mostly Chinese immigrants there. He was found by a busboy who works at the restaurant, who'd been out having a smoke in the alley. Near the garbage cans, Cloe notices the remnants of a homeless person's bedding. Someone else, not the victim, Cloe thinks.

The area filled with homeless who are living in the alleys and, at night or even day, on stoops of corporate or government buildings. They have their dogs with them as Cloe strolls Van Ness, four-lane lines of cars streaming, and turns off of Van Ness into the alleys.

A gel-spike-red-hair-cut showing small mother-of-pearl ears, Cloe's mouth a soft smile speaks clearly and kindly. But no one recognizes the first boy, nor later, the other one.

Cloe had knelt there beside her corpse (of a homeless woman, once) while the priest, interviewed by the press, stated the episode would be forgotten immediately.

People will get over this in a couple of days, he'd said, as if he were dismissing sensationalism, they should get over it. Not give sensation or life attention.

So much for church, she stings inside a year ago.

Strolling now, she interviews homeless on Mission Street (the Hispanic neighborhoods of San Francisco). She asks first with one picture, then both. A boy darts away from her when she asks if he can identify the boys in the pictures. He sees the corpses in the photos and his face changes. Hey, she calls and runs after him but he disappears into a construction site.

Walking home passing by a fruit and flower stand on 16th and Valencia, Cloe forgets the day and is in only one moment in the evening. Then it's night black with lights.

The present is the same and so is different at once. In that there is war all the time.

Is everything being the same everything is different and is then romanticism one time—is that all the time? In that there is a war all the time.[1]

A man riding a bicycle as if on the open sea in that a wave traveling five hundred miles an hour is not visible in the other waves is in evening. He is barely visible. At the same time as he's swathed in evening, the hills carry him and the bicycle fast as the bicycle is in the other waves. Cars in the waves perched hanging at lights crawl or hang down on the hill.

---

1. Gertrude Stein's view of change had to do with composition. Our composing: separation and simultaneity of action and fate. "This then was the period that brings me to the period of the beginning of 1914... Romanticism is then when everything being alike everything is naturally simply different, and romanticism... Everything alike naturally everything was simply different and this is and was romanticism and this is and was war." —Gertrude Stein ("Composition as Explanation," page 527 in *Stein: Writings 1903-1932*, The Library of America, New York, 1998).

Around 5:00 Thursday evening, Jonah Winter is dumped in California Street in front of Grace Cathedral. The corpse is naked with cuts everywhere on him. Covered in blood and curled, he resembles a cocoon.

He's been flayed quiet. His clothes were found a few yards away. The patrol cars blocking traffic which is stalled everywhere in rush hour anyway standing cars panting, Grace walks from her own car to the scene and kneels examining his cocoon. (I had a dream of someone dying then after, wet capillary case.)

She examines the clothes and wallet.

Perhaps he's aware of the very slow wave now rather than the cars that are carried invisible in it. The moon races outside the slow wave. Until he's completely outside the wave there.

Officer Andrew Chen rings the bell outside. The doorman answers. Showing their police badges, Detective Grace Abe and Andrew pass the doorman (who's calling upstairs) and take the elevator to the level of Jonah Winter's apartment.

There is Dahlia Winter, jet black hair, the mouth blurred opening Where? in Grace's sentence. Grace says, Mrs. Winter, we regret, your husband is dead, California Street Why? he's been killed.

Grace had changed. Four years earlier a meeting of occurrences had precipitated, or suddenly there was a man who had been a marine dead who was in her. She would be running out, it would be him running. But she would never leave her body or her own mind when he was there. He'd been Special Forces, an assassin when he was alive; she hadn't known him but she would feel the presence of his activities, 'ghosts of actions she had done' which were apparently his, or hers. Though she hadn't acted (when he had killed someone, before entering her).

First addicted to Ibogaine, a drug used by Indian hunters, causing illness of vomiting followed by elation and an utter lucidity in hunting, she'd spiraled with the marine being there erratically. Then addicted to a Peruvian drug derived from frogs, the secretion applied to burn marks on one's chest or arms. Cloe, Andrew, Jasper Frank were aware of her use of drugs. They were not aware of the marine who might suddenly begin and be there in her. She didn't tell them. Andrew murmured Don't Grace, finding her in her underslip burning her chest. She changed. The marine, who really was a particular unknown person, did not return.

Yet there were still flickers as if she'd known people before, whom she was now seeing. She stared at Dahlia speaking seated on the sofa in the old elegant Russian Hill apartment. Dahlia Winter rose her face splitting in a mask. Tears poured on a stretched face which appeared furious. She split apart then coldly.

She burst out but is always contained. After he'd died, one is walking across a field of high grass that is white in the sunlight and is changing to orange-rust in the wind. A trail has been cut through the grass and one hears the sound of a motor far ahead through the swaying high grass, which moves in the wind. Powdery white fog is boiling on the top of the high grass ahead, a wall of grass that sways. Dahlia Winter had repressed in being a servant pretending to be that to blame and to corrode with attack so that a man with whom she was was soon silent cringing. An image of a wrathful deity with a larvae-like figure in its mouth, Dahlia held in her mouth the bleeding cocoon, burst capillaries threading it that's him—held in her mouth, her suffering because her life was closing (his was closed)—which had never dilated to be love or to do other than close malevolence in a recurring pattern. Hearing the sound of the motor as if he's grinding by the sound in the waving field ahead. That one is or will be there to grind. Being who grinds. On the cut trail the sound enlarges as one walks and is a tractor mowing, the powdery grind of white grass flying in the fog on the white high sheets of uncut field turning orange-rust in wind.

I was always having to be a servant in pictures as a child, Dahlia Winter explains to no one. I'd wait on him too. He worked all the time like a drone, she snaps.

Grace murmurs I think you should call a friend to stay tonight, perhaps to stay a few days, Mrs. Winter. Dahlia Winter rises, in the entrance hall makes a call murmuring. They hear her return in the icy silence, her face flexing repressed.

Mrs. Winter, where did your husband work? Inventions dot.com Inc. Were you aware of him being in trouble, of there being anyone people who would kill him? No. Had his mood changed, had he appeared disturbed? He was always silent. That hadn't changed. He worked constantly. Mrs. Winter, what kind of corporation is Inventions dot.com? Dahlia Winter stares stinging Grace. Pretending she Grace had no intellect, Grace thinks. The room is lined with bookcases, filled with books. In the pause Grace feels Andrew Chen stir calmly seated beside her. Information, Dahlia Winter says suddenly losing attention and wavering. We're sorry to have to ask you these questions now, Officer Andrew Chen interjects leaning forward kindly so that Dahlia Winter's shoulders relaxing slightly shake and tears rush from her eyes.

Grace wonders is she speaking of the marriage? as if his death were nothing, or she can't comprehend his death yet.

Grace crouching in the midst of California Street on the cocoon, a curled ball of webbed bleeding capillaries—is the first instant it occurs to her to wonder if the marine had been addicted. He'd first appeared in her dead in the caustic anger of someone who was Grace's friend then.

He'd transferred into her. In the same period, Grace became addicted to Ibogaine. Events appear entwined but occur separately. Sometimes the same event appears to occur again.

She had a dim 'memory,' always in the present only, of the marine's activities but these were separate from her own actions (she did not do his actions or any resemblance of his at the time the marine was in her, or before he was in her). And these were not dreams of something she *wanted* to do either. She had no impulse to do his actions hunting killing people (though she had no specific information about his life either) regardless of her job as a police detective. He was entirely separate troubled. Running, she would find herself weeping, but as him.

Excruciating physical pain finally dazes so the person is still in their flesh. One's still, while the flesh feels as if it is existing in the outside separated. The flesh does not seem to *be* that one, yet is theirs only and enhanced delirious.

The door to Dahlia's apartment opens. The friend apparently, the one she'd called. Who lets herself in. Mrs. Winter introduces her to Andrew, Mabel Jet. Mabel Jet without words, a shocked expression there already, warmly embraces Dahlia.

They leave her with Mabel Jet.

The white field of high grass now completely mown close to, in the sense of touching, evening—where silent it's utterly white-yellow evening, the air also becomes dark, one to grind there on the mown white will occur anyway. No space of time on the completely mown white grass at evening yet grinding of the person there/people there—in visibility—will occur though it's silent white mown.

> What is the relation of character to action? In "The Storyteller," for example, Walter Benjamin views fate as being character. So one's fate is not determined, is not outside oneself, because it is one's character.

But one's fate is tied to or alongside many people's characters simultaneously. This simultaneity occurs in the separation of the storyteller's speaking and the listening of those present.

Actions (physical motions) occur in between or amidst, or one's motions *are* character as fate at once?

One's movements in events and in time transpire separately, are not one's character—though *later* appear to be one's character. Is movement of being (physical motion even) something other than character or fate?

One's actions (motions in events) and character transpiring separately simultaneously, is the present-time repetition only?

DAHLIA'S IRIS

Dahlia's iris may have only action in it. Or the action in any present instant not visible (any sight is only a photograph of what *was* seen) may be only visible there after the action has passed (just as the light from dying stars is seen much later)—so an action isn't visible ever.

Dahlia appears to be separate, seated at lunch at Zuni's, dressed as if she is waiting for someone. She taps her fingers on the table at her place setting, a second place setting empty beside her.

Her apartment has an iris in a vase, but Cloe hasn't been there. Dahlia has not seen Cloe before.

Cloe has been following her, seats herself at a table nearby. The young officer muses Surely Dahlia has seen her (Cloe thinks, of seeing herself in third person through Dahlia's green iris). But there is no flicker in Dahlia's eyes, as if she's so abstracted that nothing passes in front of her, after her husband's death. Or did she see this blank way before? Cloe wonders, but she does not have the thought recur over and over the way Grace would.

Dōgen's sense of time and being is that present, past, and future are simultaneous; they occur at once separately and do not impede each other. A possible way of seeing this: a person who has died, is not 'dead' except when they are 'in death'—at other times, viewing their lifetime in space as also time, they are not 'in death.'

A book might be a simultaneous past, present, and future. To find out a relation that doesn't occur before, in the text.

Introduce motion and interior is in it. Only.

The order of the chapters of *Dahlia's Iris* is: to see character of people, character of an individual, at random, an invisible thin weight, prior to streams of events or a huge event—character of ordinary people, who have no impingement on those events in history—and see their weight/their relation to it. It's not a sense of seeing character as either good or bad but as if shining thin weight whose composition is grasped 'at once,' in one instant here.

To see the relation of character of people and the present instant, in every instant. That is, seeing character while (or as part of) continually staying on tracking every present instant. Even trying to track every instant changes an instant.

In the comic strip, one is separate—sight and reading are separate. Reading is unseen, is below or above and calm.

FROM EVERYDAY PSYCHOKILLERS: A HISTORY FOR GIRLS

BY LUCY CORIN (2004)

EDITOR'S NOTE: Lucy Corin's *Everyday Psychokillers: A History for Girls* is a novel composed of generic parodies—myths, histories, rumors, local legends, news reports—that present a troubling subject: the sadistic murder of young girls. The novel poses a question about why this brutality seems so pervasively sexualized, and it blocks all ready answers by foregrounding the reading experience of the novel itself. As I explained in my report to our editorial board, "*Everyday Psychokillers* frequently strikes a tone that seems generically incongruous with the narrated action, creating a surreal, dreamlike atmosphere. Most often this tone results from the juxtaposition of preposterous or comic everydayness with horrific brutality. The death of Rhonda, for which the narrator feels responsible because of her injured thumb, or the remarkable scene in which D (variously Donny, David, Dominick, Derek, Dennis) 'sympathizes' with CiCi because her assailant *wasn't* Ted Bundy, or the spectacle of Gwen meticulously pointing out the places on a road map where the parts of Adam Walsh were found, all seem generically unstable, resulting in an extraordinary tension." In a phrase, sadistic murder has become a genre, and nobody knows what to make of the fact that so many of us find it thrilling. If only literature were empty artifice! No other first book published by FC2 from 1999 through 2009 sold as rapidly.

—RMB

"I don't feel certain about very much for very long, and I think of being political as requiring a form of conviction that I really don't have. But stories can have conviction because writing and reading approximates (or dramatizes) stopping time. I can sustain a sense of conviction for the space of writing a story and within the conventions of fiction as a pursuit. Also, the kind of conviction it takes in real life to take action or tell people what they should do or think creeps me out and makes me feel very suspicious. Conviction is closely related to madness. In a way, all writing has to do to be political is call people (the culture/me) out on their (its/my) bull. So that's what I do. Then, in life, when I want to be political, I do stuff like volunteer, give things to people, and try to be helpful to people in pain, etc."

—Lucy Corin

CiCi arrived distant, grumpy, in a floaty sundress. It was close to seven and still light out and still hot. We went inside to greet her and she flung her bag onto the kitchen counter and said "Jesus, Ted, why don't you get a damn air conditioner?" We followed her to the balcony and squeezed together on the threshold of the open sliding glass door, holding our grins, waiting to make her day.

"Nice try," she said when she saw the chairs, and tipped one over with her foot. She was wearing her slim white tennis shoes and holding a pair of high-heeled sandals by their heels in one fist, the way you hold a bouquet of flowers, but in the way that holding a bouquet of flowers is like holding them by their necks. With her foot, she lifted the airy beach chair and kind of kicked it into the corner of the balcony where it clattered and then collapsed into a square heap. Then she sat on the other one with her knees together and her elbows on her knees and her fists to her temples. The strappy sandals seemed to come right out of her head like a trick dagger. Their straps flopped and dangled.

"I want take-out, Ted," she said. "I want greasy, ground-up chicken smushed into a patty and boiled in oil. No goddamn tomatoes. Extra mayo. Go. Fetch. And fries. And a shake."

Ted mussed the top of her head. I think it was one of his favorite things, when CiCi played baby. He said nothing and went off happily, jangling his keys.

Now here's one thing I knew about CiCi since I first met CiCi, which was right when she started going out with Ted, which was right around when I turned twelve, which was over a year before this time with this guy in Miami. Ted told me this thing, or CiCi told me, or they told me together, swapping off, my point being that it came up all the time, it was no secret and we all knew it had everything to do with whatever magical connection there was between those two. So what we all knew, the background information, if you want to call it that, was that a couple years before I met CiCi, before Ted met her even, back when she was living with her parents in Tallahassee and just starting high school, one day CiCi was finished taking a tennis lesson and sitting on the curb in the parking lot by the courts, zipping her racket back into its case, waiting for her mother to pick her up. The sun was pretty low, a really dense rosy sun coming at everything sideways, and CiCi sat there on one of the parking spot dividers redoing her ponytail. She pulled the rubber band out, shook her hair out over her head, and then, with the band clutched in her teeth, she closed her eyes for a second and flipped it back and ran her hands over it to put it back into its ponytail. She opened her eyes and in that moment a man appeared before her, a looming shadow in front of the sun, and she squinted up at him with her hands holding her hair and the rubber band still in her teeth.

She was so tired from school all day and then the lesson. She was pretty dizzy in fact, and as her eyes worked on adjusting, trying to see him against the sun, her head was tilted, because the man was standing not directly in front of her but to the side a little. The world was a little tilted, and she could see the man, in a glowing silhouette, with the sun making stratified rainbow bursts over his shoulder. The sun made sparks fly from the bits of glass and shell ground up in the blacktop everywhere except where the man's shadow fell. So the shadow was dull and flat, and everything shimmered around it.

And remember her angle, which made the man himself so hard to see. The silhouette and the shadow he cast, it was hard to tell which was which. It was like seeing two shadows, bound at the feet and leaning away from one another. Like a moment before, he'd been one man, but he'd been sliced crosswise down the center, and as he was hinged at the feet, one of him fell one way and the other of him fell the other. She felt giddy and giggled briefly at her private image and how silly it was.

When she fixed her focus the man was smiling and pointing at his ankle.

"I'm such a klutz," he said. "I twisted it." He held a racket, but he wasn't sweating. She put her hand to her brow so she could see him better. She could see little glinting lights in his hair, but mostly he remained a shadow. She stood up, and then she could see him. He was really good-looking.

That's what she thought, and that's what she said to me: He had medium brown hair, but he'd been in the sun a lot and when the light hit it you could see reddish and golden strands.

Like her own hair, in fact, a worn sorrel shade, but his was hollow, without gloss.

He was kind of tall, she said. He had normal features, his eyes were cool-looking, he was good-looking is what she said.

The man's shadow loomed, and he said, "You're pretty good out there."

"I am not," CiCi said, smiling despite herself, and I could see the funny half-blushing look she'd make with her face, because it was true, she was lousy at tennis, but when he said it she thought for a second that maybe he was right, maybe she looked good out there. I knew the face I made when I felt like that, part embarrassed that anyone had noticed me, that I'd been unaware of being watched, part hopeful that maybe I was wrong, maybe I was good.

He said he had an old racket in his van, that it wasn't as good as the one he used, but it was a damn sight nicer than hers. He said he thought she had a lot of potential. That he'd like to give her the racket because a good racket made all the difference.

"I don't even like tennis that much," she said.

"Oh, you should," said the man. "It's not right to waste your gifts."

She walked with him across the parking lot to where his van was, carrying her racket and her duffel bag, and he limped at her side, carrying his. He opened the sliding door and put his duffel bag on the van floor. He was standing to her side and a little behind her, and his hand touched the small of her back as he leaned past her to put his tennis racket on top of the duffel bag. "I'm sorry," he said, sounding truly sad.

"I'm such an idiot. That other racket's at the pro shop. I'm having it strung."

"Well that's okay," CiCi said.

The man said his name was Mark, and he offered her a ride home if she needed one. CiCi was mad at her mother anyway, so she said yes, she actually did need a ride. They drove off. They chatted. Then after a couple miles Mark started to sound stuttery. Suddenly he pulled onto the shoulder and stopped the van with such force that it rocked. He leaned across her and opened her door. "Get the fuck out of my car," he said, and shoved her. And he left her there on the side of the road.

CiCi stood, empty-handed, on the shoulder of the road, and then she walked. By the time she got home, her father was out driving around looking for her and her mother was standing by the telephone, unraveling the fringe on a dishtowel, frantic. She'd called the police. "I want to strangle you!" she said, hugging CiCi. She said the police were out looking for her, that they'd relayed her description to patrolmen all over town.

But I don't know, maybe the police said they had to wait forty-eight hours, that's what I hear they have to say.

But CiCi said her mother said the police had her description, so maybe CiCi's mother lied. Or maybe the police lied to CiCi's mother.

Either way, she clutched at CiCi and wept, and then she held CiCi at arm's length and yelled and said, "Where on God's green earth have you been? The police are out using their resources right now!" So CiCi told her mother a strange man had tricked her into his van. She said he took her duffel bag and her tennis racket and then he left her on the side of the road, and as soon as CiCi's father came home, they all got into the car and drove down to the station and made out a report.

Two days later, five sorority sisters at the Chi Omega House at the State University were variously raped, beaten, killed, mutilated, and a couple weeks after that, twelve-year-old Kimberly Leach was abducted in Lake City, and eight days after that, Ted Bundy (who'd abandoned the white van he'd been using) was pulled over (in what turned out to be his second Volkswagen Bug, an orange one this time; the first one, some less interesting color, he'd used all through what you call his "string" of killings in Washington, Colorado, and Salt Lake City) and arrested.

A few days after that CiCi was called in and interviewed about Mark and his tennis rackets, his ankle, and his van. They interviewed her for hours, she said. She said at times there were eight to ten people in the room taking notes. She said there was a one-way mirror in the room and that at one point a lady psychiatrist came in and asked her about whether "this Mark" touched her here or there, and she just knew tons of people were behind the glass, watching. She did the lady psychiatrist's voice in a sort of fake-British accent, in a kind of tea-party voice. "Well my dea-h Beatrice," that sort of thing. She pretended to be the British psychiatrist and pointed at my chest the way a schoolmarm might point at a blackboard or a disgusting lump of mud on the floor.

"Did he touch you hea-h?" she said, and then pointed to my crotch, "Or did he touch you *hea-h*," as if that then must be the case.

They tape-recorded her, and there was a stenographer on a little chair in the corner the whole time. After the interview, the police called her parents' house once or twice, to ask one more question or to confirm one more detail (So how sure are you about the color of that van? Anything, for instance, that struck you as *suspicious*? So again, please name the *items* you remember seeing in the back of that van. You say he hurt his *ankle*. Did it seem to you that he *had* hurt his ankle? You say it was *stratified* sunbursts?), but then she didn't hear from them any more. They just stopped calling.

She figured for sure they'd need her to testify in Miami, where the trial took place. In her diary she wrote out what her testimony would be. She wrote out all the possible ways she could be cross-examined and wrote out her responses to every one. And right about that time—way before I met CiCi, when I was states and states away, complaining to my teacher at recess that retarded John Crumb was sitting in the outfield with the dandelions, hunched over his foot, licking the heel of his sock, and he wouldn't come in, even though I told him it was time to line up—right about that time, when the trial started and CiCi had not been called to testify, CiCi flung herself on the morning paper, reading it and wringing it, weeping in the breakfast nook, and CiCi's mother said, "Thank God it's all over. No more Ted Bundy." She told CiCi under no circumstances was she to watch the trial coverage on television, but CiCi went to friends' houses or to Dillard's at the mall even, and watched there. "It's true he's good-looking," she told her friends, "but in real life, he's not as good-looking as everyone says."

She read about him, she watched him, she imagined him, she remembered him. She felt a pull of greatness. She felt she was on the edge of being unearthed, she felt the possibility of going down in history.

One time CiCi showed me in the paper how they were getting ready to make a TV movie about Ted Bundy, about who might get to play the leading man, the Matinee Idol Murderer, the High I.Q. Killer, the Stranger Next Door, the Promising Republican, the Murderous Prince Charming.

"How do you think you got away?" I asked her.

"I dunno," she said. "I guess he didn't like me."

On Ted's balcony, the air remained stiff and so filled with liquid it took effort to breathe. CiCi leaned back in the beach chair. She let the strappy sandals drop to the floor and folded her hands in her lap. She closed her eyes. I looked at the new polish on my toes. It looked dumb. Then I watched her face for a little while, knowing exactly what it's like to sit like that in the dusk, to feel like you've disappeared, like you might as well be anywhere. I could see how tired she was. Her complexion was off a little. A little pale, a little puffy, a little uneven in color. Like she'd been sailing all day. Like she'd come home from that much wind and then washed her face over and over. She looked like she could be sleeping; her face held that extremely peaceful expression that's as close as it gets to no expression at all. Then as I watched, although I swear it didn't change a bit, I could see sadness in there, and pensiveness, and a kind of fear, too. I mean look at a doll's face sometime. It's all there.

"CiCi," I said, when watching her overwhelmed me. "Will you tell me what happened with the guy in Miami?" And she did.

Heat shone and coated the highway, its pavement, its tin guardrails, its heaving trucks and darting cars. On the bus, CiCi changed from her sneakers into her heels and put the sneakers in a big canvas bag. At the bus station she put her wallet and her lipstick into a white leather purse the size of a grapefruit, locked the canvas bag in a locker, and slipped the key to the locker into her bra. But you could see the key poking at the material, so she took it out and put it in the purse.

Outside, she worked her legs hard to keep her stride long in the shoes and among the people. The city towers felt bottom-heavy, with people on their lunch breaks spinning in and out of lobbies on revolving doors. Higher up, the windows were like closed eyes, and it was hard to imagine anyone in there. The thin upper stories seemed hollow, like metallic husks, and it looked both bright and silent up there. A flock of small birds, the kind of birds you might find anywhere in the world, one version or another, a flock of plain little birds, zoomed in unison in front of one mirrored tower and then behind the next, silvery, each blinking, wings in, wings out, like mirrors turned toward you and then sideways, flashing, full-on bright and then invisible, fast. Dazzling. A shifting shining cloud. They could have been white birds, or they could have been dark birds. It was impossible to tell, each was so alternately shiny and invisible. As a mass they twinkled in the hot sky. When CiCi looked up the flock was there, like the crowd of sparkles that the tips of shallow waves make in a lake. They were like nerve endings, like a cross-sectioned antiseptic limb, the electrode nerve endings pulsing, tongues licking air for what seemed like ages, and within a second the flock was gone behind a wall of pink marble. Her purse bounced at her hip as she walked, so she put her hand on it. The strap crossed between her breasts. Her skirt fluttered at her knees, and her stomach fluttered in her skirt.

As soon as she entered the café the guy spotted her and he gestured to her as he rose from his seat by the window. She'd actually noticed him on her way into the restaurant. She'd seen him in the window as she walked past it to get to the door, and she actually thought it'd be too good to be true if this was the guy, because he was so sharp looking, with a linen jacket and a silk shirt and one gold chain you could just see where his collar opened. He pulled her chair out for her as she approached and touched her arm to guide her into it. CiCi lifted her purse strap over her head. It took her several tries to get the strap to stay on the rounded back of the tippy chair.

The guy introduced himself. His name was Dean, or Daniel, or Dylan, I don't remember. As he was talking, saying, "Wow, CiCi, I'm glad you made it, I'm so glad you agreed," he took a mini tape recorder from his briefcase and showed it to her with his eyebrows raised, acknowledging to her that he was turning it on, that she could object if she wanted, everything out in the open, on the record, super-professional, all via eye contact, like he did it every day and like she did too. He placed the mini recorder on the café table next to the vase with its one ruffled flower. He said he was so glad they'd be working together, and then he gestured to the menu and said, "Anything you want."

When the waiter came, he ordered her a glass of white wine without even asking.

The vase on the café table was white, and the shape of an egret, of a lean bowling pin. It had a thin blue ribbon around its neck, a decorative noose. The waiters scurried around in black-and-white and the whole room hummed with its mirrors and flamingo pink and aqua everything.

Then she told him. She told him exactly what it was like to be in a van with Bundy, she told him just as she'd written in her journal she'd tell it. How his hair sparkled. How he touched the small of her back. How he held her hand to help her balance as she stepped into the van like it was a gleaming white carriage. Yes, she said, his eyes devastated her. Yes, he seemed truly wounded when he remembered the racket was in the shop. His hands quivered on the steering wheel as he listened to her tell him what she was studying in school. His face turned to something ravaged and rageful when he shoved her from the van. Yes, she was frightened. Like there was a beast inside him, she said. Like Jekyll and Hyde.

The guy shook his head, overwhelmed, it seemed, with sympathy. He was eating bowtie pasta with curled-up shrimps. "And you were just a child," he said.

"I know," said CiCi. "I was pretty naïve. But you have to remember, Romeo and Juliet were thirteen, right?" A busboy came by and filled their water glasses. CiCi watched the ice cubes rock to the lip of her glass, ready for water to spill, but water didn't spill and the cubes rocked back into place.

"Funny thing, though," the guy said. Donny, David, Dominick, whichever it was. "As I'm remembering from my notes it was, what, the twelfth? For your incident? Thursday, right? I mean, look at the dates here," he said, pulling a small spiral notebook out of his briefcase.

"Yeah," she said, not quite getting it.

"Well, it doesn't make sense," he said. "Because, I mean, he didn't get that van until right before he left. So, if he had the van, you know, that'd mean he'd have to be over in Lake City killing Kimberly Leach. Look," he said and handed her the notebook. She held it in the palm of her hand. He'd drawn a little map in blue ink, showing Tallahassee and the Chi Omega Sorority House and Lake City and the Holiday Inn where they'd come up with a receipt. He'd made little x-marks-the-spot marks in red ink, and put the dates next to each x in purple ink. "Because see that was a Saturday, with Kimberly," he said, pointing with his fork. CiCi looked at the notebook in her hand and it looked like the map of that day: the tennis court, the parking lot, the stretch of road through the newly constructed stretch of strip malls, the anonymous shoulder where he pulled over, her parents' house, the police station. Change the names and it could be a map of anything.

In the air conditioning, she suddenly felt cold in her sundress and her face got hot. When she looked at him, she couldn't help it, her eyes, as they say, swam with tears. Once, when she was a little kid, she'd rescued a baby rabbit from her cat and held it in the palm of her hand, where it crouched, in shock. She held it, trying to figure out what to do, in wonder at its fur, at its eyes, its immaculate feet. She bent her knees and crouched there, in her backyard, watching the exquisite animal breathe, so caught with it that when the creature stopped breathing it was the first she'd noticed time passing since she'd flung the cat away. In the café, she held the notebook like that, and when she let herself realize what it meant, that it had never been Bundy in the van at all, that it'd been just some guy, any old guy, and that suddenly she couldn't remember what the man at the tennis courts looked like at all, he was nothing but a shadow in the sun, in that moment it was like the notebook died, and she reached her hand across the tippy table, palm up, holding it out for Derek, or Dennis, whatever his name was, to take.

At that point, CiCi told me, well at that point she's just letting it be obvious how upset she is and the guy really slimes up to her. So that's a little better, in a way, she said, to have him be all comforting and sympathetic, especially out there in public where everyone in the restaurant knows how good-looking he is, and they don't have to know he's a fucking slime. But then he does something scary. He says he'll take her by the bus station to pick up her stuff and then take her home, but first he takes her to a hotel. It's a fancy hotel, and he takes her there in his amazing little red convertible, which she'd actually walked by on her way to the café and thought what a cute car it was. But in the room, he gets obsessed with making her come. He says it's *criminal*—no lie, CiCi said to me, his exact words, it's *criminal*, he says—that she doesn't orgasm and then it's all fucking afternoon, he's doing this, and he's trying that, and she tries faking it twice, but he catches her and says, "Relax, relax, baby, it's no hurry," and then a little while later he says, "Give it to me," which she heard about guys saying but never thought they actually said. She says finally she thought she maybe did come, but she was so mad she didn't change her face at all and pretended she didn't, and finally he gave up and said she shouldn't worry, with some girls it took them years to learn how to get turned on, but at least she knew now it took a real man to be patient with her and she should expect no less ever again. No lie, she said. He said *real man*.

After the hotel, she's drained, and raw in every way. Her eyes hurt. In his red convertible she can feel the air on her eyeballs. The sun is getting low in the sky and it creeps her out. She makes him stop at the bus station, and she takes the key from her little white purse and unlocks her stuff and it looks damp and sort of rubbed-out. She puts her purse in the canvas bag and looks at it lying on the bottom of the bag, with her tennis shoes. It's a cheap thing, with cheap gold-tone-plated clips that attach the strap to the body.

He drives her all the way back from Miami. "No way you're taking a bus, babe, not on my watch." He shows her how there's cocaine in a little tube in the glove compartment. At a stoplight, he taps a tiny amount into his palm, licks his finger, dabs his finger in it, and puts his finger in her mouth to rub it on her gums, above her front teeth. He licks his palm and says, "See how it gets all numb? You like it?" When they pull into Ted's apartment complex, CiCi is ready to jump out without saying another word to him. She's careful, of course, to have the guy pull up to this one side of the building, the side without the balconies, but she still feels like she can imagine Ted watching them pull up. The guy stops the car, but then he takes hold of her elbow. He says, "One more thing, CiCi. Really. Look at me." He takes the mini cassette recorder from the pocket of his linen blazer. He pushes the rewind button with his thumb, and then he pushes play. CiCi listens. At first she can hear only the hushing mechanical sound of the cassette tape moving. Then she can hear herself breathing. She can hear her own noises. "Give it to me," says the man on the tape. She breathes and breathes, and sometimes she makes little vocal breaths. For a while she sounds like herself, but then she starts sounding like anyone. She sounds like any animal. The closer she listens the less she is listening to herself.

"Now don't be mad," the guy says. "I'm showing you this for a reason."

"Let go of my elbow," CiCi says.

"Now listen to me," he says, leaning, and lets his hand slide down her arm to her wrist, which he holds. "Listen to how you sound. Listen. And don't you tell me you weren't in heaven, girl." She listens to the sounds on the recorder and they might not even be the sounds of anything alive anymore. They're the sounds of a river in wind. They're the sounds of a door, opening and not-quite-closing on bent hinges.

So then she gets out of the little red convertible and climbs the stairs past seven identical doors to seven apartments. She imagines maybe lying on a couch and watching TV, thinking that might be what she can imagine herself doing, but then she remembers they have no couch and the TV is so crappy you have to lie right next to it so you can adjust it every second. As soon as she steps inside the apartment everything looks incredibly dingy. She thinks about what it was like watching Bundy at his trial, smooth in his suit, passionately defending himself, wild with fiery intelligence and demonic arrogance. When she sees him through the glass doors to the balcony, and he rises and strides inside to greet her, her Ted looks dim. The limp curls in his hair, the blurry charcoal color. In a comic, black hair looks dense and sharp blue-black, with windows drawn on to show you how shiny it is. Ted's hair looks washed-out, like a comic left in the rain, and then dried out, and then left in the rain again. His square hands are like blocks of wood. When he leans in to kiss her hello, the pores on his nose look big. Mostly, his place is crappy. And then when he finally returns with her dinner and they spread it out on the balcony floor—because they have no table to go with the two chairs and there's three of them anyway, there's CiCi, Ted, and me—when they spread out the dinner, the lettuce is weak and frayed, exhausted in her sandwich. Her french fries are splayed on the flattened white bag that carried them. There's no sign of the potato they came from. They came from millions of potatoes. They're Humpty fucking Dumpty. But lots of Humpties, lots of Dumpties, tossed together, strewn and heaped.

You know how they say in the Old West how Indians didn't want their pictures taken because they thought it would steal their souls. Then there were all those famous photos of the chiefs who went to Washington and dressed up as themselves and had their portraits done in exchange for this and that trinket or reprieve for their tribe. This is history. CiCi said, don't they have those pictures in your history book at school? I said yes they did. Men who looked like beautiful women with skin the color of eggplant. "Well, it does," said CiCi, ignoring Ted, who kept trying to catch her eye. "It steals your soul."

FROM THE WAVERING KNIFE

BY BRIAN EVENSON (2004)

EDITOR'S NOTE: I had admired Brian Evenson's *Contagion* when it was first released, so when Jessica Treat introduced me to Brian at the 2002 AWP convention, I encouraged him to send FC2 his work. That following summer Brian sent the MS of *The Wavering Knife.* In my report to our editorial board, I noted how, because of its abstractness, Brian's fiction "flirts with allegorization but refuses to come into consistent alignment with any familiar structure of ideas." For me, this estrangement of interpretation, the separation of reading's form from its context and aim, foregrounds writing's irreducibility to meaning. I had come to believe that the late twentieth century abandonment of modernism, at least by mainstream literature, was implicated in the xenophobia that had brought Bush to power in 2000, and so I considered FC2's social mission to involve the sort of alieness that radically ambitious writing formerly revealed. In Brian's work, this unrepression usually exposes literature's materiality, its refusal of our human interests, a refusal that Brian's texts manifest in their extraneousness to the characters' obsessions. The abstract form of allegory, with its projection of a hidden key or secret code, tempts us in reading to replicate the action of the characters, imagining our real interests to lie beyond our grasp, while the words in their fixity dispel this aspiration. The result is that our own finitude becomes newly interesting. In my reading Brian's fiction consistently reorients attention in this way.

—RMB

"A good portion of my work is about destabilizing existing structures of all kinds, including patriarchal religious structures and the political structures that these imply (and which we're feeling particularly strongly and painfully these days). 'White Square' strikes me as a somewhat anarchic text, about a man (the detective) caught between a system that has very fixed rules and a man/killer with his own set of rules. The detective is trying to serve as a conduit between the two...but finds himself in a position increasingly compromised, a reasonable man being ground down between two different sorts of insistence."

—Brian Evenson

WHITE SQUARE

The black square on the table is meant to represent Gahern's estranged wife; it is presented as such at Gahern's request. The gray square beside it stands in for the black square's new husband, also presented as such at Gahern's request. Though Hauser has offered him the full gamut of shapes and colors, Gahern insists upon remaining unrepresented. Nothing stands in for him. When Hauser suggests to Gahern that the investigation might proceed more smoothly were a shape allowed to stand in for him as well, Gahern simply refuses to reply. *Perhaps a green rhombus?* suggests Hauser. Gahern asks to be returned to his cell.

The investigation, Hauser repeatedly reminds himself, is progressing poorly. Gahern will only speak when both the black square and the gray square are on the table before him. Even then he says little, if anything, of use. When questioned concerning the whereabouts of the gray and black squares, Gahern says nothing. He will not indicate whether these squares represent persons alive or dead. *These are meant to stand in for them, they are symbols*, is all he will indicate, gesturing to the squares. When Hauser hides the squares in his lap and asks Gahern where they have gone, Gahern only says, *They are in your lap.*

Such are the facts as Hauser has recorded them:

- Individuals represented by gray and black squares both disappeared, 12 October. Said individuals absent three months now.
- Said disappearance preceded by Gahern's own sudden disappearance, 17 August. When, 8 November, Gahern reappeared and returned to former workplace to request reinstatement, he cited his reason for being absent as *continued persecution by my estranged wife and her new husband.* Said persecution, he indicated to lathe foreman, had concluded, was not to be resumed.
- After Christmas, Gahern found to be living in black and gray squares' residence (Gahern's former residence before estrangement from black square), with both squares having disappeared. This last fact compelled Hauser, at Commissioner Torver's request, to open an investigation.

The additional information Hauser has amassed through interrogating Gahern is marginal at best. Hauser's investigation, Gahern insists, is a form of persecution somehow perpetrated by black and gray squares from a distance—their persecution of him has unexpectedly resumed. He is certain they will never leave him alone. He fled to escape them, came back only when he had taken steps to assure his escape. Now, he can see, he escaped nothing.

"What steps did you take to assure an escape?" asks Hauser.

"It is of the utmost importance," claims Gahern, "that I be provided a new identity and be allowed to leave the city immediately."

"Of course," says Hauser. "We will assign you a new identity: Rhombus, Green. Just answer a few questions first."

In Gahern's private world, Hauser thinks as he sits in stocking feet, a cup of hot water before him, *there is only one shape. Square.* There are, however, two colors. Or rather two shades—gray and black. Each of which admittedly might be described as a lightening or darkening of the other.

Through the window, through square panes of glass, he can see down into the central courtyard. The courtyard consists of eight rectangular slabs of concrete, of a slightly lighter gray than the gray square meant to represent the new husband. Beyond, he can see the even façade of the North wing of Branner B. Hauser's office is in the South wing of Branner B, a building designed by one Edouard Branner if a plaque on one marble corner of the building is to be believed. In his travels about the city, from crime scene to crime scene, Hauser keeps an eye open for Branner A, the precursor of Branner B. He has never seen it. Perhaps Branner A was torn down to make way for another building, perhaps even for Branner B. Whatever the crime that presents itself to him, Hauser's first question is always the name of the residence or residences attached to the crime.

Yet this crime is different. There is no crime scene to visit. He cannot ask his habitual question. Instead, it is just he and Gahern, in a narrow room, a table between. Only words. Or as now, just he himself, in his office, alone. Only thoughts.

One shape, he thinks. *Two shades.*

Why is it that Gahern will not take a shape and color to represent himself?

Can I force him to accept a shape and color?

Was it prudent, wonders Hauser, *to have allowed this game of squares and shades to commence?*

"Shall we try again, Mr. Gahern?" asks Hauser. "Where were you during the month of October?"

"Fleeing the persecution of the following," says Gahern, and reaches out to finger first the black squares, then the gray square.

"Of what did said persecution consist?"

"They constantly disturbed me," says Gahern. "They appropriated my residence, interrupted my sleep, impeded me on my path to work, insulted me, interfered with my operations on the lathe in my place of employ—"

"—Yet, Mr. Gahern, curiously enough, I have a sheet of paper before me which claims that the reverse of what you say is true. On seven separate occasions complaints were filed against you by your ex-wife and her new husband, the last culminating in a restraining order."

"This too is part and parcel of their persecution of me."

"Where are they, Mr. Gahern? What have you done with them?"

"These are meant to stand in for them," says Gahern, gesturing to the squares.

"I'm afraid that doesn't answer my question," says Hauser.

Gahern folds his arms, tightens his lips.

Hauser receives a telephone call. It is Commissioner Torver. *How is the investigation?* Torver wants to know.

"It seems to have become a sort of geometry problem," says Hauser.

"Yes," says Torver, "so I hear. Or a child's game. Do you think it wise, Hauser? Shall I step in so we can have a word?"

Hauser assents and recradles the headpiece, awaits Torver's arrival. As he waits, he looks at the square panes of glass in the window. *Surely*, he thinks, *I will be reprimanded.*

He realigns the already aligned piles of paper on his desk, picks up the gray and black squares. *If Torver were a square*, he is starting to wonder as Torver enters, *what color square would he be?*

Yet, he suspects in looking at the man's face, in watching his lips move, that a square would not be the proper shape for Torver.

Hauser has two days and then the investigation will be taken from him, Torver seems to be saying. The gist of his words comes to Hauser as if from a distance. *Like Gahern*, thinks Hauser, fingering the squares, *I myself prefer to remain unrepresented.* Apparently Hauser's methods are most unorthodox, but Torver is willing to let him extend said unorthodox methods for a short period. Hauser must not let him down. *Perhaps a rectangle*, Hauser thinks of Torver, but soon discards this in favor of a simple oval. By the time he has settled on a dirty white for the color, the simple oval has finished its admonishments and is just going, leaving Hauser alone to wonder what the Commissioner's shape and shade signify.

Perhaps, thinks Hauser, *I could produce a series of squares moving in almost indiscernible increments from black to gray and substitute them in consecutively for each square on the table.* After a number of careful substitutions, the black square would wither to gray and the gray square would have ripened to black. Gahern might realize something was happening, but perhaps would not understand what. Suddenly he would perceive that the square he thought gray was black and the square he thought black, gray.

And what, Hauser wonders, regarding his reflection in a pane of glass, *would be the point of that?*

Anything could happen, one of them suggests, either him or his reflection, perhaps both.

But nothing significant ever does.

Something could.

You have two days. You haven't time to experiment.

Perhaps, one of them thinks, *both squares could be gradually changed until they are nothing but two pieces of slick white cardstock, squares of light shining up from the tabletop.*

He closes his notebook, turns each square face down. Time has passed. He has learned nothing. Gahern is still there, just on the other side of the table. Unrepresented, still himself. *I, too*, Hauser insists, *remain unrepresented.* He holds his hand before his face, assures himself it is still a hand.

He watches the hand remove a cigarette from a pack, extend it toward Gahern.

Cigarette? he hears his mouth offer. He knows that the voice he hears in his head sounds different to him than it must sound to Gahern, listening outside the head that speaks. Who is to say who hears the voice correctly?

Gahern takes the cigarette, tucks it into his breast pocket. "You look tired," he says.

"What do you know about Branner A?" asks Hauser.

"Who?"

"Not who," says Hauser. "What. And A, not B."

"I don't know anything," says Gahern. "I don't even know what you're talking about."

"Look," says Hauser. "Let's forget everything. I don't care what you did with the squares. I'm willing to forget all that. Just tell me where to find Branner A."

Gahern does not answer. Instead he regards his fingernails. To Hauser, from the other side of the table, the fingernails appear to be normal. There is no reason that he can see for anyone to be looking at them. Yet he cannot stop looking.

Hauser's time all but gone, his methods failed, he has let Torver down or is about to. *A final effort*, his reflection tells him, *gird yourself.*

He brings in a piece of paper, blank, places it on the table between the black and gray squares. He sits across the table from Gahern, watching him.

He lets nearly an hour slip by without speaking. He looks at Gahern's face, trying to will it into a simpler shape.

He takes a pencil from his pocket, draws a short line on the paper. Carefully he tears up first the gray square and then the black square.

"Care to add anything?" asks Hauser.

"You're guessing," says Gahern.

"Am I?" asks Hauser, and standing up leaves Gahern alone in the room. He leaves behind the scraps of squares, the pencil, the paper.

Outside, he takes a place looking through the mirrored wall. Next to him are four people whom he chooses to represent in the following fashion: oval, triangle, rhombus, triangle. Through the mirrored wall, he watches Gahern sit at the table, head in his hands. He seems, for once, shaken. Hauser goes to fetch a cup of hot water; when he comes back, nothing has changed.

"Now what?" asks one of the shapes beside him.

Oval. Red, Hauser thinks, *perhaps orange.* Hauser holds one hand before his face to assure himself it is still a hand, then shrugs. "Wait," he says. "Nothing to do but wait."

He watches through the glass. Having sipped away his water, he goes in search of another cup.

When he comes back he finds Gahern has pulled his chair

about to bring his back to the mirrored wall. He has taken up the pencil, is hunched over the paper, his arm moving furiously. Hauser wishes he could see Gahern's face.

Gahern remains hunched over for some time. At last he puts down the pencil, brings both hands together before his body to do something with the paper. Hauser finishes his water, but does not go back for more.

When finished, Gahern pulls his chair back to its usual place at the table. He has folded the sheet of paper into a white box, a simple cube. The pieces of the squares are nowhere to be seen.

Something has happened, thinks Hauser. *Something always does.*

But what?

Once Gahern has been returned to his cell, Hauser enters, sits alone with the box. He examines it, draws a picture of it in his notebook. It is the sort of box that children make, and having made them himself as a child, he knows which seam he must unfold first. He knows what to do.

He turns the seam and the box cracks open. Inside are the scraps of the black and gray squares. Dumping them out onto the tabletop, he forms a little heap. He unfolds the next seam, then the next, until the box lies flat on the table, nothing but a creased piece of paper.

There is nothing written on the paper. Indeed, all that remains of Hauser's original mark is a thinness in the paper where Gahern has fastidiously rubbed said mark away.

An hour later, Hauser is still staring at the blank sheet of paper, at the pile of scraps. Perhaps it is a denial, perhaps a confession, but in either case, he is no closer to understanding anything. There is no point, he knows from past experience, in asking Gahern to explain further.

He looks at his watch. He begins to piece the squares back together, the black one representing, he can still bother himself to recall fleetingly, the wife, the gray one representing her new husband.

Soon the investigation will be taken from him. He will pass along the evidence—the fragments of squares, the folded sheet of paper—and then he will tender his resignation to a dirty white oval. Leaving Branner B for good, leaving the unrepresented Gahern, he will walk into the street and lose himself in the crowd among shapes of all kinds. Until then, there is nothing to do but wait.

FROM BORGES' TRAVEL, HEMINGWAY'S GARAGE

BY MARK AXELROD (2004)

EDITOR'S NOTE: What initially interested me about Mark Axelrod's *Borges' Travel, Hemingway's Garage* was its faithful documentation of reality's contamination by literature. This is an old topos, but in *Borges' Travel* the contamination seemed unusually material, having little to do with fictions. The places and objects shown in the accompanying photographs had all been found, not invented, and they remained locatable in the quotidian world that I and other readers inhabited. They were, after all, garages, toothpaste, flowershops, etc. In fact, reality's contamination appeared more historical than imaginary. Mark's prose merely elaborated the associations that those of us familiar with the history of Western literature would in most cases have already made. What had given rise to the contamination was the simple accident of naming, a random and contextless event. The names surrounded each business or product with an aura that the facts of commodification rendered preposterous, but confronted with this irresolvable conflict, neither material reality nor literature would give way. The result is, I think, equal parts funny and astonishing. I should also say that *Borges' Travel* is one of several recent FC2 works in which visual images have an especially interesting relation to text. The photos in Mark's book are neither illustrative nor decorative. They are intrinsic. Without them, there's no story.

—RMB

"Much of my work is politically incorrect, written in a blackly humoristic way. It often deals with...the plight of the artist in a society that is bent on subjugating creative impulses in lieu of the reign of superficiality."

—Mark Axelrod

SÖDERBERG'S FLORISTS
MINNEAPOLIS

It is widely accepted that the famous Swedish writer Hjalmar Söderberg was greatly influenced in his shorter writings by both de Maupassant and Anatole France, but his genius lay in his tiny masterpiece, *Dr. Glas* (1905), a small work which raises the moral question: Is it right to take the life of a useless or dangerous human being? The lonely physician in the story becomes a murderer in order to free a young woman from her husband, an unsympathetic clergyman; however, the wife is abandoned by her new lover and in the midst of the horror a sharp, ironic light is cast upon the doctor and his attempt to remedy the arbitrariness of life. This arbitrariness was to haunt Söderberg throughout his own life and it wasn't until he gave up writing for the floral business that he could be at peace with it.

Though Söderberg loved Stockholm, the smell of the city and

the city life, its Bohemian cafés and his life as a *flâneur*, it was his growing marital difficulties that forced him to leave Stockholm for Copenhagen, where he lived a kind of self-imposed exile. Söderberg had a keen eye for the weaknesses of humankind and most of his works were marked by a mixture of laconic irony and a deep sense of the tragic. Curiously, most of his major work was written prior to the time he left Stockholm, and when he got to Denmark he began to write more spiritual and philosophical works, such as *Jesus Barabbas* (1928) and *Den förvandlade Messias* (*The Transformed Messiah*, 1932).

It was also at that time, in the early 1930s, that Söderberg wrote scathing articles which were highly critical of Fascist and Nazi thought and the regimes that professed them. But the ensuing horrors of the Nazi occupation tended to debilitate his senses and eventually led to a complete loss of interest in the meaning of writing. So what does a socially conscious writer do when weariness and emptiness weighs so heavily upon the senses? When the bleakness of the Scandinavian landscape is only intensified by the bleakness of the inhumanity of man? Flowers.

It was on an autumn day in 1933, shortly after *The Transformed Messiah* was published in Denmark, that Söderberg had a chance meeting with Hans Christian Andersen. Now the two of them had known each other through their respective works, but they had never actually met until they were invited to a party given by Axel Käpp, yet another writer who, like Söderberg, was a student of the Scandinavian *fin-de-siècle* school of humanistic pessimism. Käpp was a highly opinionated Jewish novelist famous for his ironic novels and scathing wit, who had lived in Denmark all his life and who was high on the Nazi "hit list" because he had written "disparaging remarks about the Führer's sexual preferences." Käpp had close ties with many German writers, including Alfred Döblin, and he knew exactly what Jewish horrors were transpiring in the minds of the Nazis as early as 1933. But it was Andersen who, upon hearing about Söderberg's depression, told him a story about a friend of his who, after opening a flower shop, had discovered it altered his life. "Nothing was quite the same after that," Andersen told Söderberg. "His entire world-view had changed. The role of nature in the universe, the role of man in nature, the role of God in man, were all resplendent ideas seen in the variegations of a leaf or in the petals of a flower." Söderberg didn't need much convincing and soon thereafter opened a flower shop in Frederiksberg Allé (presently the home of the internationally known film director, Henning Carlsen) and began the life of a florist.

Indeed, Andersen could not have been more right. Everything was progressing grandly for Söderberg until the Nazi invasion of Denmark and upon hearing of Käpp's execution by the Gestapo (a most violent and grotesque death), Söderberg could neither arrange sentences nor carnations and felt compelled to escape the continent. But to where? Then he recalled a meeting he once had with Knut Hamsun (long before Hamsun's own Nazi affiliations) about America, specifically the Midwest of America, and Minneapolis in particular. He recalled that Hamsun, though not very complimentary about Chicago, had gentle praise for Minneapolis and its natives as a place of "warm and compassionate people, as tolerant and progressive as their winters were long" (*Hamsun in America* 115).

With little reluctance (and with Andersen's financial assistance), Söderberg crammed all of his belongings into the backseat of his Saab and sailed from Copenhagen to New York, from where he drove to Minneapolis where, without the threat of Nazi persecution, he opened a new flower shop on Lake Street just across the river from St. Paul. It's a flower shop that specializes in the Butterfly Pea, an homage to his friend Axel Käpp. The flower shop thrives to this day.

BORGES' TRAVEL

TUSTIN

One only needs to read such magnificent short stories as "Tlön Uqbar, Orbis Tertius" or "Death and the Compass" or even "The Utopia of a Tired Man" to realize that Borges would eventually expand those artistic interests in travel into something less metaphysical and more lucrative. That's clear from a 1973 chat Borges had with fellow Argentine writer Julio Cortázar at the Café Tortoni in Buenos Aires. At that time, Borges reminded Cortázar, "Let us admit it. Selling short stories is not going to help our retirement. As for me, I have always been fascinated by travel, especially to exotic lands, and I can think of no better kind of vocation than to become a travel agent" (*The Tortoni Chats* 1973). Knowing of Cortázar's interest in music, especially jazz, Borges recommended that the younger writer look for a rock band which would make him some "retirement money." Cortázar heeded

Borges' advice and after writing the short story "The Axolotl," founded a pop group with a similar name. But it was soon after the Tortoni interview that Borges founded his travel agency in his old Buenos Aires neighborhood among "los calles" Guatemala & Serrano, Paraguay & Gurruchaga.

Originally he called the agency "Averroes' Search," but soon after changed it to Borges' Travel when too many people confused the name with a lost-and-found service. The business flourished and actually helped pay for a number of publications of Borges' short stories, including "The Garden of the Forking Paths" and "The Circular Ruins," both of which have travel components to their textual apparatus. Not long after the agency opened, the "travel bug" hit Borges badly and was responsible for his many labyrinthine journeys which took him into and out of "El Aleph" and, according to Dr. Brodie's Report, was responsible for many of his extraordinary tales. But it was on his first visit to Disneyland™ in 1966 (which, by the way, was the origin for the creatures in his *Book of Imaginary Beings*) that Borges decided to franchise the agency when he fell in love with the sleepy little village of Tustin, California. Though there were, at first, a number of problems to be ironed out by the store manager, Don Isidro Parodi, once those six problems were solved, the agency boomed.

According to the chronicles of Bustos Domecq, in keeping with Borges' passion for visiting foreign places, the agency eventually booked a plot for *el maestro* in La Recoleta Cemetery in Buenos Aires, but Borges, always a plot innovator, opted instead to be buried at the Cimetiere des Rois, in Geneva, Switzerland, because those who were to live among him were, he said, better travelers.

To this day, the original store remains in the sleepy village of Tustin, California, and in keeping with a kind of poetic solidarity, books all trips for all artists not only included in this collection, but in the sequel, *Balzac's Coffee, da Vinci's Motel.*

AXELROD'S TOYS
LA JOLLA

Doubtless it was out of both professional and economic frustration that after his 50th birthday (more or less the same birthday that suffused Von Aschenbach with the need to escape to Venice and Don Quixote to depart La Mancha) and with little to show for 30 years of literary effort, Axelrod decided to give up the literary life altogether and enter the toy business. Toys, of course, were a natural extension of the kind of work Axelrod had been engaged in for over three decades since most of his work was considered, by those who knew it best as "light, playful, and jocular," so the transition from writing fiction to peddling toys was perfect. Works like the feature novel *Bombay California*; the Castles Trilogy (*Cardboard Castles, Cloud Castles, Capital Castles*); the innovative *Neville Chamberlain's Chimera and Dante's Foil and Other Tales*; the uniquely postmodern *The Posthumous Memoirs of Blase Kubash*

and the memorable *Borges' Travel, Hemingway's Garage* (not to mention all the fiction that was yet unwritten, including *Balzac's Coffee, da Vinci's Motel*) all reflected the extraordinary playfulness of his work. Though the majority of the minority of literary critics who have even read Axelrod's work have all overlooked the political nature of it, that oversight was due to the fact that everyone ignored him anyway. However, if they did not ignore him, they would have concurred with Axelrod's former college English professor Melvin Plotinsky, who once called his work "witty" and his former comparative literature professor Claus Clüver, who once asked him, "Did you really write this stuff?"

In the now famous *Esquire*™ interview with Hunter Thompson, conducted at a tide pool in La Jolla, California, when asked about his decision to abandon writing fiction for selling toys, Axelrod, who, at the time, was walking a battery operated lobster on a pink leash, responded in a Nervalian way, "Toys don' t bark and they know the secrets of the sea. Besides," he continued, "unlike editors, agents, publishers, and most readers, toys are dependable and can be trusted to be there when you need them. More important, they do it without taking a commission. They may not have life as we understand it, but toys have heart."

Those familiar with his work know that it was not only ignored, but spurned, and that his fiction and graphic work were among the most imaginative in the late twentieth century. Asked by Thompson if he held any grudges, Axelrod replied, quoting Beckett when he was asked in the early '80s why he wasn't considered by *Passion* magazine as one of the top 100 authors living in Paris, "I forgive them."

Though Thompson claims he actually witnessed Axelrod walk into the ocean with the toy lobster, disappearing in the festered foam, witnesses claim to have seen him walking the same lobster on the streets of Santiago de Chile (actually in Providencia, specifically outside the Café Tavelli). Others have claimed they've seen him with Raymond Federman at La Coupole plagiarizing material for future unwritten texts, while still others claim he is actually living in Buenos Aires, having seen him imbibing Malebec at the Café Mahler and consorting with Argentine novelist Louis Valenzuela, under the alias Macedonio Fernandez, at the Café Tortoni. Regardless of where he is, or what he is now doing, the store itself remains in La Jolla, California, ironically on Girard Avenue, the street where he was born in Philadelphia, which is nestled between the pathos of the Pacific and the pines and the peripatetic breezes that render fiction writers innocuous.

FROM A HISTORY OF THE IMAGINATION

BY NORMAN LOCK (2004)

EDITOR'S NOTE: I found Norman Lock's *A History of the Imagination* in the FC2 "slush pile" in October of 2001 and recommended it to our editorial board. In my reader's report I characterized its subject as "the relation of cultural memory to the unconscious," saying that it literalized the mythic geography of early modernism. My phrase that now stands out is: "making Western provincialism and ethnocentrism into the precondition for recreating the world as image of desire." It strikes me as uncanny that in the immediate aftermath of the World Trade Center attack anyone could've written those words, but at the time many of us at FC2 were resisting the demand for representational immediacy that the memory of collapsing towers had made so intense. Attention to language, to form, had suddenly become suspect, almost decadent, and in such circumstances insisting on fiction's otherness felt like fighting for freedom. What I wanted to emphasize was the way Norman's fiction attracts readers, not like realism through the recognizability of its descriptions, but like dreams through its tantalizing elusiveness. The work's premise, that it explores modernism's imaginary before the colonial revolutions scandalized it, aligns its form with our subjectivity. "Is that what you want?" Wilbur Wright repeatedly asks the narrator, a question to which neither negative nor affirmative answers seem satisfying. Placing readers in the paradoxical position of 21st century Western artists and intellectuals, Norman's writing locates our very wish for expression, for a City of Radiant Objects, somewhere between nostalgia for lost innocence and a guilty desire for forbidden fruit.

—RMB

"My fiction can be said to be political insofar as it posits a world beyond politics or—say, rather, that it demonstrates the uses of power obliquely, in situations that only appear to have a tenuous relationship to the real. The flight from an unlovely present in tension with an involvement in the present—therein lies the necessary tension in my writing; there, too, lies the guilt that gnaws the conscience of this 'apolitical' writer."

—Norman Lock

THE CITY OF RADIANT OBJECTS

The first thing one sees on entering the City of Radiant Objects is a field of white beds. It is here that all the trajectories of the walkers converge: mysteriously as it came, the walking sickness leaves them, and they lie down and sleep for days. It is here also that the sleepers awake at last from the sleeping sickness. My God, they say, have I been asleep so long? They cast off the dreaming in which they have been mired, many for years—cast it off without interpretation, so great is their joy in the sudden clarity of the air.

In the City of Radiant Objects, things are free of the obligation to signify. It is this that makes them radiant. And it is for this I have been searching so long in Africa without knowing it.

"It began with a vision of an iron stairway," he said, fingering the silver plumb he wore around his neck. "It made a graceful S in the air above Alexandria where I was engaged in scholarly research at the great Library." To illustrate, he traced with a finger a graceful S in the air above the tiled esplanade.

I was giving praise to the Architect of the Radiant City beneath a perfectly formed plane tree. The reason I was giving him praise ought to be obvious. Isn't it? Well, consider who he was and may very well be yet. Standing in the Alexandrine gardens of the third century AD, he had imagined this place—imagined it, then caused it to be built here in equatorial Africa, with a single stroke of genius. What else if not genius for he used no tools. He created ideal forms out of nothing with not so much as a speck of dust left over to mark their making. Was he not worthy of my praise?

"I started with a spiral stair and ended with a sill on which many since have placed their elbows in rapt contemplation of perfection."

"Why here?" I asked. "Why not in some more temperate zone?"

"I wanted a place devoid of associations," he answered. "And one in which objects would cast no shadow."

He lifted his arm and the wide mandarin sleeve fell back, revealing a hand that cast no shadow under the vertical tropic rays.

"It's a property of the equatorial sun," he said. "Only shadowless objects can be radiant."

He looked down at my shoes, scuffed and dusty with the journey.

"You must keep them well polished," he said of them.

I walked through the City, inventorying its architectural features: Window.

Fluted column.

Architrave.

Proscenium arch.

Plinth.

Oriel.

Stone balustrade.

Golden dome.

"No," said the Architect, ripping the list to pieces. "This is not the way to experience objects."

He called for the movers.

"You must immerse yourself—not entertain them one at a time."

The movers arrived with numerous objects and piled them on top of me. Because the objects were light, they did not hurt me.

"It is the meanings people give things that make them heavy," the Architect said from outside the mound in which I lay buried. "Objects in themselves weigh nothing at all."

I rummaged in them a while.

"Do you see the radiance of the whole?" he asked.

"I see it," I replied.

I pillowed my head on a soft catafalque and rested.

"You know the phrase 'shades of meaning'?" he asked, pursuing his catechism.

"Yes," I said, stifling (I confess) a yawn.

"It is literally true. Shadows are meanings made visible. Radiant objects cast none. They are light."

I permitted several small objects to enter me for my spiritual well-being. While there was no pain, neither was there enlightenment.

"Chairs will float if one has never thought of sitting on them." Indeed, I had seen a dozen or so chairs high above the Museum of Exquisite Machines as I approached the City.

"A sea is vast, cold, and desolate; but it is only thinking that makes it so."

"Yes," I said. "There is a sea here with me now, and it is very pleasant, and so are the fish swimming in it."

"Do you fear drowning?" he asked, testing me.

"Not at all," I answered confidently, for I really didn't.

"Good," he said. "The sea in itself is not in the least frightening. It is only the idea of drowning that makes it so."

"Mozart is also here," I said.

"Of course," he answered. "His music has always been here."

We were sitting once more beneath the plane tree (not on a chair!). While it cast no shadow (how could it?), I had the sensation of shade. The movers had removed the objects. And while I had felt no discomfort beneath them, I was glad to be "out in the air" again, for it was the crystalline air of the City of Radiant Objects more than the objects themselves that amazed me.

"The air is like a—"

The Architect cut me short.

"We do not allow similes here," he said, "nor any figurative language, which distracts from the object, thereby dimming its radiance."

He blindfolded me and had me identify objects by touch or smell "to strengthen you in objectness." He bid me taste certain objects, cleansing my palate each time with sherbet. Many were delicious, others foul-tasting, depending on the material. The end of all these trials was an increased sensitivity to the true nature of things that remains with me even now.

"Why are there so few people here?" I asked, looking around me, as if for the first time.

"People cannot resist giving meaning to things," he said. "*I was sitting in that very chair when the wind arrived with the fragrance of frangipani from the South.* Or, *I was holding that tortoise comb when I thought of Rachel, whom I had once loved long ago.* Or, *I leaned against that column and recalled a picnic on the beach at Crete.* And for those people, for ever after, 'chair' and 'comb' and 'column' adumbrate qualities foreign to their nature as objects. Once that happens, radiance is at risk."

"And so you ask them to leave?"

"They leave without being told. We wake and find them gone. They understand."

"Cannot memory also make a thing radiant?" I asked.

I was thinking of Anna, whose face shone in my memory though she was now, like me, no longer young.

"Only falsely," he answered. "Memory is kind or cruel but seldom truthful."

"And desire?" I asked.

"Desire is a projection of one's need upon an object."

"And can there be love where there are no objects of desire?"

He turned and looked into the distance. What perfection he saw there I do not know.

We sat for a time in silence. I waited for the sun to set, but it did not.

FLIGHT

I fled the City of Radiant Objects and hurried into the waiting dark. The merciless logic of the Architect and his city, brilliant under a never-setting sun, had injured sensitive tissue so that I craved the bandages of shade and shadow. My head ached and my eyes stung. My mouth was bitter with the taste of disappointment. I had hoped to escape the weight and waste of matter, the endless variations on a theme of procreation. I had longed for the economy of the ark floating above a drowned world of useless diversity. But the purity of the City was intolerable, its idealism inhuman. I could not live without desire, love, and night—without the sweet disorder of Anna's hair.

"Hello," said Wilbur as I entered the clearing. "Would you like to ride in my new aeroplane?"

"Why yes," I said.

He was leaning against a juniper tree, eating a sandwich.

"Where is Orville?" I asked, for I understood they were inseparable.

"In Dayton," he answered, "looking after the shop. I came to Paris to drum up money for our machine. The night was so beautiful I thought I'd fly to Africa."

"They will wonder where you've gone," I said.

"Paris is asleep. All of France is asleep. Only Wilbur is awake."

He slept little, he said, because of his mind; it revolved constantly with diagrams and formulae. His mind, he said, gave him great pleasure. His mind, he said, wrought the most elegant science.

He sang a jaunty song, accompanying himself on the piano-wire braces of his aeroplane. In return, the jungle performed a delicate score for winds and nightingale.

Silence once more restored, we stood under the moon, smiling at one another. I was tempted to go off into the trees with him, but only for a moment.

I coughed instead, to break the spell.

"I flew through the night," he said. "I felt the land under me and then the ocean. The ocean was blacker than the land and lit here and there with the tiny lights of ships. And then Africa—its welcoming darkness. I landed my machine here among the thorns without a single tear to its paper wings. How do you explain that?"

I couldn't. Instead, I quoted Victor Hugo: "'The enigma in which being dissolves.'"

I admired aloud the various features of his aeroplane.

"The engine's a dream," he said. "I have only to close my eyes."

I began to cry for reasons I have never understood. Perhaps the softness of the night, the strangeness of the machine, the beauty of science and the moon.

The wild forest people came out from behind the trees and began to dance. My friend Pennington, whose throat had been cut by the porters, was with them. His face was white, but that may have been the effect of moonlight. Wilbur looked on benevolently. His oiled sandwich paper shone in the grass. How lovely everything was at that moment! The imaginary Haha bird sat on a pine bough just as it did on the Chinese scroll hanging in Quigley's tent. Where is Quigley? I wondered. And Carlson, Hanby, Stephens, and Captain Slade? What has happened to the journey upon which we embarked with full hearts so long ago?

I took off my clothes and joined the wild forest people in their dance.

"Is this what you want?" asked Wilbur, getting into his machine.

"I don't know!" I cried in an anguished voice.

He started his motor.

"That man is dead, you know," he called above the noise. "In a little while he will start to stink."

I tried to leave the dance, but the dancers had formed a charmed circle around me.

"Goodbye," said Wilbur.

"Take me with you!" I shouted. "To Paris. To America and to Anna in the Hamptons!"

But the aeroplane was gone—I won't say "vanished," although that is the impression with which I was left. I heard the roar of the motor, the humming of the wires, then silence. The wild forest people went back into the trees, carrying Pennington with them.

I dressed quickly and left for Mombasa.

A herd of zebras rushed through the streets of Mombasa. I stepped into an alley, so as not to be trampled. They did only minor damage to the streetlights and the steeple of the Episcopal church. The people of Mombasa leaned out of their windows and cheered them.

"Hooray!" they shouted.

"*Qua-ha-ha*!" barked the zebras.

A woman waved to me from a house across the street.

"Come and drink with me," she called.

I waited for the zebras to pass, then crossed the street to her house. She was French; I am an American. We drank bumpers of champagne in honor of democracy.

"I am Madame Tussaud," she said. "My husband went into the jungle to discover a new orchid and never returned. I am hungry for kisses."

I kissed her. Why should she go hungry?

We opened the curtains and encouraged the moonlight to fall on the bed. Particles of it got all over us as we rolled on top of the sheet. Outside in the Mombasa night, the zebras whinnied joyously.

Night, I said, is what I like best.

She told me her house: Sagittarius; in China, the Monkey.

I fell asleep and dreamt I was flying in Wilbur's machine.

"Is that what you want?" asked Wilbur.

He was standing at the open window. His teeth flashed, his eyes sparkled. Stardust and broken bits of moon clung to his hair.

"What a handsome man!" exclaimed Madame Tussaud from the depths of sleep. Her face was white, but that may have been the effect of moonlight.

"Is that what you want?" he repeated.

"I don't seem to be able to leave!" I cried again in anguish.

"How did you find me?"

"The zebras. Get dressed; we're flying to Dayton tonight. You'll work in the bicycle shop, tightening spokes. Anna can join you there."

I dressed and followed him out into the street. The wings of his machine trembled lightly in the wind. The wind strummed the wires.

Kassitura! I said to myself. How can I leave your magic harping?

Wilbur laid his hand on my arm. He spoke kindly: "We'll be there in no time. I've reshaped the propellers to a new equation. You have only to close your eyes."

We rolled down the street and jumped into the sky. The motor dreamed; the varnished propellers scarcely disturbed the sleeping town. The zebras drowsed under the mimosas. Madame Tussaud floated in the dark waters of sleep, and I was in flight from Africa.

Is this what I want? I asked myself.

I could not answer. For the second time that night I wept.

FROM THE BODY PARTS SHOP

BY LYNDA SCHOR (2005)

EDITOR'S NOTE: Lynda Schor is probably the only writer in America whose fiction has regularly appeared in both *Playboy* and *Ms.* That her writing could satisfy these contradictory audiences is a first hint of its interest. Like so many writers considered postmodern, Lynda creates fiction that's hard to situate morally or politically, often treating topics at the center of controversies while undermining the reified oppositions of so-called "public discourse." Such writing is a political act irreducible to a political position. In "Still the Top Banana" Lynda demonstrates a characteristic procedure of this activism by simultaneously demythologizing and remythologizing a pop culture ikon, Tarzan's companion Cheetah. The interest of such work is avoided by talk of postmodern irony or parody, for Lynda's writing dispels the aura surrounding animal celebrities, not by caricaturing it, but by literalizing it. The fiction of Cheetah's bourgeois domestic life brings to the surface a significance already there in the vapid enthusiasm of her bolded journalistic prose, a combination of nostalgia for lost innocence and compulsive destruction of it. That our Flickas and Flippers and Lassies could suffer the same identity confusions and economic anxieties as their audiences seems to us both monstrous and right, the preposterous yet literal meaning of their represented humanity. It's as though the two proses of Lynda's text, her celebrity mag reportage and its fictional elaboration, were the incompatible halves of our national culture and individual souls. In her work, when we meet our adversary, it's always us.

—RMB

"I consider my writing to be very political. Every story I write is about gender, class, or both, whether or not it's also about something else."

—Lynda Schor

STILL THE TOP BANANA

Cheetah, the chimp who starred in Tarzan movies back in the 1930s, is still hanging around. The beloved animal actor turns 63 in April, making him the oldest chimp in captivity.

Cheetah sits in his cage drinking a Bud from the can. His girlfriend Suzy, much younger than he, lopes over and begins chattering and nattering at him for drinking beer at his age. Frankly, he's lived longer than he'd ever thought he would. He deserves a beer now and then. He's worried about his daughter, and his grandchildren. Jeeter seems to be growing into a ne'er-do-well just like his father, Cheetah's son Peetah, who disappeared years ago. He knows Jeeter is living in a condemned building with some other homeless youngsters, and believes he might be using. On top of that, it seems his daughter Sheenah is pregnant with a third child. She's on welfare, and there's no man around, it seems to him, except when she's in heat. Chimp family values have really gone to hell. He sips his beer and wonders whether it's urban life that's at fault.

He pays no attention to Suzy's complaints, just brushes her away with an enormous leathery hand the way he'd brush annoying flies from his face.

"Cheetah is happy and healthy," says animal trainer Tony Gentry, who cares for the 4 1/2-foot-tall, 175-pound chimp. The trainer is the talented chimp's original owner, who brought 1-year-old Cheetah back from Africa in 1933 and launched the animal's Hollywood career.

Cheetah hates to recall old, painful memories, but he can't seem to control them. It's strange to him how early memories seem more vivid, more important, even more part of his life, now that he's reached old age. It's as if his life is turning in on itself like a snake eating its tail. Whether Tony really brought Cheetah from Africa he can't corroborate. In his memory, he is not on an ocean liner, being carried around by Tony, as he's been told. He recalls the hold of a steamer, packed full of chimps, each one, like him, in a crate. He couldn't move much. He doesn't recall how he was fed. He still remembers the smells. He remembers his cries as an empty tune in his head, but his mother's angry roar as her baby Cheetah was carried away remains in his body, so that whenever he roars, he can't help thinking of her. He can practically smell her milk. Perhaps the person who pulled him from her weakened arms was Tony.

The tree-climbing movie idol played second banana in 50 films before leaving the Hollywood jungle. He now lives a cushy life of retirement in Santa Monica, California.

Cheetah moves from one spot to another, back and forth, in

his enormous cage in Tony's yard. He can feel the arthritis in his shoulders and the joints of his fingers.

Suzy lies on her side, one knee over the other, smoking a long strand of grass. He knows she gets impatient with his obsessive wandering back and forth. She always wants something from him; she seems always to be in heat. Suzy knows he's in a ruminative mood, and that usually makes her want to roughhouse. He realizes he shouldn't be with such a youngster (Suzy is only forty years old) but just looking at her lips spreading and contracting flexibly around that straw in her mouth, even when she's annoyed at him, like now, makes his old knees quake.

The cuddly creature debuted in the 1934 movie "Tarzan Finds a Mate" starring Johnny Weissmuller and Maureen O'Sullivan.

At first Cheetah had enjoyed being part of the Tarzan movies. First of all, they filmed in locations that reminded him of his home. He got to shriek, pound his chest, and swing on vines. (Chest-pounding is something gorillas do, not chimps, but people loved it.) He'd begun to feel like part of the Tarzan family, almost as if he and Boy (Tarzan and Jane's son) were the children of the family. And he usually got to save Tarzan from something horrible, like vicious headhunters, or Europeans who wanted to destroy the jungles. He didn't realize the movies were fantasy. Then suddenly a picture shoot would end, and he'd have to leave his family once again, to stay with Tony, his owner. Not that he didn't love Tony. But it wasn't the same.

Cheetah also costarred with Weissmuller and other "Janes" in a string of Tarzan movies.

Though Cheetah enjoyed making movies, and loved the attention he got, it wasn't easy. He worked really hard. He had to do whatever was asked of him over and over again. It was painful for him when they wanted him to act silly or stupid. The sillier he acted, the more people seemed to like him.

It took him a while to realize that though the characters remained the same, the actors and actresses changed, so that, though he was part of the Tarzan Family, the humans he'd become attached to would suddenly disappear, and others appear in their places. He recalled acting very spitefully, throwing food and feces, and not doing what he was told, when there was a new, a different Boy, but he just got a wallop across the butt from Tony.

Cheetah enjoys watching his old movies on TV.

Tony and his friends love it when Cheetah watches his own movies and sees himself and points and jumps around. So he does it to make them happy. But what he really feels is a mixture of shame and nostalgia. Looking at these old films that he made when he was just a kid, he studies them and deconstructs them:

Tarzan is a white European, who comes from a wealthy family. His parents, who are anthropologists studying simpler cultures, are murdered by natives who live in the area and don't give a hoot how wealthy and handsome this white couple is. The precious (rich, so good looks and intelligence are in his genes) baby is saved by the indigenous animals (apes), which have just enough human characteristics to bring up the little boy. Now there is a switch. Suddenly evil white men (hunters and exploiters) begin to murder and capture these apes (noble savages). Tarzan's adoptive family is killed, and some apes are trapped to be sent to zoos. Though he cleverly hides, these hideous humanoids finally find him, and recognize him, with difficulty, as one of their own. He is sent home to England (the imperialist owner of that section of Africa being pillaged at the time) to live with a wealthy relative, so that he can be educated to his full potential, and taught some manners befitting his noble class (like how to use silverware and napkins, as well as toilets and baths, and hairbrushes, and how to say please and thank you, and how to properly court the female, etc.). But somehow, while he has incredible sensitivity, certain potential is already down the drain, and he never progresses as far as he might in communicating with his fellow humans. "Me Tarzan, you Jane," is about as verbal as he gets. Neither the English boarding school nor the private tutor makes him happy, but he learns enough to understand the problems of humans, the problems of animals, politics, imperialism, anthropology, and the politics of the rich and poor. Needless to say, he never feels at home, and perhaps this is why he reviles the hypocrisy around him and decides to return to the jungle (the simple, honest, noble culture) where, because of his special skills swimming, calling aaa-eeee-aaaahhhh-ooooo-oooooo, pounding his chest, climbing trees, and getting across large distances and formidable landscapes by swinging on vines, he can act most nobly, and with the greatest integrity.

Though Cheetah can see those movies objectively, they still move him, cause his eyes to sting, his nose to run. He understands very well the pain of belonging to two cultures, but not really belonging to either one.

The chimp's no chump.

Eventually he gets tired of making the same old movies with slight variations in plot, but Tony says he has to keep doing them because of the money. Also because people love him. "Would you want to deprive people of the chance to see the most talented chimp in the world?" he'd cajole, cooking up some flapjacks, Cheetah's favorite food at the time. One day Cheetah realized that he was earning quite a bit of money from his movies. He'd heard a joke…well—he can't recall it now, but it ended with, "I'd be happy to earn as much as Cheetah."

"I have a lot of money now from my movies," he told Tony, one glorious California evening when the sun was reflected in the swimming pool. "I want to join Actors Equity. I want to handle my own money. I want to go to school to learn how to read and write."

"It's my money," said Tony, "not yours." Though it was evening, sweat ran down his chest. He snapped the waistband of his swim shorts. "I mean, some of it may be yours, but who trains you? Who coaches you? Who feeds you, and buys your clothes, and gives you a nice home? All that costs money."

The chimp's no champ.

Eventually Tarzan movies go out of style. When Tony uses up all their money, he sells Cheetah to a group of scientists at a university who want to prove that they can teach chimpanzees to speak using sign language, and to write using computers.

Tony wept when he handed Cheetah over. The scientists, all of whom had beards (except the two women), had to hold Cheetah down. He felt betrayed by Tony, yet he longed for him too. "You wanted to learn to read and write," Tony said. Cheetah's shrieks were so loud the women scientists both put their hands over their ears like hairless earmuffs.

Chimps learn to speak. Five chimpanzees learn sign language. They not only learn words, but also put them together creatively.

Cheetah falls in love with his teacher Ivy. She holds him, hugs him, feeds him. When he learns to ask for things, she gives them to him. She kisses him on his wide mobile mouth and his small eyes, and massages his long fingers and the wrinkled brown bottoms of his feet, which makes him smile from ear to ear. She combs his hair for hours with the blue brush. Ivy teaches him to sign by making the sign herself. He loves the nimble way she moves her tiny fingers. She then takes his long, leathery digits in her warm hand and moves his fingers for him. He can feel a sign throughout his entire body when he is successful. It feels something like Ivy combing him straight down his back—like a long, exotic chill. He learns how to sign: *me*, *you*, *want*, *hungry*, *face*, *hug*, *eat*, *banana*, *out*, *sleep*, *I love you.*

Talking chimps tie the knot.

Even though he was in love with Ivy, Cheetah found himself responding to some strange thing that caused him to notice Chloe. Ordinarily he had nothing to do with her, but at certain times he found himself following her around, becoming obsessed with her. Ivy encouraged them to groom each other, and soon the scientists hugged each other excitedly while they watched Cheetah and Chloe sign to each other. Chloe had very long, straight, orange-brown hair, a slender, smooth butt, and long, hairy legs. The inner corners of her hazel eyes looked like black grape pits. Cheetah was at first concerned about theirs being only a physical relationship, but that worry dissipated. He learned to sign: *hot*, *estrus*, *horny*, *cute*, *smile*, *bed*, *banana.*

The two years of their grant had almost run out, but the scientists were far along with another grant proposal describing their successes, and requesting a renewal. "I hate this grant stuff," said Phil. "Did I get a PhD in Biology, and another in Psycholinguistics, so I could write grant proposals?"

Babies born to famous talking apes.

Cheetah regrets being far from the best father in the world. He spent all his time on his thesis, which was called "Jane: Gender and Culture in the Tarzan Series." He read all the Edgar Rice Burroughs Tarzan books, and reveled in their complexity. He loved the baroque language and descriptions. The stories were gut wrenching, political, and full of rage, so different from the movies he was in.

Talking gorilla project successful, yet funding is withheld.

The scientists wept. They couldn't believe that, just as they were achieving real success, their grants were denied. "This country is going down the tubes," wept Ivy. "No one cares about humanistic and scholarly pursuits anymore," said Chris. "Not what this country's about," said Barbara.

Cheetah couldn't believe that he was being deserted once again. Ivy held him, wept, and said they couldn't afford to keep the chimps they'd taken care of so lovingly. She signed, "My baby," to him, and whimpered, running her finger around his eyes, where the hairs are very short, and his cool nostrils. He stroked her long, wavy banana-colored hair, trying to comfort her, while tears ran down his face and tickled his nipples. "We are trying to find zoos for you, or other projects where you'll be taken care of," she said, hiccupping, her nose all rosy. "There's nothing else we can do."

Cheetah couldn't find a publisher for his thesis, and became morose. If he hadn't been removed from his native Africa, he'd be able to live naturally, by climbing trees, foraging for food. "Stop feeling sorry for yourself," said Chloe.

Former trainer saves derelict chimp family. "I'm so glad I found them just in time," says Tony Gentry.

By the time Tony discovers Cheetah, they've been living on the streets for nearly a year, surviving by sleeping in parks and subway tunnels, and dumpster diving for food. Chloe, addicted to drugs and alcohol, had disappeared. Cheetah is afraid she'll die, or be killed. His son disappears soon after. Cheetah and Sheenah and tiny Jeeter are in bad shape.

As soon as Sheenah, Cheetah's daughter, is well, Tony and she agree that she should be on her own. She takes tiny Jeeter, her brother Peetah's little boy, with her. Cheetah, who can't take care of her, regretfully lets her go.

Cheetah, the Tarzan ape, becomes an artist. "He's very good," says Tony.

Tony buys Cheetah all kinds of paint and canvas, and encourages him. Suzy, another chimp belonging to Tony, paints too. She helps him, but his work soon surpasses hers in intensity and complexity. Tony is soon selling almost everything that Cheetah creates.

Both Tony and Cheetah are upset because, while Tony has to ask for a fairly low price for the paintings, the wealthy collectors who buy them cheaply sell them to other collectors for huge amounts of money.

Some reviews of Cheetah's artwork:

> Highly charged as a Tibetan tanka. Though Cheetah's work can be confounding in its variety, this show, more black and white chronicle than spectacle, seems to communicate the essentials.
>
> —*Art Views*

> Moves from a quiet, perceptual realism into a self-consciously symbolic mysticism. Cheetah's present style is an open echo of Vincent van Gogh's without seeming directly imitative. Using a darker, more primary color scale, he paints in thick, richly colored strokes meant to convey an immediate and emotive response to a resplendent natural world. Cheetah's paintings are, in a sense, offerings to the sources of his own enchantments, even as they are public expressions of a private sadness. Fortunately

> they are executed by a talented hand with sure intuitions about the craft of painting.
>
> —*Los Angeles Chronicle*

Before long Tony can't afford to buy Cheetah or Suzy the art supplies they need to work, much less food.

Cheetah goes bananas.

Cheetah discovers that his daughter, who has two boys, Cheater and Cheetos, is pregnant, on welfare, and that his grandson Jeeter, who'd been in her care, is off living on his own. But just as he thinks life can't get any worse, he finds out that he is going to be in the *Guinness Book of World Records* for being the oldest (longest living) chimpanzee, surpassing a female chimp named Gamma, who lived to the age of fifty-nine. What a thing, finally, to be known for.

Chimp-rock star, son of Cheetah, strikes it rich.

That night Tony gets a call from someone who says he's Jeeter's agent. Apparently Jeeter is making tons of money recording and giving concerts with his band The All-Chimps, formerly The Eating Death. The agent is making a celebration party at the new mansion he's bought for Jeeter and himself. "It's Jeeter's house, really it is," he says. "Jeeter wants his relatives there."

The party is out by the pool, which seems to be carved out of one side of the highest of the Hollywood hills. Quite a bit of attention is being paid to Jeeter's family. Sheenah, looking kind of dumpy and depressed, and beginning to show that Cheetah was right about her being pregnant again, has brought the boys, Cheetos and Cheater. They've been giving her a lot of trouble lately, never listening to her, and running around with a fast crowd. But watching them swim in Jeeter's new Olympic-sized pool, they look like they should—like carefree little chimp kids having a good time.

When the crowd thins, Cheetah tries to get Jeeter alone for a moment. "Why not give Sheenah some money, and get her a place to live," he says, rejecting the caviar canapés the caterer is sending around, waving his creased leathery hand. "You have enough for fifty or a hundred chimps to live well." "Careful of the palm plants," Jeeter says. "Want a drink, Pop?" Cheetah presses, "Well, what do you say?" "I don't know," says Jeeter. "She's a fat, lazy slob. I earned my money myself. It's a free country—let her strike it rich herself. I'm getting a drink." "Jeeter," Cheetah pulls him back, "she has all those kids." "I should give her money to take care of them?" Jeeter's eyebrows practically go over the top of his head. "She made her bed, let her sleep in it." "She took care of you," pleads Cheetah. "You were just poor and homeless yourself. We need to help each other." Jeeter scratches his head with his huge hand, and stirs his drink with his index finger. A woman who reminds Cheetah of Iris thinks it's cute and giggles.

Cheetah watches his grandson pulling at the three earrings in his pendulous earlobes, enjoying his wealth and his new mansion, and thinks how Jeeter doesn't yet realize that his agent owns him, and how much of his good fortune was just that.

"Don't splash each other," Sheenah yells at the boys. She looks down at herself, with her slumping shoulders and protruding belly. Then she looks at her boys again. Drops of water sit in their terracotta fur like silver coins. When they dive into the clear aqua their thin, dark limbs create a crude calligraphy. They haven't looked so happy or behaved so well since they were small. She looks over the pool and down at Santa Monica below. She sees blurry layers of color that someone told her is really pollution.

Is that all it takes to make everything better? she wonders. Just lots of money? Her eyes begin to sting and tear, until she has to wipe them with the back of her hand. She's not sure whether she's weeping or if it's just the smog.

Cheetah looks down, then out toward the mountains in the distance. If he looks out at the horizon, at the lavender, vermilion, and rose sunset, and then squints his round eyes, he can imagine he's looking out across a dry African savannah. He can almost hear Tarzan call, "Ohhhhh-eeeeeehhhooooohhhhehhh-eeee-ooooo."

FROM FORGETFULNESS

BY MICHAEL MEJIA (2005)

EDITOR'S NOTE: Michael Mejia's *Forgetfulness* is representative of recent work by younger American writers that adopts a more complex attitude toward the high modernist past than its postmodern predecessors. Although critical of modernism's insularity, *Forgetfulness* nevertheless positions itself as modernism's successor, a work of comparably high and uncompromising ambition. Written in two distinct parts, it recalls the life of Austrian composer Anton Webern and his struggle amid the rise of Nazism to create a spiritually pure musical expression. Its second part, "Triologue: For Soprano, Composer, and Archivist, May 1, 1986," contextualizes the first, implying that overcoming this past is more difficult than presently imagined. Our reader, Harold Jaffe, described it as a "tour de force," a polymorphous work that deals with one of the twentieth century's most passionate episodes. What originally excited me, however, was Mike's success at not retelling this episode. Presented in a collage of quotations, newspaper articles, language exercises, musical scores, and songs, his novel's meaning does not result from its narrative, its representation of character and action, but from its form. History in *Forgetfulness* is just a mess, a deteriorating archive in the basement of the triologue's final voice. Its nature is to be lost on those who claim it, to be repressed in being told. By contrast, Mike's polymorphous text embodies the struggle, not *of* history, but *for* it, making reading replicate the problem Webern's work tried to solve. Is our ambition to purify expression of its accidents, to free present understanding from old blindness and lies, bad faith or progress? There's simply no telling *Forgetfulness's* answer.

—RMB

"If there is a central politics in my fiction, it emerges mainly from a self-consciousness of the politics in all fictions (the extra-literary as well the literary), that is, the inescapable presence of 'narration,' of an arbitrarily authorized voice.... Consequently, I've become much more interested in disrupting narrations and forcing them to fail than in fulfilling traditional expectations of narrative coherence, expectations of entertainments and pleasures, of assurance."

—Michael Mejia

In the Attic Style

This is the concept of World.

Fragments in the walls, on the floors.

Some cross over to other slabs.

Let everyone be a Greek in his own way, but let him be a Greek!

—Johann Wolfgang von Goethe

Is this history?

A procession. A simple repeated form.

Horses with riders, chariots, men, women, animals.

What has been lost?

Arms. Legs. The torso, the tunic, the shield, the pitcher, the pipes, the beckoning hand.

Is this allegory?

Faceless riders. Horses without eyes.

Decoration depends on variety; in writing and in buildings it provides a change for the intellect and the eye, and when decoration on architecture is combined with simplicity, the result is beauty: for a thing is good and beautiful if it is what it ought to be.

—Johann Joachim Winckelmann

Identical forms, but features unique to each: speed, laziness, unruliness, intelligence, anxiety, humor, pride, friendship, respect for position, respect for the gods, an impatience for those lagging behind, an expectation that others will follow.

Some nude, some clothed, some helmeted, others bareheaded.

Beyond is blank stone.

Is this forgetfulness?

On a spring evening in Vienna, as the bells toll five o'clock, Dr. Florian Mittermayr, a music critic with political aspirations, enters the Café Sperl. He is greeted by Otto, an affable giant of a lisping, white-haired waiter. Otto's black suit and vest show few signs of wear.

Conversational German: Chapter Review

Part I: Greetings!

—Good evening, Herr Dr. Mittermayr!

—Good evening, Otto.

—Would you like your usual seat?*

—Of course I would. Why would I not?

—Yes. And will you be dining here alone tonight, Herr Dr. Mittermayr?

—Yes. Yes. The old bitch is up at the sanatorium again.

Part II: Ordering Food and Drink

—I will fetch the menu.

—There is no need for a menu. What is the special?

—We have a very nice Chicken à la Marengo tonight, Herr Dr. Mittermayr.

—Chicken? Good God. Well, I suppose that will do.

—Wonderful! Would you like tea or coffee, Herr Dr. Mittermayr?

—A beer. Gösser.**

—Excellent!

Otto nods politely and goes to check on a young woman in the corner who has been trying to attract his attention.

* Always use the polite form, Sie, when addressing a superior or someone you don't know very well.

** In general it is considered more polite to say "please," bitte, when ordering something to eat or drink.

Part III: Compare and Contrast

Near the door, two women enjoy dessert.

—Do you like the Sachertorte, Hanna?
—Yes, I do. It is better than the Hotel Sacher's. And how is the pudding?
—I am afraid it is a bit thick. I prefer the strudel much better, though the Napoleon is also quite good.

Another woman approaches carrying a small box tied up with string.

—Hello, Hanna. Hello, Wilma.
—Good evening, Katrina. What is in your box?
—A cat. His name is Ludwig, but I call him Pickle. Pickle is a gift given to me by my neighbor, Dr. Schrödinger, from the university.
—How sweet. What kind of cat is it, dear? May we see him?
—Oh, no. I am sorry. Pickle may be dead.
—Heavens!
—He may also be alive. As long as I do not open the box, Pickle is both dead and alive.
—All at once?
—Yes! Isn't he adorable?
—Yes, my dear, yes! Pickle is very handsome! He has such unique and beautiful markings.

Part IV: Shock, Surprise, and Unpleasantness

Dr. Mittermayr stands, squinting at the newspaper rack. Another man, Dr. Karel Bilenski, a Bohemian veterinary surgeon, runs into him, almost toppling Dr. Mittermayr over his table.

—Damn you!

The large glass ashtray slides off Dr. Mittermayr's table and falls to the floor, bounces once, spins and glitters like a trout, then hits the floor again and shatters. Everyone stares.

—Excuse me! Ah!
—You damn… Ah!

The two men recognize each other.

—Florian!
—Karel! You are as clumsy as ever. Damn you!
—Please excuse me. Were you leaving?
—No. I was going to get a newspaper when you trampled me.
—I said excuse me.
—Yes.
—Yes.*

Part V: Express Your Opinion!

A young Czech student is unable to pay his bill. The cashier is annoyed by this and also by the student's poor German.

—German! We speak German in Vienna!

Overhearing this, Dr. Mittermayr offers his opinion:

—That is correct, young man! German here! German throughout the empire! Damn you Slavs and your Slav-language schools! Communists! Atheists! Degenerates! Call the police!

The young Czech turns on Dr. Mittermayr and begins to sing a song that was popular in Prague during the uprising of 1848.

---

* Awkward pauses will be covered in the next chapter.

Part VI: Sport

Two young men emerge from the billiards area and drag the Czech out into the street for a beating. The one says to the other:

—We must go cycling very soon, Christian! And perhaps do some shooting, as well.

The other replies:

—What a wonderful idea, Franz! And such timing. Just yesterday I bought myself a new Mannlicher.

And the young Czech chimes in:

—Hunting is a fine pastime. I enjoy it very much. I also enjoy cycling, climbing, hiking, and swimming.

Part VII: Issuing Orders

Otto arrives at Dr. Mittermayr's table with a small whisk broom and dust pan.

—Please excuse me, gentlemen. I am very sorry.

He sweeps up the shards of the broken ashtray.

—Where is my beer!
—Ah, yes, Herr Dr. Mittermayr! I am very sorry. I will bring it immediately.

Otto leaves his sweeping and heads toward the order window.

—Bring another ashtray!
—Yes, Herr Dr. Mittermayr!

Part VIII: Time and Space

At the center billiards table, Ernst and Benjamin discuss their plans for the evening.

—Tonight I am taking my Lisl to the opera, where Herr Mahler will be conducting Lohengrin. I must meet Lisl at six o'clock on the east side of the east pavilion on the Karlsplatz.
—That is very interesting, my friend, as I have to meet my Nadja on the west side of the west pavilion on the Karlsplatz, also at precisely six o'clock. We are going to the Konzerthaus, where the Gustavus Quartet and Herr Thomas Reismann of Salzburg will perform Herr Schubert's "Trout" Quintet.
—Wonderful! Let us all meet at the Café Central afterwards, at fifteen minutes past ten.
—That is an excellent idea. Isn't it interesting that we will be kissing our young ladies simultaneously at six o'clock?
—Interesting, yes, and rather arousing. But if we cannot observe each other, how can we be certain that we are kissing our young ladies simultaneously?
—We both have watches, do we not? And are they not of the same or similar design? We can kiss our young ladies and observe by our watches that it is exactly six o'clock. As we will both leave the Café Sperl together, we can be sure that neither of us is late. Therefore we can each enjoy this secret arousal simultaneously without either Lisl or Nadja knowing about it. Secrecy itself is rather arousing, isn't it?
—It is. But we cannot judge simultaneity by our watches, despite their similarities, as this method is not very precise. Perhaps we can enlist a third party as an observer, who will carry a watch exactly like yours and mine, and who will signal us when it is six o'clock. Or perhaps we can leave early and construct a system of mirrors in which we can watch ourselves as we kiss our young ladies and look at our watches, thus eliminating the awkward intrusion of the third party.
—I rather like the idea of a third party.
—No, no. It is all too complicated, I am afraid. It seems, my

friend, that these days both love and architecture have become overburdened with ornament and, as you can see, this is dampening my enthusiasm.

—Yes, I suppose you are right. Perhaps a more direct approach is necessary. The only way to fulfill my erotic fantasy is to skip the Café Central altogether and go to my flat and kiss our young ladies simultaneously in each other's presence, perhaps in front of a large mirror. This eliminates the aspect of secrecy of which I was so fond, but I believe we can make up for that through other means.

—Yes, perhaps we can achieve simultaneous orgasms.

—That is an excellent suggestion. That sounds very pleasurable.

—I would like to kiss you.

—All right. But let us go into the toilet where you can do so in secret.

Part IX: Members of the Family

In the kitchen Greta, the waitress, is pregnant and feeling ill. She retches intermittently into a small bucket while the French-Romanian chef, Zoltan Villeneuf, prepares Dr. Mittermayr's Chicken à la Marengo and suggests names for Greta's baby.

—Emperor Franz Josef is the older brother of Ferdinand Maximilian, emperor of Mexico, who was executed in 1867. Their mother was the archduchess Sophie and their father was Archduke Franz Karl. But, because Sophie hated Franz Karl and had not given him any children after six years, when her sons were finally born, in 1830 and 1832 respectively, it was rumored that Franz Josef and Ferdinand Maximilian were the illegitimate children of Archduchess Sophie and her favored companion and nephew, by marriage, Napoleon II, or Napoleon Franz, as he was never crowned emperor of France, whose mother was Archduchess Marie-Louise, Franz Karl's sister, and whose father was Napoleon Bonaparte, tyrant and emperor of France, who had defeated Franz Josef and Ferdinand Maximilian's grandfather, Marie-Louise and Franz Karl's father, Francis II—last of the Holy Roman Emperors, also known as, after 1806, Francis I, Emperor of Austria, King of Hungary and of Bohemia—in the wars of the First, Second, and Third Coalitions, including humiliating defeats at Marengo, in 1800, and Austerlitz, in 1805. If this rumor were true, of course, it would mean Franz Josef and Ferdinand Maximilian were not only heirs of the Holy Roman Emperors but also descended from the most celebrated military mind since Attila, from whom I myself am descended.

—Thank you, Zoltan, but my husband and I have already agreed to name this child after one of his great-grandparents.

—Well, it was only a suggestion. And now for a unique Slavic touch to Herr Dr. Mittermayr's supper. Please hand me your little bucket. What are the names you and your husband are considering?

—If she is a girl, Caroline, and if he is a boy, Augustin.

—Ach, du lieber Augustin!

They sing.

Au-gu-stin, Au-gu-stin!
Ach, du lieber Augustin,
Alles ist hin!

All the patrons of the Café Sperl sing along.

Money's gone! Girlfriend's gone!
It's all gone, Augustin!
Ach, du lieber Augustin,
'S all gone to hell!

Part X: Numbers

Anton Webern, a young music student from the southern province of Carinthia, enters, counting his coins to see if he has enough money for one beer, a packet of cigarettes, and a ticket for tonight's concert at the Musikverein.

—Five, six, eleven, twenty-one, twenty-two, -three, -four, thirty…

Dr. Mittermayr, red and raging and spilling Gösser all over himself and his friend, Dr. Karel Bilenski, shoves a handful of coins and bills into the young man's hand, grabs him by the collar, and exhorts him to:

—Sing, you little shit, sing!

Which Anton Webern does.

Ach, du lieber AU-gu-stin,
AU-gu-stin, AU-gu-stin!
ACH, du lieber AU-gu-stin,
IT'S ALL GONE TO HELL!

Part XI: Reading Comprehension (optional)

In Heiligenstadt, a train whistle sounds, waking the gypsies who descend from their nests in the chestnut trees. A goat is slaughtered in the Tenth District and the eastern workers give three cheers for the newborn child. Streetcars, red and white, rattle around the Ring, hurtle off into the outer districts, come jingling from the Prater.

Light the lamp now, tune the string as the imperial capital turns aside in the interval to rest its faces, to change into its evening wear. Atop the Kahlenberg young lovers settle in the grass to watch the sunset.

From the full teat of the first star the thick, sweet milk of fantasy cascades over the city, pools in the Stadtpark, the Augarten, the Central Cemetery, tides and eddies around the Stephansdom, the Michaelertor and the Burgtheater, the Rathaus, the Riesenrad, the Arsenal, floods butcher shops and wurstel stalls, haberdasheries, luthiers, and papeterie, churns through the alleys and lanes of the inner districts, overflows bridges, railbeds, stairs, seeps into crypts and coal cellars, rolls in deep, frothy waves out to Hietzing, Simmering, Döbling, Floridsdorf, the vineyards of Grinzing, and beyond, into woods and meadows.

Doves and nightingales slowly circle, counterclockwise, above the rising, reddening waves, while bats glide out of spires and attic spaces to feed on sluggish mayflies. Their prehistoric shadows terrify the citizenry.

Light the lamp now. Tune the string.

Fat and quivering in their catacombs, the entrails of the Habsburgs convulse in ecstasy.

FROM PUBLIC WORKS

BY CHRISTOPHER GRIMES (2005)

EDITOR'S NOTE: Christopher Grimes's writing, like that of so many FC2 authors, involves a continuous invention at the level of its form or concept. The aim, for both writer and reader, is to see what can create wholeness, how far a voice will sustain conviction, or simply whether *this* makes a work. In a sense that I don't find equally true of mainstream literature, Chris's fiction almost always shows me what's staked in writing it. In their reader's reports Lidia Yuknavitch praised the "formal defiance of the tyranny of the traditional short story" and Elisabeth Sheffield described the writing's "idiosyncratic and associative quality," as though the author were "bemusedly following language's direction, one eyebrow raised," wherever it led. The result for me is a peculiar tension, a sense of apprehension and excitement, best likened to entering a foreign country. Boundaries take on significance, since missteps and presumption are likely, and one's natural inclinations are transformed into encumbrances, obstacles to further discovery. In this sense Chris's experiments seek to overcome parochialism, but this requires penetrating the interior, an approach every border guard tries to control. There's the risk of meaninglessness since, like the typing of monkeys, such forays may appear random or ridiculous, but also a risk of transgression, of violated norms, sanctuaries. Whether the risks are worth taking is each reader's decision, but surpassing the limits of one's own past, group, or nation occurs in no other way.

—RMB

"As both a citizen and a writer, I like to think that I celebrate contamination, the mongrelization and neo-cosmopolitanism created when discrete cultural preferences, mythologies and aesthetic sensibilities contaminate one another. I despise fundamentalism—the impulse toward cultural and intellectual purity—and its prescribed preferences, mythologies and aesthetic sensibilities. I value patois over fatwa."

—Christopher Grimes

CUSTOMS IN A DEVELOPING COUNTRY: A PREFATORY STORY

...Alas, who is there
we can make use of? Not angels, not men;
and even the noticing beasts are aware
that we don't feel very securely at home
in this interpreted world.... —*Rilke*

If you've arrived with animal, vegetable or mineral, declare the full name of the animal, vegetable or mineral that you have arrived here with. Zucchini was once individually wrapped in tissue paper and imported here from Japan in beautiful cedar boxes like Havana cigars. Now we stink of zucchini. Where did it come from? Who can answer? An elegant Japanese girl carries the seeds stuck in her molar for ten thousand miles, spits it out onto our native soil, and boom, *bloom!,* an invading species, a predatory plant. Now open your bags for me.

We're considering having this printed up and distributed during the final descent on in-bound flights. You'll read no pleases, no thank yous, no pretty colored snapshots of places that simply can't be missed, just *The Facts: Courtesy of Our Municipal Government*, which reminds you to watch yourself, keep an eye on your things. Recall here *The Honeymooners* with the stars Audrey Meadows and Jackie Gleason, wherein vacuous Ralph Kramden says to pragmatic wife Alice, *Don't say it, don't say it, don't say it, Alice!* and her reply, which she must repeat over and over again to pierce the darkness of his terrible selfishness: *I told you so!*

Listen to someone who knows. Experience tells me that pragmatism is still the most viable of philosophies. Stripped from your shoulder, your camera will just as easily image another's memories as your own. Personal identification can be defaced with a pen knife in thirty seconds flat, your name associated with the concussion and heat that one hundred out-bound passengers welcome as the Epiphany while plowing a fiery furrow into a field of sorghum. Picked from your pocket, your money will surely be spent on things that you would go your whole life denying yourself. In one such story, a woman's house keys are lifted from her and couriered overnight to a contact in her place of origin. Her home is ransacked, and everything she owned finds its way back here by means of shoulder bags, millet sacks, tennis balls, prosthetic limbs, parcel-post agencies and several combinations of the nine orifices. In another story, things don't take nearly as long. A man's address book is rifled through, phone calls made, household appliances charged to his account.

Once removed from your person, your most private possessions will be fondled by any number of questionable characters and absorbed—taken separately they are only bits and pieces after all—into our local economy and general public at large. Have no hope for recovery. You will think you recognize your pajama bottoms worn by someone as pants, but you will not be able to say with certainty that they're yours. So many people will have fingered your things with so many different intentions that they will become nearly unrecognizable things. Foreign things. Things, as I've said, that are no longer yours. The faded movie starlet Zsa Zsa Gabor on holiday here many years ago stole from her chambermaid our traditional toast and salutation—*ta!*—but in her mouth, even to our ears, it is nearly unrecognizable.

None of which is to imply that we are crime-infested. On the contrary, we have very little crime, what might be called *petty crime*, because our prisons are used prophylactically. Indeed, there are many among us who believe that we should pass what's been termed the *Criminal Year* legislation now before our Justices. This law would make it mandatory that the young and simple-minded are incarcerated for exactly one calendar year, or until such time that the voices in their heads subside. The voices speak through their mouths and say such things as it's no life, this life they lead here with us, and that they are off to live the lives they see available to them on the television, for example. Worse yet is when things are quiet, because it's now that the voice is convincing our children to steal away in the middle of the night, leaving us in bed listening to the sound of a broken muffler fading into the darkness and wondering how in the world we didn't hear it coming.

Once imprisoned, the criminals will be wakened by a specially appointed warden in the small hours of the morning with simple, nagging questions: How are you doing? the warden will ask severely, So how's everything?

The warden will only show kindness if bribed. Advocates argue that this is sufficient for those too young or simple to feel what it's like to have the infinite possibility of their dreams reduced to the singularly ugly and hard business of living. If it's reality they want, in short, we intend to give them a taste of it.

If the legislation passes, the day of arrest is expected to be a time of great excitement for the criminals' families. At its climax, tenderloin of beef will be served, and there will be a special bread for the festival—our traditional cracker—which is similar to, I believe, the British biscuit. Relatives of the criminals will gather at the family's home to repair any structural damage that might have occurred during the arrest, while their hosts serve medallions of tenderloins of beef on crackers. In their absence, no one will talk about the criminal because the family will be officially entering shame—an as-yet undefined period of intense sorrow and longing.

Until these measures are implemented, our misdirected juveniles and simple-minded ship-jumpers are best ignored. Simply cross to the other side of the street to avoid them, making sure to look both ways before stepping off the curb, as traffic has the right of way. This might seem uncivil, but we see it as subscribing to the greater law of causality, the logic of which takes into account the pedestrian body pit against one of our drivers driving a car. You of pliable flesh and brittle bones versus one ton of amoral metal. If these odds alone fail to impress you, then at least embrace the common sense that a people foreign to you will live in a manner that is foreign to your sensibilities. You are somewhere new. Perhaps try to appreciate its novelty. Our toilet paper is blue, our water pressure low, our telephone exchange improving.

In turn, we would like to get to know you. All we ask is some measure of consideration, no matter how small. Ours is an insatiable appetite for consideration, a simple vanity that no doubt comes from pride. We are perhaps haughty as a matter of fact. And if we, a proud, haughty people feel that you are disappointed in us, we'll find it hard to recover from the blow. In short, don't insult the natives. We hold grudges.

I am reminded once more of Ms. Zsa Zsa Gabor, whom we mistakenly made an honorary citizen during her holiday here many years ago, and who, relatively recently, we mistakenly invited back to marshal in the opening of our Municipal Airport. She stood on a platform erected right here in the atrium for the proceedings, as expressionless as a statue. Her lack of interest was palpable, her presence among us clearly a justification for the hefty honorarium she charged. Moreover, while she stood there on the platform, she did not look one of us in the eye. I could go on describing this humiliating and dark portrait of Ms. Gabor, but I strongly recommend instead that you visit our Municipal Art Museum where the portrait hangs. In it, the blue ribbon winner of our all-schools exhibition perfectly captured the spectacle: the artificial gloss of her skin, her dangerously high-heeled shoes, pink jumpsuit and all. Our museum also contains the most complete collection of Rodin casts of any museum in the world.

Our women, you'll notice, are Rodin sculptures come alive. Aesthetically speaking, of course. Their thin skulls and round bottoms immediately call to mind the sculpture of Rodin. They are famously beautiful. Our women should be in museums. One would think that our men should be accustomed to the apprehension of such beauty, and yet they can often be heard to profess the critical observation that a woman's nipples are like what both we and the French call *bon-bons*. I try to prevent the consternation of our female visitors by saying this: Don't be frightened. You will not be touched, unless this is in fact what you desire. Our men are typically sheepish when confronted, and, on the whole, otherwise well-mannered. They live with their mothers until marriage and can thus be easily dismissed as clotheshorses when misbehaving. This is the warning that I give to each and every man that passes through here: mind your manners.

In all respects you'll notice that we are always working to improve. We work very hard. We have a humorous saying: working hard or hardly working? I might make the sweeping request that you please pardon our appearance as we renovate. It seems that we are tearing things down now faster than we can put them up so that nothing looks the same the next morning. So if you should find yourself lost, simply ask for direction. We are abundantly approachable and patient. The customary closing salutation in these casual encounters is, as I've said, *ta.* This expression, an abbreviation of *to you*, is also our traditional toast of appreciation. We raise our glasses and exclaim *ta!*, and, when parting company, simply bid *ta.* Of course elsewhere the *ta* has become followed by another *ta*, which is accompanied by hitting the higher registers in the voice: *ta ta.* This redundancy—directly attributable to Ms. Gabor—is also in our vocabulary. But let me sternly warn you against its usage. In our language, the first *ta* is equivalent to the simple salutation good-bye, no more or less. The second *ta*, however, perverts the first so that the one addressed is bid farewell twice, the translation being: *good bye, I am anxious to rid myself of you.*

As such, Ms. Zsa Zsa Gabor and her kind understandably lack for admirers here. A glance at any recent tabloid photograph of her reveals the hopelessly artificial creature she has now become. One can't help being repulsed by the poor craftsmanship lately exhibited in her nose, the obviousness of her plastic chin, hairpiece and silicone bosom. One can't help wincing at the estimated eleven percent of her so apparently composed of man-made material, to say nothing of being the source of countless many social blunders that have led to who knows how much alienation every time she opens her mouth. But like everyone else who passes through here, there was no way to know where her visit was going to lead. It's ironic, a vicious, vicious irony that we are made to labor under. You will please keep this in mind as you strike out now amongst us.

THE PUBLIC SENTENCE

Speak of the devil, if it isn't our young Doctor defiantly taking his lunch break downwind from the Willet Loop Sewage Plant, secondary source of his catastrophe some thirty-three and a third days ago, now bench-ridden in the Municipal Gardens before a terrace of white gladiolas, staring at his khaki-trousered knees while his Indian counterparts in Delhi are undoubtedly hard at work composing yet another addition to the thick ream of facsimiles providing oblique descriptions of their impenetrable customs, misleading and nonsensical analyses of their archaic municipal histography and sketchy explanations of their unfathomable appetites, all of which, sheaf by onionskin sheaf, churns the young Doctor's thoughts into foam while a limp rooster's tail of hair dangles from the crown of his head toward the back of his collar, itself cinched tight by a tie that he is too weary to loosen, as Ella, the young Doctor's wife of a month, attested this morning ("You are tossing and turning, do you understand me? and biting your teeth all night") in the timbre of innocent assessment because, as she pointed out immediately after the back-flush, as one of our newest immigrants she was least represented in the sewage now being contained by the Army Corps of Engineers in our beloved river, was, in point of fact, culpable for precisely fifty-seven days worth, a teeny-tiny drop in the bucket that she began contributing the morning she touched down at the Municipal Airport, her dry, frizzy hair the color of bark still carrying, it seemed to the young Doctor when they awkwardly embraced on the tarmac, something of the smell of the autumn corn husks that fill the fields down there in Sioux Falls, where the two had been coupled as freshman physics lab partners at the University until, eventually, they found themselves not only sharing the lab table, but whole days together, then evenings and finally dormitories, as pressed wood and Formica refuges against what they both thought to be a temporary condition during their remaining three years of college, namely their persistent sense of alienation, of being utterly alone without each other in that strangely expansive country, until they both graduated and she returned to Buenos Aires and he, not to the deep kettles and rolling moraines of his native south-central Wisconsin, but here, Bismarck, this Great State's Capital, which employed him, and from where he posted short, type-written notes that *crescendoed*—a term used by Ella in a letter describing Paco D'Martine's voice in *Jupiter y Juno*, within which Zeus does the deed with Hera, his wife and sister, as recalled and related by Ella from her stint in the orchestra pit of the *Teatro Colón*—into a one sentence invitation ("the Bismarck Municipal Symphony is looking for musicians") that prompted her subsequent descension from the sky as dramatic as a stage prop, bassoon in hand, a sheaf of operatic orchestrations flowing from memory to her fingertips unabated during an audition for the symphony, which, in preparation for the forthcoming summer-long festival of opera, immediately offered her a contract, withdrew it upon discovery that she had neither a work permit nor a Green Card, and offered it again when, two and a half months later, well within the Bureau of Customs and Immigration's three month term-limit on tourist visas granted to Argentine Nationals, they were married, so that there she was this morning, leaning against the bathroom sink, informing him that he is tossing and turning the night through and pointing out, before he could attempt to explain the seemingly unspeakable source of his nocturnal restlessness, the discrepancy between the color of his black belt and brown socks to which he, in turn, resisted the impulse to give her a brotherly punch in the arm—an astonishingly new impulse altogether, he being raised without siblings—and found himself staring at her, this *wife* of his, without any idea of what to do next, as a *husband*, but change his socks to rectify this slight fashion guffaw made in the distraction of the ever-present memory of the first harbinger turd, black and swollen as the plague itself, that surfaced on the Missouri at precisely 2:07 p.m. on a pleasant Saturday exactly thirty-three and a third days ago, thereby ushering in this state of mind we now find him in, sitting on his park bench, unbuttoning his cuffs and disheveling his collar and tie, oblivious to the flock of pigeons scattered around him, grounded themselves by the shimmering thermal folds of heat that have been slowly baking the river into a wretched, turtle-infested casserole, its warm, flatulent aroma wafting through the rusty links of chain and rope-burned bollards of the river port, blowing through the broken windows and open doors of the abandoned Customs House and the dilapidated Intercoastal Navy Mechanics School's barracks, across Pioneer Park, Grandview Heights, the Bird Arboretum and Divide Avenue, through Tom

O'Leary Golf Course, Hanaford Avenue and 3rd and 4th Streets to dump its sour load of odors inside the shallow brick walls here in the Municipal Gardens, where it converges *counter-punctually* (Ella again) with the sweet theme running through the young Doctor's head in the form of last year's Christmas Program, exquisitely performed by our Municipal Choir, which included John Francis Wade's 1743 composition *O Come All Ye Faithful* and its penetrating refrain which asks that we *come and adore Him* (repeated three times), effectively uniting us—you and me and the young Doctor himself—in the dark of our Civic Center then miraculously filled with a spirit altogether different from the one now displayed by us all, each one of us now, who haven't the vaguest notion of how our public waste is directed through a system second in complexity only to that one posteriorly balanced above it, who have, until this moment, been perched blind as bats on the great public commode without *once* having occasion to think past our ankles, down the wrought iron throat that connects us to the municipal digestive system, the intestines of tunnels, conduits and channels, the brick-lined bowels that release into the newly vulcanized slag tanks churning the corporate volume flowing from our homes and businesses for, *individually*, we are more concerned with by whom the sound of the soft scrape of toilet paper is being heard than we are with the workings of the sophisticated mechanism to which we are just then affixed, its product, coupled with the bad advice given to the young Doctor by the Indian Municipal Government in Delhi, being the true and primary source of the bespoilment of our beloved river and the burgeoning turtle population first, under the direction of those Indians, purposefully seeded and now swarming on our river's banks, their collective shock to our senses matched only by how shockingly quick we are to lay blame when, truly, no one contributing factor can be blamed, neither the impoverished Indians with their appetite for turtles, nor the summer of opera suddenly thrust upon us and the subsequent rush to prepare the infrastructure to receive it, which is undoubtedly taxing all of the municipal services, including the Division of Water Works, one component piece, albeit an important one, to the larger composition that makes up the Public Works, employer of the young Doctor, our Assistant Regulator of Flowage, who opened the grit chamber, but failed to close the outflow seals of the sedimentation lagoon, our raw sewage overwhelming the tertiary system, the charcoal filtration unit, lime clarifier and recarbination filters, so that we find ourselves with a very large helping of our own offal stew belched back into our river in its undigested state, now contained by the Army Corps of Engineers with gaudy yellow floats and buoys that keep the discharge stationary, but not the turtles from migrating, as the Department of Natural Resources pointed out, pronouncing both the spill *and* turtle population a biological hazard, thus provoking the overly-hasty adoption of the ill-conceived Indian model first posited by the young Doctor, who, drawing on his Comparative Municipal Histography curriculum, directed the Emergency Advisory Committee's attention to the confluence of the Ganges and Yamuna Rivers, where the Indians in general and Hindus in particular pilgrimage to wash their feet in waters endowed with the mystical power to wash away both sin and sickness and the tribulations of the dead who, cremated if the mourner can afford the wood for the funeral pyre—the Indian soul apparently being designed to leave through the head, which is apparently signaled by the skull cracking in a shower of sparks—and cast into the river, are assured liberation from the cycles of life and death, the inference being that, not at all unlike us, those Indians love their river and therefore can't keep themselves away from it, the consequence of which is that it swarms with cholera, tetanus and typhoid, that a statistical analysis of a tear drop of its microbiotic life yields cosmological proportions, and that its flow has grown sluggish with human silt, a fact that does not dissuade in the least the pilgrims from immersing themselves in the symbolically charged but unspeakably polluted river roiling with their beloveds' ashes—in itself not problematic, as estuary muck is estuary muck—but it's the impoverished multitudes, however, who are unable to afford the wood for a proper cremation, and their alternative ritual of chanting then simply dumping in their corpses, beads and all, like a sack of spoiled yams, that, when we multiply this act by the millions, conveys a sense of the problem's severity, and, hence, the simple genius of what by all accounts is, or *was*, a seemingly infallible solution, of which even those in the various Indian Municipal agencies in Delhi could not help but be awed by the centrifugal force of life and death at the heart of its populace, namely that the turtles released into the Ganges year after year—a species that subsists on decaying matter, particularly fond of the flesh—are eventually poached and eaten, the turtle population therefore controlled by sheer appetite alone by those same pilgrims who dampen out the sun with their breakfast fires before wrapping up their dead for their big send-off, thereby obscuring what appeared by all accounts to be a useful test case for an environmentally efficient, low-cost clean water program with similar impurities, a model so compelling, in fact, that the young Doctor himself tabled it without ever imagining that the turtle population would, as anyone can now plainly see, reach the thousands, if not tens of thousands, such that the sheer congestion of the shells on the surface of the Missouri admittedly gives it, if not a hallucinatory, then at least a menacing aspect, so much so that while no immediate danger to the operational infrastructure of our city is predicted, the Department of Public Works, equally alarmed at the negative *aesthetic* impact that the turtles may have on our visitors and residents alike, offers two, possibly concomitant solutions, the first one being that we effectively eradicate a controlled portion of the turtles by, for example, injecting sides of beef with a toxic, non-leaching substance in an effort to target the species without jeopardizing the life of the river itself—the one significant drawback here involving an understandable reluctance to floating sides of beef down the river (an unsavory prospect for any stroller to happen upon)—which brings us to the second proposition, a more community-oriented approach, whereby a sum of money is offered, or perhaps a ticket, or coupons towards the cost of a ticket to some of our community events like, for instance, the forthcoming opera, or the art museum, in exchange for a turtle brought to a particular location, which might be called a "return station" and may be affiliated with our recycling stations, the outcome being, it is hoped, that the ever-burgeoning turtle population is curbed while, simultaneously, cultivating interest in our community events, and, as an added bonus, it is further hoped that the turtle "return" will be particularly attractive to our youth, who it is believed will see it as a "game," and as consequence receive a "prize," thus fostering participation in these cultural events, suffering, as they are, from lack of at least local interest, all of which should reveal both the enormous obstacles confronted by and far reaching substance of the young Doctor's counter-proposal, and might, therefore, silence his critics who more than suggest that his Ph.D. is a Ph.Demented, a Ph.Dummy, and—in the halls of the Public Water Works—his pH's unbalanced, though even *there* a tendency exists for misrepresenting the complexity of the system, so that he is sorely tempted to abandon us to the pathogenic diseases which generally dwell in our digestive tracks, as well as the malodorous gases created by the decomposition of our solid wastes, while, in his newfound free time, the young Doctor might instead enjoy becoming acquainted with his wife and finally writing a review for the seventh edition of the excellent four-volume series *Sewerage and Sewage Disposal* written by the engineers Metcalf and Eddy (though, indispensable as it otherwise is, there's not a word printed on *this* subject), to say nothing about the real problem with criticizing and laying blame, mainly knowing when to stop, because all are finally blameworthy, including the most innocent seeming among us, like Ella, for instance, for whom the young Doctor made explicit his requirement of one hour of solitude before leaving for his office, so that she was free to lunch to the accompaniment of a military marching band, puncture the fall of darkness with fireworks and sparklers, and in all hours in between (except six to seven in the morning) waltz about with bone china tea plates strapped to her feet while tooting her infernal bassoon if she was so moved, but *this* exact hour was to be a peaceful hour, the only one that he fully relies upon to unfold *peaceably* in order to execute the responsibilities of his part of the Public (which Ella is no doubt part of now) Works, the complexity and contemplation of which requires, in both strict and vivid language, to declare that if she is so inclined to use the toilet during this time, that she would please avoid flushing, as, his study being situated below the bathroom, his skull is filled with its vacuous suction, thereby drawing his attention from the task at hand, away to the opposite wall, inside which the sewer pipe is hidden, and that pre-empting this constant interruption by clasping his hands over his ears serves, since the physics of plumbing are in no large degree different in the human and municipal forms, little good, as the sound of the flush perfectly mimics the sound of one, with his hands over his ears, swallowing, but he does not blame Ella, no, on the contrary he hears the sound of the waste water falling through the pipe and is reminded of their connectivity, how each is plugged into something larger, how the many make up the one, and how the German composer Schiller himself defined the bassoon as the instrument of hunger and unquestionable optimism, so that we too might do well to listen to Ella's transformation of gases into music with her alchemist's instrument right smack on top of our young Doctor's head and recall Schiller's odd axiom that *one bassoon doth the symphony make*, and not be surprised when, after taking our seats, after the lights are dimmed and we hear Ella's throaty bassoon lumbering out of the woodwinds during the *prelude*, we find the young Doctor sitting there in the darkness next to us, and the choice will be ours, to up and leave our seats or remain, pretending to ignore him, yearning for the last note to fade, concerned not with the painted faces, colorful costumes and booming voice before us, but instead our tailbones pressing further and further against our skins, thus reminding us of the young Doctor's presence and therefore possibly missing the moment when we might be otherwise filled with the emotion at the heart of every tragedy ever written, acted or sung, which is that our hero, having made his mistake in water, finds that nothing remains to wash it away.

MY IMMORTAL WORKS

Among the physicists of our late century who practice the art of the commonplace analogy, Andres Cerebria gives us the story about an infinite number of monkeys pounding away at an infinite number of typewriters. Given such odds, the theorist states, there will be monkeys among the multitudes who will write Shakespeare's sonnets; in the parlance of science, the event is a statistical inevitability.

As, of course, is the extinction of the human race. While it might not occur that a virulent pox is born from some madness in this age of millennium, it will happen eventually. Everyone says so. We can infer here that it is at this time, in the vacancy left by our extinction, that the monkeys will accidentally stumble into the Pentagon, universities, Small Business Administration, IRS, and all other places where typewriters are kept in deep storage. Given enough time, they will begin poking at the keys and composing the infinite combinations that include the line, *That thou art blamed shall not be thy defect,* and the other 13 lines that follow.

Likewise, through infinite combinations, these monkeys will hit upon an efficient office hierarchy: one monkey writing cogent inter-office memos, another creating an effective marketing strategy while still another composes the copy on a publicity brochure. Included among the squirrel and fiddler monkeys will be the chance filer monkey, the competent mimeograph monkey. One monkey will pull a folder with my name on it which another monkey had filed alphabetically, and through infinite combinations, this folder will necessarily contain my entire body of work, including my recent letter of complaint to American Airlines, every draft of my resume updated over the course of my lifetime, a faked permission slip to leave grammar school early on the afternoon of April 11th, 1975, a grocery list dictated by my wife on October 28th, 1997, the obligatory sentence "when everything was said and done, one word hung in the air" that I had to use in the writing of a story of exactly 500 words (excluding title), and it will also contain these choice phrases: Chimps are chumps, a monkey smells as bad as a monkey, and you haven't the slightest idea of how lucky you are.

Given that all possibilities would comprise this file, it would include the finished collection of short stories that I have yet to finish. This doesn't disturb me. What does disturb me is all the possible revisions that contain better choices, better words and stories that I will forever be incapable of writing. Somewhere on a terra cotta office floor in Taipei will be a better story than I am able to write, but whose resemblance to mine is unmistakable. This more accomplished version will be scattered among other type-written pages of nonsensical key-strokes and the chanced-upon third sentence of the *Communist Manifesto.* In the middle of this will be a monkey who, after idly picking at his teeth with a tortoise shell hairpin, will begin typing again to relieve his boredom.

FROM WHAT BEGINS WITH BIRD

BY NOY HOLLAND (2005)

EDITOR'S NOTE: Brian Evenson's reader's report on Noy Holland's *What Begins with Bird* so exactly characterizes my experience of it that his words will do for mine: "The best of these pieces (such as the title story and 'Rooster, Pollard, Cricket, Goose') mime realism—i.e. on one level they can be read as straightforward narratives, but on another level there is so much going on with language, with sound, with repetition, with quiet language innovation, that they demand another sort of reading, and there are moments in all these stories... where Holland's attention to language becomes like a bolus in the throat, where one can't help but read the virtuoso performance as superceding the narrative itself.... Through such gestures, Holland creates a genuine and satisfying tension between the satisfactions of meaning and the lyrical satisfactions of language, which makes reading some of these stories a distracted, ethereal experience, the fiction *felt* as often as it is understood." For me, Brian's comment describes the spiritual discipline involved in reading Noy's work, the state of attention in which our customary acquisitiveness must be quieted and we learn to dwell between past and future, the known and unknown. This attentiveness to meaning's present unfolding discloses the world's independence from me, its refusal to conform. That's how it survives.

—RMB

"Since I have had children, my work has become increasingly overtly political, and I am more and more comfortable with this, more and more outraged and frightened about, for instance, what we are doing to the natural world, and how little of it we are leaving to the many souls who live and shall."

—Noy Holland

ROOSTER, POLLARD, CRICKET, GOOSE

We could do with him what we wanted. The old people left and left Goose here and what they left was ours.

They'd have taken him if they could. They took the glass from in the windows, they took the crib from the bend in the road. Our pa would have to drag a new crib out to keep the corncobs in. They took the cow in the wet field lowing. They took the blind pig beating the barn.

Down from the house where our ma stuck tight it went barn and barn and barn and crib and next the pond-bridge over the pond next the brocade couch in the pond where they had gone and dragged it. They left us the couch and the road paint sure from wherever cheap they had got it. They left the washer machine with its top torn loose down on its side beside the creek.

They took the knobs from the doors and the rods for towels

and what bulbs that burned they could reach out to and loose them from their sockets. Anything much they could loose they took and everything they left behind we got to keep between us. I got the doll I saved from the johnnie that simpered when I hit it. I got the trees and the wind in the trees and the pond with the couch and the muskrat traps and the green gone garish on it. Pa got the horse and the hills.

The horse, we found between the barns where it had gone up and over. It had knocked its thick head on the road, Pa said. We were sitting in the truck.

We had checked the coop for chickens. We had seen that the crib was gone.

It went Pa then me then Ma in the truck with the baby asleep on her bosom.

They had hit it with a pipe, Pa said. Else it had gone up and over.

Ma got out like he told her to and went up the hill with the baby. I heard her high shoes on the road when she went and I heard when she stopped and rested.

The horse, I heard and would hear again the queer high birdish sound he made. It hung between the barns. He was laid out between the barns.

I got the barn and the hay in the barn and the dust coming slatted through the rafters. I got the pail for corn I beat to spook the rats from the crib when I fed when I came from the bus from school. It was my job to feed the animals, to fatten Maggie cow. I got the hay and the smell of the hay and the light snapping on on the barn.

The horse was Pa's and the hills he rode and the bees he dug that clouded him when he dragged the hooked plow with the tractor. The rabbits he dug he gave to me, I kept in the bowl in the washer machine thrown out where the creek ran through.

I stretched the come-along out like Pa told me. Because the others never did have a come-along to crank the horse over the gravel with to take him off on whatever it was they had brought to move away on. So they left him laid out on the hump of our road between the high walls of our barns.

The horse was dead, Pa said, or good as dead but what was the thin long sound he made, what were the lifting moons of his eyes when Pa came close with his gun? So he was good yet good for something.

A horse is worth something, easy, Pa said, you could sell him off handsome on the hoof in a blink. They would buy him from Pa by the pound. We could haul him up on the bed of Pa's truck, sell him off quick down the hill from us to pay for what they loosed from us the hooks and bulbs and sockets. And yet I thought to ride him. Yes. I thought to him: Hum up.

I looped the steel loop around his pastern first as quick in the dark as I could. I walked the slack out. I worked the handle some.

I saw the light go on in the house up the hill and then Ma in the window passing. So they left a light with the chairs all gone so Ma could see to sit the floor and hitch up her shirt for the baby. The baby always goes to the one so I ask who is the other one for. She laughs. You are as bad as your pa. Get on.

There are chickens to feed and cow Maggie. Two cobs twice for Maggie. There are board fences sure to creosote and thistle to dig from the fields when it bolts before the purple crowns. I muck the stalls and soap the tack and vet Pa's dogs they run the fields flushing birds all day. I am his girl Cricket. I climb the big oak on the hill Pa's hill even after when it is hit and burns and the burn blacks my skin my clothes.

I work the handle some and the slack is out and I can feel the horse start to pull over the hump of gravel. He lets his long high sound. Pa says it is like a goose so Goose but I never heard a goose as that, so long as that it warbled, not a sound like that and never since from bird nor horse nor man. Not even when Pa hit him.

He hit him in his head. Then was a sound a girl-girl lets, queerly sung and pretty. But that was some time after. That was when we shod.

First Pa thinks to work with him when he is up and well enough and we walk him down in the sun in the heat on the road between the barns. First Pa thinks to gentle Goose to ride him days we do not plow, afternoons we do not need to hoe nor pick nor harrow. Pa went to him first going easy talking sweetly in his ear. *Hope hope.*

He never did hit Goose at the first the night when Ma went off up the road. She went up the hill with the baby quick her hair a knot on her brightened head he reached for when she rested. First it was me Ma reached for. Then after me she rested. I took the strength she had, Pa said, so after me she rested.

Pa gets the hills and the oaks on the hills the old people called the farm by. Ma gets the house she climbs to, her shoes tapping bright on the road. Our ma gets the boy not yet a boy for Pa to need to work the fields while he is weak and small. She gets the way he smells the way he gums her how he coos.

Goose lets his long high sound. I feel him shudder across the gravel the ratchet clicking slow. I see him rest if I rest and flutter his nose but Ma will have something fixed for us and sits her chair to watch for us and sheets on the floor she has spread for us and the light is gone from the barn. They have loosed it from its socket hung from the spavined wall of the barn. *Get up.*

I taut the line some. I bring him easy.

I haul up the traps in the muck by and by from the bank where the old people left them. The dogs come to drink from the pond.

They beat out a flattened path in the weeds in the burrs that catch and mat my hair flown loose when first I found one. First how we knew to look at all was once I heard Pa's dog. She had her paw snapped up in the mouth of the trap in the gone-by weeds that mark the pond in the rattling pods come winter. Summer coming to its close. The fescue stiffly yellowed. And in the night Pa's dog cries out from the drawn-back lip of the pond.

Be slow. Our Goose.

See the road slopes up. Take your time to calm you.

His breath comes weak and shallows. I let the line slack. He throws himself to kneeling and his bones knock against the road. He shoves his muzzle down on the road to rest so his thick head saws above. Pa touches his flank with the gun. I ease up I think I am easing up, the line gone slack to tap the road but I can never see Goose quite. I can scarcely see him stand but to see the yellow of his eye swing up and the white of his face against the road.

So he is up. I hear Pa humming to him slow and the coins in his pants when he moves to him going, *Ho,* going, *Hope hope ho.*

Pa ought to have a sugar cube, a cigarette to give him.

He throws his head up. The stripe in his head when he throws it streaks and see the dark will bleed it free, will from him in the darkness wick the whiteness clean away. It is like our pa has thrown it—how his bird dogs quake and trill.

You goose. First she called Pa so to tease him. But then Ma called the baby *goose* and by and by each name for Pa I used to hear her call him by she picked to name the baby with and mine I had forgotten. Now we are only Pa to her and Pa and his girl Cricket. Moving slowly in the road.

He throws his head up. It is like our pa has thrown it, gone from the trees from the creek where he likes to work his dogs to the field. Good dogs.

We can do with him what we want to. Sell him off quick on the hoof if we like to grind his bones to give the dogs the inly tubes and organs keep them fed and fit and strong. They are field dogs, bird dogs all. Pa throws them the wing of the cut-away goose in the falling dark and the dogs at his feet and they stay they stay, the wing dipping down until he moves his hand to school them.

And then his long high sound. And so Pa named him Goose for the goose for the wing he throws his dogs.

Goose lunges at Pa so much as he can but I have got him looped up still, Pa tripping back with his gun at his chest so I ratchet the line to hold him. I cannot hold Pa. Only watch him slowly falling. He takes a long time falling.

Pa's dogs bed down and whinge. *You quit.* But they are thinking what will happen what is next to come?

Time comes Pa thinks to ride him. Out between the barns. He rides to the oaks the lightning hits along the fence cow Maggie rubs to leaning while she fattens. Past the coop the chickens pecking slowly at their corn. Past Pa's prize yellow rooster learned to blind his favored hens.

Pa's dogs, they are bird dogs all—but are they bird enough to guess at him? At Pa's prize yellow rooster? Who appeared in a fluff in the barn—the day Goose rode Pa past and every day thereafter. And sat his back thereafter. Who flew his coop to bide his days sitting Goose's withers—could they guess at such as him?

And at the day we shod him?

And of the bees Pa plowed?

I am not one to picture it not nearly even half of it not Ma in her chair past autumn not the wrangled plow. Nor Goose. The rooster shyly by him. Pa's. And then the rooster Goose's. Only walking back to rooster pecking gently at his hens.

Nor that. I had not pictured that. And not the picked-over

eyes of the hens bright as the yolks of the eggs we take left seeping in their feathers.

Not the blood the baby lets not the milk the baby lets, Ma's shirt run pinkly through. Nor that. Him plumping at her bosom.

Time was I was Ma's. Nor that. Nor time was Pa was also.

Not Pa when I come upon him. He has dragged across the pond.

I am not cut to picture. To stand at the bank and puzzle out I am cut to cut and run.

The gun fires when he wallops the road. Then Goose is up and hanging.

The old people have come. I thought Goose had seen the old people come rolling home to claim him.

And so he hung there. What to do.

I touched the line once. They couldn't loose him. They could go on back from wherever they'd come and forget they ever saw him stood and pawing where they left him in a heap upon the road.

They could find another. There are others after Goose. There are Mouse and Pepper, Blue, Prim Sue and Candysara. Cribbing at the barn.

I tie Pa's bootstrings every morning. Did his bootstrings loose I tied for him did his pantlegs make him fall?

Ma takes one pair and me another. We hem the legs on Pa's short side from the time when Pa was a boy my size and crumpled in his bed. *Get up.* And Pa could not get up and not. And not for a long time after. So is it mine or Ma's dread cross? Who take one pair and one another. We are not much with our needles. And Pa is fallen across the road. He seems to quit there.

He seems to quit and stiffen, ready for the blow.

Goose would throw himself off from us. He would fly himself over the barn he thought come soft on his hooves in the field where he grazed with we two dumbly watching.

Then he was over. Goose flung himself on over. I heard his bones, the clatter and snap, his head a rind against the road bursted wetly open. He lay there—his legs sprung stiff, his corded neck—his body hauled in chinked from stone to mark the field the fallen dead the bloody day forgotten.

Pa softly now, "Let up."

I held the line taut. I saw I held the line taut still from the coil where I let it.

The nightsky stooped and held its breath, the trees bent too to listen—for the sputter and tick the quieting tide of Goose's reedy pipes and valves the rocking iridescent humps and hollows of his organs.

And Pa again, "Let up." Still I heard *Get.*

Pa struggled up from where he fell and knocked the grit from his pants I stitched, the sloppy hem, and he nodded. Pa came at me with his hand high up. He had never hit me yet but still I stood to let him.

The line had cut some through. I had looped it over the curl of fur above the hoof you sell them on and it had dug some through. His eye had spun wide up in the dark to regard the stars above. The moon on its slow crossing.

His burblings—mine—my cross to bear, my thin bitten birdish shrill he let, my name though Pa had thought it—*Goose. Goose* and also *Cricket.* We were named for the sounds thrown from us yes for a dream's long soured tongue.

And so I loosed it. I shook the line some. Nothing not a twitch not a nostril flared no breath no lifting brisket. So I could do it easy ease the loop the cable from his pastern where I cut him. I felt the heat rise from him. I felt the give in my knees when I kneeled by him and the heat of the softened road. So we could winch him up now. He had made it easy. We would wait for the light for the morning.

Morning. Hello, little farm.

Still we wake to him up come sunup. We are sleeping all on the sheet Ma spread and Goose is scrolloping over the road.

I snip Pa's toenails for him turn his hem and tie his boots who cannot reach to do it.

I can smell the barn. I smell in my hair the baby too he gummed it as we rode.

Pa clips the leadshank on him. He feels along his bones.

Pa leads him off between the trees me and Ma standing out in our gowns she wears to walk in time the fallen dew the hill we climb to reach her. I sit the chair her chair to watch her, watch the nightshade fill behind her see the bats loop briefly through. Her small boy nearby sleeping.

At length when once the snow has come to keep us snugly home, Ma goes sunup to nightfall gowned else sits the bath from meal to meal the latch thrown once the baby walks to keep him always with her to keep him safely in.

She has heard us at our chores by then. We have backed Goose onto the slab by then. The rooster crowing on.

Pa's dogs spooked about for the moons Pa clipped, for the tailings curled from his hooves filed flat to take the shoe and he cussed them. Cussed his horse his dogs. His girl with the mangled paw stumping in who sat with me at his knees should he sit should he think to nudge her head. Let her bump her ribs against him.

After her I found the others easy. You go by your nose through the weeds for the traps going low to the ground like a dog. Red fox I found and muskrat, coon and the paw of what I do not know in the muck cow Maggie made of the banks of the pond I would wade in the dry out into.

The old people could have found them caught in the dry time when they moved. Then I would not have had to. Would not have had to smell them then nor burr my hair to get to them nor haul them onto the bridge for Pa so Pa could see to flay or gut or what any else he did to them or sort the parts to bury.

We buried them back by the chicken coop in sight of the pond where they swam if they swam or only came and drank from. Soon the rooster flapped over the pond—his Goose had gone from the field. The rooster come to sit Goose's back flapped in his grief to the couch when Goose passed come rain come sleet come snow. Crowing on.

His hens in the coop to hear him. I lay in my bed and heard him, the moon sweeping past, the stars.

Cricket you Cricket you.

See the white of his face swung up?

His bright eye webbed and curdled?

And then when we had blinded him and set him out in the field to browse I saw the skin seal and crumple saw in the cold it was blent and gathered.

They will do it to a baby too a rooster will give him half a chance he does it to his own. And his hens' eyes are small.

I lay in my bed and pictured it.

Pictured Pa when I came upon him.

I came upon him in the wet months yet the flying leaves the sinking grass the geese dropped from their wedges yet and scudding across the pond.

I had come on the bus from school. I skipped. I swung my feet through the fallen leaves to smell the sweet wet smell of them to smell the wind the needling rain that in the night had felled them. The leaves flew up and clung to me to the ratty flounce of the skirt I wore the bitten ridge of my shinbones. I stopped at the pond to peel them from me.

I could hear the tractor then. You turn the fields to fallow them. I liked to listen for Pa to know where he might leave the harrowbed the plow.

I heard him. But I did not think *Pa* at first I did not think *listen.* I sang my song the coming home song against his note I had not heard and hope again to never. Still I looked about and saw him. He was wallowed up on the couch in the green with the yellow bead the pond was deep on the couchback scarcely showing.

He could not be Pa. He was something in the wet the old people left that had loosed itself from the muck as it went and yet it spit my name. With still our barns to pass between, the hill to the house to run. I ran. I ran the day the bees got Pa and ran the day I held his Goose in the washroom where we shod. But I did not run far. I heard him bellow. You try it try to run. Drop to your hands if the grass is high and dream he cannot find you there with your heart knotted small as the rabbits new-born he brings to you in the crown of his hat the days he plows to calm. But I have never saved one. I have never saved one yet of all the ones he brings to me I have lost them all.

I lay on the bank and watched him. The longer I kept away from Pa the harder it was to go to him.

And yet I went to him. I knocked the bees from his neck for him Pa gone in his hurt not hearing me not a place on him to hold him by I held him by his hair. Through the green I swam him. I could have walked the pond but it took my shoes from my feet the silken bottom. Me and Pa dragged a stripe in the green where I swam where it folded against Pa's head. Pa Pa.

Once we grew a pig so fat even its eyelids fattened, ear and jowl and bursting cheek and by and by its eyeballs—squeezed—stood away loose from its head.

Then Pa. Bellowing out of the wallow. The cow to her teats to cool. The tractor run up on a stump and stopped and still at its ticking idle. I made my hands a stirrup—Pa's legs were too swelled to bend. *Swing up.* And from the time of riding shotgun years I knew which stick to muscle, which to back to raise the plow when once we had it scraping up loud against the road.

Ma in her chair past autumn. Us come up come dew come snow. The baby let to his knees at the screen to scream the day the bees swarmed Pa and Ma came out to swat at us going *Gracious lord above.*

Think back to when time was in her—my soft head broken through. Before that. When time was she was Pa's. Before my hair I grew in her that made her retch and swoon.

A girl. And her boy sick and small. I took the strength she had in her. I kept them up nights nights in her: their Cricket. Chirruping in the swill.

Boy, her boy, her funny runt. He could not be Pa's. Who came before they thought his name and stayed they had not thought he might for such a long time after. *Boy*, she called him. *Goose, you goose*, and *mister*—Ma thinking not to choose a name to have to have to call him by should he be taken from her.

We never took him from her. Even when he crawled. Nor say I ever came to her to cut my name most fine in her not before nor after Ma swelling as he grew.

I was all Pa's girl. The barns were mine and the hay in the barns and Pa and the trees and the cows. Cow Maggie leaned against me. The birds flew south by the stars. Barn and barn and barn and pond the road climbing out through the fields. Mine and Pa's, my pa's. The high quiet wobbledy stars. And Ma where she sat in the window was ours and sat in the shut-away buttery gold, the dogs at our heels the stars. Should you wish.

Ma's shirt bled pinkly through.

The seed-blown fields the wickerings. The slickened births and murders, ours, the fierce wide blowing day.

I tended to him gently. Pa wallowing in the tub. He would swell to fit it. And swell till he could not budge from it and I would spoon a mash to him and keep the water cooled for him and nest his head in my pillow. His eye unloosed like a doll's. Fetch a sledge. Break him duly from it.

Pa's arms puffed out to float from him and seep in milky puddles, his skin so hot to touch it scalds. I did not touch it. I worked the coughing spigot, churned the cold to sap the heat slowly not to hurt him. And made as not to hear him his voice not his no voice at all—a green sea grief a great whale culled and keening in its traces.

I daubed a paste where he was stung a curdly dull against his skin I first swiped bright with butter. Pa. Who plowed the bees it comes to me to see if Ma would see to him to see if she would tend to him but Ma would not have come.

Why seem at last to hear him? Ma would not have come.

And who was it came upon him?

And so I took it slow. I made Ma's clucks and muddlings and swabbed and slowly doctored him. I had no Goose to think of no price to fetch no mouths to fill no deed to hide the doing of.

No day yet when we shod.

It's me Pa Pa it's Cricket.

Get.

I was not her. Not Ma and never Cricket quite but proof she had not come.

I took to sleeping in the barn else the sinking grass in the leaves unhinged in the wind. Pa's rooster nightly crowing.

Pa when he was up again and shrunk into himself again rode Goose unshod through our honeyed woods our creeks our windfall autumn. Among the lowly creatures named and ours to daily tend. We are sloppy in our tending. Our swallows catch in the raftered dark our rabbits are turned from the fields. Fox we trap and whistle pig and the spotty domes of our turtles crush in the wet upon our road. And in our hay we gather. And too the narrow fellows sunning lazy in the stubble catch—snakes pressed between the flakes of hay as though we mean to keep them, and faith by them in the shut-away days the snowbound weeks we wait to breathe that the fields are strewn and rooted through with bees with bodies sleeping.

Pa wore Goose away his hooves split and curled and then a day I came from school Pa brought him to me saddled and swung me up to ride him. Pa gave me a whip to run him with. Goose could not walk it looked to me he seemed to wince to stand there.

Up the hill I ran him.

We ran until Pa could not see and then we let him come to us come gimping up the hill to us to snap the lunge line on. Pa swung me up again. So he could run us. So we might see she watched him run us. He stood at the hub of the circle we ran in whatever dusk was left to us and Ma appeared in the windowlight in her sorry robe. *Hup ho.*

The night closed in the early cold. Goose beneath me frothed and steamed and still my hands my skinny arms grew thick to me and shook. My bare legs burned beneath my skirt against the sweating saddleflaps and so I tried to hold them off so that when Goose tripped he threw me, he would throw me, I would fly through the trees like a doll. Soon enough.

Quick the snow the brittling cold. As quick the thaw comes on.

I trick Goose into the trailer then his blinkers on to calm him and grain in the bin to steady him after we have beat at him and cussed and poked and whooped at him till Pa has gone off for his gun.

After the day we shod this was. After the snow the thaw had come.

No bird for us no Christmas.

The snow slumping against the barn. "You load the cur before I'm back else I am going to have to—"

To have to. Pa could do with him what he wanted—he was toddling off for his gun. I did not try to stop him but to think to walk Goose in.

Ma gone from her chair the tent jerked down we had hung at the hearth to snug in. Yet we were not what kept her. It was not in us to keep her.

And so I walked him in.

The first I saw I ran from him. I did not think *Pa* at first but is it dead or living.

This was before we blinded Goose before the time we trailered him our Ma going off with her wheelbarrow her boy in a bunch in the wheelbarrow how small against the road.

Before any of that. Before we shod this was. Before the rooster flapped onto the pond.

And yet I ran from Pa. Crept back. Before the bees died off I did. Before the fescue yellowed. I lay on the bank to look at him. The pods of the milkweed swelled and split and the seed by its silken feathery plumes as it was meant to do broke away.

And then we shod him.

The day was dull the day we shod him and cold before the snow had come and Pa sent me out to fetch Goose out of the withering grass where he browsed. I walked through the gate with my pail at my knees and called to him over the field.

He came to me.

He let me come to him, whinnying, that day as any other.

The days were dry then. The corn a stubble. The apples blew into the fields, a glut that year—I could find him. It was easy enough to find Goose—he was feasting beneath the trees. He quit to look at me. Pa's rooster pecking lazily a drubbing on his withers.

Pa had fired the forge in the barn the barn dark to me but for the embers there the shadows rayed and flinching the cottony raftered dark. Goose was shy of it, I brought him gently in, he was skittish.

I backed him into the washroom into the crossties where we shod. I leaned my chest, a boy's, against him. I felt my heart at the bone in his head his breath the wet of the grass he ate and sweet against my belly. *Hush.*

I kept it to me.

At the first even Pa was kind. He clipped away where the hoof began at the end to hook and tear. He kicked the shards the cut-away moons to his dogs to take to nibble at at the end of the barn and hide. He rasped the hoof flat, he picked a small stone from the frog.

The shoe nested in the forge on the fire—outside, winter's early winded dark advancing slowly on.

The rooster stood to crow for it. That day as any other. But Pa when the rooster crowed jerked up and let his hollowed sound he made the day I came upon him swarmed. He jabbed Goose in his brisket. Goose already lunging. Pa gone to his knees on the slab.

The rooster flapped to the rafters. The sparrows swept from the barn.

He filed the hoof flat. You have to rasp it flat to take the shoe to ride the wash and hillside slopes to pass the house and Ma in the house to pass the coop the chickens.

He pinched the shoe from the forge—it was flaring, a shaking liquid yellow. He hooked the shoe over the anvil then over the battered nose—you have to turn it. Pound it to make a fit of it bore the slim squared holes.

I knew Pa's knees were swelling—I had heard them knock against the slab. His long face pinched and fallowed, I saw, who saw ahead as I knew he must the bruisy syrupy blue of skin the selvage pressed of the pants I hemmed sloppily upon it. I would have to cut Pa's pants from him—from the burl the knotted sickened joint and ice or lance or sit to bend or what any else Pa thought to show he could bully through the doing of and so we two kept on with it so we two said nothing.

He punched the nail through—once, three times again, on the one shank and then on the other. To keep the shoe fast. To drive the nails through—square and blunted. Eight in all. I knew the sound and counted.

Pa held the shoe against his hoof. The shoe was hot still it was hissing and the stink of hide of hair or hoof the twangy burning smell rose up and Goose threw himself against me. Pa held him. He did what he could to hold him Pa he kept him wedged against the wall we hang the tack the leadshanks on the picks and forks and shovels.

Tell her that.

He tapped the nail in.

Tell your ma I tried to calm him. That at the last we twitched him. To make it easy. I meant to calm him. I put myself between you tried to keep you safe from harm. No harm meant. You could not trust him. He was game but you could not trust him. He would throw you into the trees he would he would drag you across the fields.

I let Pa twitch him. So I could hold him. So the day might come I thought so of the weeks I sulked to school.

Pa drew out Goose's lip where the stripe blazed through the velvet soft that veered across and snatched down the twitch the silver bars upon it hard and twisted. It was easier then to hold Goose shaking quiet on the slab. I drew his head down slowly and pressed my face to the white of his face how soft where the stripe swept through.

Pa tapped a nail in. He went hoof to hoof in the graying light. *How quick the dark came on. Tell her that.*

But I could not yet think of Ma of what we would need or not to tell but thought of the day I would ride our Goose in my boots to school. I would tie Goose off on the chalky racks the city kids lash their bicycles to, would come to him between the bells to curry him to feed him.

Hey horsie girl.

Of course they teased me. Would. Who wished to be me.

How I pressed my heart to his brisket.

Pa wedged each hoof between his knees his shoulder thrown against Goose hard to keep him tipped against the wall we hang the leads and halters on the shoe for luck to hold him. I felt his breath against my chest a wind drawn rough across my throat and felt the cool the whips of spit the snot swept down from his nostrils yes and of his mouth the velvet there where the stripe blazed through.

You get. And the rooster too. *Get get.*

I kept the loop of his mouth pinched fast the twist in the loop that made him wheeze that Pa had stopped to show to me that made him drip and gurgle. And still I could not hold him. I was sick in myself to hold him so so Pa could shove and cuss at him so Pa could treat him roughly.

He swung the rasp back.

It would not be long.

We would leave our tools and the cooling forge and make our way up from the barn. Soon enough.

Then I could cut Pa's pants from him. Who cannot reach to do it. Who have not kept him from it. The selvage dug well in.

Pa kept on as I knew he must who knew by him the way of things who knew to watch him swing his rasp he swung at Goose's head his knees enough to think *he's mine. He is mine he is mine he is mine.*

Will be.

I will cook and clean for him and sew and scrub his feet for him and shine his boots and buckles.

Keep him safe from harm.

Say that.

That it was easy, it would have been easy—to lose an eye on the washroom wall on the hooks and nails we hang tack from he could do it to himself tell her he could do it easy.

That he is fractious. He is meant to be worked and strong tell her. How quick the dark came on.

It came on.

Pa beat at Goose about the knees the rasp struck in behind and hard where you can hear the bones in him where you can make him buckle.

I would not have pictured it—that you could make him buckle. That Pa could fell him in the crossties hanging ready for the blow.

Goose dropped to his knees his rump yet high as if to let me throw my foot my leg across and ride him. My hat flying up to school. *Wheeo.*

He quit there—to let before Pa came at him his last breath ratchet through. And then Pa came at him.

I thought how the white swept up. Pa fallen across the road. *Wheeo.*

Because Pa could not have rolled from him. Pa could not have moved.

He swung the rasp back. He brought it hard across his head his rolling curdled eye I saw.

Cricket you Cricket you.

Quick a girl's sweet wurbled note. Quick as that the wettish thuck the jellied seep of his eyeball burst the flies the puss like honey.

We set him out then. When it was done then. I walked Goose out on his blinded side and set him loose like Pa had said back in the back and hidden field the deer came to to lie in. We walked up the hill and washed our hands and sat and ate our supper.

She had fried three eggs for supper for us as Ma had come those weeks to do no matter what Pa said of it and three again come morning. And Pa said nothing of it and not again when light had come and Ma went out with her boy in the snow that as we slept flew down. Her tracks went out to the fence I sat the days Goose ran the sloping field and turned toward the barn and quit there well shy of the bend in the road.

She came back then. I put my mind to it—to the tracks I had to go by. There were two of them going she left in the snow and not a step she came back by.

She had gone away twice down the hill, I thought. She had gone away once the mother we knew who sat for us in the window. Then look on her heels came the other. Here came the one from before the boy we had forgotten was hers to ever be or ever was ours to know.

I liked to think of it—that she could walk herself out away

from us from what we did or did not do she could call herself out on the road going out going out in her boots in the unbroken snow that we would know at the last we had lost her.

And yet the tracks quit.

She would find Goose in the barn she thought. She would see him she thought from the bend in the road see what we had done to him who sat at her table after and ate the meal she cooked for us and slept in the beds she made for us and so she quit well shy of it and came away back to home. She walked herself back up the hill to us walking backward her back to the wind to keep her boy from the snow.

The snow climbed in the trees in the fences. A night would pass a morningtime and soon Pa would set upon her again and break what eggs I brought to her that the hens before the rooster quit still had in them for laying. After that I did not bring the eggs. After that they did not lay them.

The rooster went from the field and back to sit the broken back of the couch stood up in the ice of the pond. No thought in his head to rooster. No eggs to bring for Pa to break for Ma to fry for supper then even should we want some.

I thought I would not want some. I would break an egg in his socket I thought let the yolk freeze bright and round. Should Goose lie down.

And then he lay down—the night of the day the wind came warm and the thaw set in the sudden melt and the birds appeared and bickered and swerved in the steam twisting up from our farm.

We hitched the trailer then. That we might use him. Sell him off quick on the hoof down the hill in the warm while we could move.

I had kept Goose's tail in a braid for him and kept his head in a hood for him so the wind could not eat at the socket. The last of our sorry apples dropped I had kicked to him in the field where he lies where he pawed at the snow for what grass there was and picked the leaves he could get to yet from the beech the oak the whippy trees at the edge of the woods that held them. What he did not eat the deer took to and to the cobs of corn I brought and his coat grew thick and ratted in the wind and his hipbones stood out from him.

We kept our heads down. The cold had deepened. I tramped a path past the coop the failing hens the rooster would not when the cold had come leave the pond to rooster.

I thought at first he would ride with me out in the pail with the corn to the field. And so I stopped at the bank to cluck at him. He turned his tail to me. I brought his prize hens to the bank to see and scratch to spread to tempt him. Before the pond was skinned with ice I ferried him back through the muck the weeks yet never once did I see him eat nor seem to think to rooster, never once did I pass the crib to climb the hill to the house to Ma but that he hadn't flapped back out to the couch to announce what we had done.

This was when the freeze augered in, this was in the thaw.

In the thaw of the year when the water rose Pa's bird seemed to walk upon it.

I went the while before the thaw before the hillsides snicked and steamed and then the once thereafter after Ma had gone. I knew to call to him, picking my way once the creek froze through between the spindly boles of trees the needled limbs of the buckthorn there where yet the small dark berries clung the beads in rimpled clusters. I shook in my pail as I went to him the corn I was not to bring to him. I brought cigarettes and sugar cubes crumbling apart in my pockets.

Hope hey. Hope hey. I meant to tend to him, to swab and slowly doctor him. To sweep my thumb through his socket. A day came I came upon Goose there forgetting myself to speak to him and stood upon his blinded side and he swung away and kicked me. I let him kick me.

Then it was easy. Then I could quit then.

The field was hidden. I tossed my pail back to the back of the crib and the rats there shied and scuttled out and trotted away to the barn.

So it was easy. The cold had deepened.

I went the once Pa sent me out when the thaw set in to fetch him. I saw his head rise up to see me. Otherwise I went no more.

We snugged in when the worst of the cold had come and fashioned a room with the blankets we had with the tablecloths Ma kept to spread should a guest appear should Christmas. I rode Pa's back to drive the nails to stand in his hands in the stirrups he made and hit at the few ruined crooked nubs the old people left to hang the walls. We brought our sheets our pillows in and ate and slept in what warmth there was from the fire we nursed and prodded. Ma ripening in her gown. Our shadows should we sit in quiet there yet flinching against the walls.

Ma kept her eye fast on her boy. Sitting her silk chair.

"Time was I thought the milk teeth came to make the women stop it," Pa said. "Let them rest a time—for the next to breed. Give a man his chance abed. Time was."

She set the baby down on his feet at her feet. Should he squall she swung him up again.

"But it makes your ma keep at it, same with that boy as you."

Her boy. Him lolling yet at her bosom.

We woke for weeks to snowfall the curling drifts the wind

banked up to pin our flapping door. The hedge disappeared the leeward fence cow Maggie walked out over to find her way to the barn. No school for weeks no place we went our tractor left with the broken plow on the road where Pa sprung off from it come up on him and over until all but the lip of the highside tire the wind picked clean seemed gone.

Then of a night a velvet wind and foreign swept our farm.

Pa legged me over the windowsill. He heaved me out in my mucklucks onto the slope of snow. The slabs of snow of thickened ice already in the pooling glare crept across the rooftops. I took my list to go by: cigarettes sardines D-con cheese.

Barn and barn and crib and pond and on the pond Pa's rooster—spun—our grudging weathervane. I think he thought to crow at me who never crowed by morninglight and so I waved my cap at him and waved as I went at his baffled hens, sunk to my peep in the snow.

"How you?"

They had lights at the store and the woodstove burned and the wind flown hard in the blackened pipe sucked and moaned and tumbled. I gathered my goods and bagged them. The girl held out her hand for the money she knew my pa would never send me with and quick I turned for home from her the thaw sunk deep upon us.

Every stone and matted leaf and fence and sloping fallow steamed. The ice on the pond broke soft when I passed and soft the newts the spotty frogs the dull fish frozen in. The barn the mossy pond I smelled and in the wind the flowers bloomed where it had crossed to reach us. It came on.

Ma went back in her blotted gown to the back of the house she had happened from and found her hat her dungarees her chalky split galoshes. So quick I went to fetch Goose. He lay in the field on his blinded side in a patch pawed free of snow.

I let him stop for a time for the apples that dropped and palmed him the last of the treats I had kept the months for him in my pockets.

We took the path past the crib. I knew no other way to go so as not to pass her. She would go on. She had her bag at her knee her hat on. Her boy in a bunch in the wheelbarrow.

I led him along his hood pulled free him lathered in the sudden warm his brisket gaunt and heaving. *Cricket you Cricket you.*

It would not be long. I knew as much to look at Ma her flicks and starts and sudden flush her voice like something burst in her should she gap her mouth to use it.

I went on. I led him up between the barns where Pa had drawn the trailer up and stood the high gates open.

Ma turned back the once and once again to bring herself to go. We stood on the road and watched her. The road black in the wet in the sudden thaw in the steam that dipped and gathered grown so thick to squat upon our pond that it seemed not our rooster there but the air itself yet crowing.

Stay. Stay. So go.

I gave Goose his head to lunge at Pa to beat the air to strike at him should Pa swing past where Goose could see else think to speak or touch him. To see if she would tend to him. But Ma was going on.

She went up through the lopped and pollarded trees I kept as she went a count of. Pa's dogs at her heels since the barn. Good dogs.

I leant against Pa's legs with them. I licked his pants when I was small with them with him not looking. Quick.

You get.

Pa toddling off for his gun.

Goose scraped at the road the piddling stream with the shoe those months he had not thrown that I would pry for luck from him and clip the braid of his tail from him hung fat with the mud we had hauled him through, the slickened clay and loamy sweet, and thinking I would go there yet where Goose yet lay in the sun and moon I found a tree a buckthorn near and deep against it hung them.

I blinkered him to calm him.

I walked on in ahead of him and we could hear Pa coming back, I was backed against the trough with him wedged away under the bars from him and Pa had creaked the swing-gate shut and Goose went back to thrashing. I felt my head flung back. Pa stood up on the running board and the shaft of the gun pushed through.

So it was Pa shot him.

It is for my sake Pa shot him.

I was in the stall beside him and the trailer shook and ringing quit and the blood of my face where Goose opened it ran free in my mouth and warm.

Enough for me. *No matter.*

Ma looked back the once and went on.

All that she had left to us and what is yet to come to us the oaks on the hill the lightning hits the fox in the field in the weeds I keep gone red to gray come autumn—it is enough for me. *No matter.*

I will sing Pa her song the getting up song she sang to me in the morningtime when she leaned to me to nudge me and the baby was in her hair.

I could smell him from her hair.

I slip through the muck the gone-by weeds the flatted grass the dogs bend down and think *if I could run from him* else think *I never came on him wallowed up on the couch in the green suppose Cricket supposing.*

We sat on the shore and watched him.

I did not know in myself what to do for Pa nor what there might be in tending him to call so even gently. To say: I tend him gently.

Pa would have me poke at him. He would have me pinch and twist at him.

Yet to say: *I tend him gently.* And ever in the dusk in the sinking light I knead his feet his withered legs to move the gout and feed him.

Am I not his girl Cricket?

Enough for me. No matter.

I sing Ma's song to him.

Our blessings count.

Enough for me to keep our Goose and in myself the truth of him and the dogs grow fat and eat of him and by the silken sweet of glue we spread across our palms to peel the skin I feel him with me and feel of the seeds that split in me and of the living harvest, shell and hide and cloven tongue and of the fruit and fowl we strew the yolky eyes the deer we cull the great whales flensed for blubber.

Ever so. Ever so gently.

I lie in the field and picture it. Who have come to be one to picture it. How long it was Goose hung there. Such a time it was he hung there pawing softly at the stars.

FROM MICHAEL MARTONE

BY MICHAEL MARTONE (2005)

EDITOR'S NOTE: Michael Martone's work turns on the errancy of form, the tendency of forms to go their own way independently of our consciousness of them. This is especially true of quotidian forms, those everyday, subliterary patterns of practice that make our expressive behavior recognizable. In *Michael Martone* Michael investigates one particularly negligible form of this kind: the contributor's note. As I wrote to the FC2 editorial board in 2003, "This work continues Martone's earlier investigation of the marginal and overlooked material accidents of literary works (i.e., their 'bookishness')…. What Martone does is transform these ordinary accessories of meaning into meaning's embodiment. Material that elsewhere stands outside the work here *does* the work. This has the effect of making us aware of how much of our lives, in particular our reading lives, is spent looking past, through, or beyond every page we confront." Readers will readily perceive Michael's subversive intent in *Michael Martone*, the entangling of every attempt to identify the author in new problems of self-representation and imposture. Each contributor's note becomes another fiction requiring its own contributor's note, ad infinitum. However, less obvious is how Michael's repetitions foreground the cultural function of this subliterary form: its attribution of words to something putatively less manipulable than words. Contributor's notes have become conventional during the same period in which literature has become marginal, and *Michael Martone*, with its tantalizing promise of authority, continually demonstrates why.

—RMB

"I like fictions that are viral, that infect readers without the reader knowing that they have picked up a fiction. The purpose, I suppose, is to inoculate the reader to the politics of fact and fiction in the world of information and disinformation, as well as to reveal the constructed nature of the world…. Question everything. And find a way to break out of our functional fixedness that only appears to be 'real.'"

—Michael Martone

CONTRIBUTOR'S NOTE

Michael Martone was born in Fort Wayne, Indiana, and was educated in the public schools there. His first published work, a poem titled "Recharging Time," and a character sketch, "Tim, the Experience," about his brother, appeared in the *Forum,* an annual literary magazine produced by the school system featuring contributions from its students. His mother, a high school freshman English teacher at the time, in fact, wrote the poem and the character sketch, signing her son's name to the work and sending it to the editor, another English teacher at a south side junior high school who had been a sorority sister, Kappa Alpha Theta, in college. Indeed, most of his papers written for school were written by his mother. Examples included English research papers, history term papers, translations from the Latin, speeches, and lab reports. It began innocently enough with his mother writing his essays, the prose supposedly dictated by the son to his mother, whose penmanship was far and away more legible. This arrangement, her son sitting across the kitchen table, in a sense thinking out loud as she transcribed his thoughts with the same pen she used to grade her own students' papers, engendered in her a very active editorial intervention, which began to shape the spontaneous utterances emanating from her son. Soon this situation evolved to the point where her son sat silently while she wrote an original response to his initial prompt. Once she finished the first draft, she read it back to her son, who made a few minor suggestions as to form, style, and content. It was at this time and under these conditions that Martone began thinking of himself as a writer. His mother promoted that view in other ways, announcing to her friends at the local chapter of the educational honorary that her son had an aptitude for writing. The collaboration continued through college, where assignments were mailed home and returned or, in some extreme cases, the prose response was communicated via the telephone and copied out in a rather cramped and illegible longhand in the dormitory phone booth. Most of Martone's first book of stories and his occasional essays on the subject of writing, published under his own name, were written by his mother, who learned, finally, to type in 1979, the year she wrote his graduate thesis. Today Martone receives microcassette recordings his mother has made of his future work with the hard copy arriving by fax or courier and little or no interaction between the collaborators prior to the work's appearance. Martone is hard-pressed to tell you what exactly of his published work could truly be said to be his original contribution, if any, including this contributor's note and the contribution published somewhere else in this volume.

CONTRIBUTOR'S NOTE

Michael Martone was born at St. Joseph's Hospital in Fort Wayne, Indiana, in 1955. It is interesting to note that the attending physician was a Doctor Frank Burns, Major, United States Army, retired, and recently returned to Fort Wayne following service in the police action in Korea. It was the same Dr. Burns, it turned out, who years later served as the model for the character "Frank Burns" appearing in the novel *MASH* authored by Richard Hooker, and in the movie and television versions based on the book. Martone recalls the modest premiere of the Altman film in 1970 and its initial screening at the Embassy Theatre in downtown Fort Wayne. Dr. Burns, who had continued, after Martone's birth (it had been a difficult one, sunny-side up, where forceps were used), to be his mother's gynecologist, arrived at the theater, the guest of honor, in a 1959 Cadillac Seville provided by Means Motor

Company on Main Street. Sally Kellerman and Jo Ann Pflug also were there. All during the run of the television series, Dr. Burns, now in semiretirement, happily appeared at strip mall ribbon cuttings and restaurant openings, a kind of official goodwill ambassador, and took the ribbing from the public whose perception of his character had been derived from what they had read or seen in the movies and on television. His son, Frank Jr., was two years ahead of Martone at North Side High School. Frank Jr. anchored the 4x440 relay for the Redskin varsity track and field club, where Martone served as team manager. Martone remembers Dr. Burns, team physician, coaching him in the use of analgesic balm and the scrubbing of cinders out from beneath the skin after a runner fell on the track. It was Dr. Burns who, later, diagnosed Martone's mother's ovarian cancer in 1979 and performed the failed hysterectomy that led to his mother's death that summer. It was Dr. Burns, still in his surgical scrubs, who met the family in the waiting room of St. Joseph Hospital in Fort Wayne, the same hospital where Martone, twenty-four years before, had been born, delivered, by means of forceps, by Dr. Burns. The television was on, of course, an RCA model made in Bloomington, Indiana, and Martone remembers how hard it was not to watch it while, in a strange way, he also felt that he was watching himself listening to Dr. Burns rehearse the final few minutes of his, Martone's, mother's life.

CONTRIBUTOR'S NOTE

Michael Martone was born in Fort Wayne, Indiana. He attended Indiana University in Bloomington, where he lived in Brown Hall, one dorm in a quadrangle of buildings each named for nearby counties—Brown, Greene, Monroe, Morgan. His dorm was part of the Living Learning Center, which operated as a small, more intimate college within the much larger, anonymous university. At the Living Learning Center the self-motivated and ambitious students that the program attracted put on plays, published their own newspaper and literary magazine, and maintained a darkroom and an art gallery. Weekly, the students held poetry readings in the coffee house they converted from the old television lounge. A future governor of the state of Indiana, who later became a United States senator mentioned frequently as a vice-presidential candidate, lived right down the hall from Martone. Martone lived with the sons and daughters of university professors and lawyers and doctors, but the dorm also housed a contingent of varsity swimmers, just as obsessive as their nonathletic neighbors. The swimmers were part of the famous team coached by Doc Councilman. The pool was nearby, arguing for the billeting of its users in the Living Learning Center. Martone would be awakened very early when a pod of swimmers banged down the hallway and stairwell on the way to train. Next door, Martone's neighbor, who played on his record player, constantly and too loud, Gordon Lightfoot singing "The Wreck of the Edmund Fitzgerald," was washed up at eighteen years old as a competitive swimmer. He had taken up intercollegiate water polo to remain eligible for his scholarship as his splits for the individual medley had fallen off. Martone knew that he still shaved down, trying through the ritual to coax a few more tenths of seconds from his hairless body. Also on Martone's floor was Jack Donahue, who would become an assistant secretary of labor during the first Clinton administration. One evening Jack invited Martone to his political science class being held in the dorm's coffee house. The teacher was conducting an educational game that simulated, Jack said, the dynamics of world politics and international economic systems. The class was small and needed bodies for the simulation to work. Martone, who wasn't doing anything but listening to "The Wreck of the Edmund Fitzgerald," was quite happy to participate. Once in place, Martone was assigned a role of a small, poor African republic recently liberated from a colonial past. The professor had actually dealt out cards to all the students and their dragooned volunteers to see who would be what nation-state. Most of them were small, poor countries, though some were large, poor countries. Only a few got to be countries like the United States or Germany or Japan or France or Great Britain. Those countries got to draw cards from a special deck while Martone and the rest received cards from a deck dealt by the professor. The cards the players received contained information pertinent to their nations for the year the hand represented. Martone learned of his country's booming population, its declining food production, its outbreak of disease, and a minor guerilla incursion on its border. The numbers indicated that famine was imminent, disaster on the horizon. After all the participants assessed the cards they had been dealt, the game called for a period of negotiation among its players. The poor countries appealed to the rich ones for assistance—aid of some metric tons of surplus food or advisers to train their struggling militias. At first the players who held the rich countries were generous with their wealth, but as further hands were dealt and the demands upon their largesse increased they became more cautious, demanding more natural resources or labor from those countries who asked, round after round, for more assistance. That was the point of the game, of course, for the students who controlled the wealth to discover how easily they became greedy, indifferent, and callous even when nothing really was at stake but these abstractions. Martone dreaded approaching the student who held all the cards during the diplomacy session. A significant percentage of Martone's population was now starving while it continued to multiply vigorously. His one liquid commodity of industrial diamonds had fallen into the hands of tribal warlords. First one and then another and another of the first-world countries had during their meetings asked him simply what was in this relationship for them. At last, after the next hand was dealt, Martone looked at his cards and realized that everyone in his country was dead or dying though babies were still being born. His country was a desert. Its forests had all been burned for fuel, its animals poached. Its polluted rivers were all diverted to neighboring countries for aborted power schemes. Its once abundant lakes were silted and brackish. The tribe that once lived on floating islands of reed, making distinctive basketry from the same versatile fiber, was now scattered or emigrated to Europe to work as taxi drivers or street vendors. Martone turned the cards back over on his desk. And during the negotiation session, as the participants milled about the room seeking audiences and making deals with each other, Martone went out for a drink of real water, deciding as he drank that he wouldn't go back in for another round. Instead he walked out onto the quad at night and made his way over to the pool, where he watched his dormmate play water polo. The bobbing rubber-capped heads of the players looked like balls floating on the surface of the water. Then the ball that was actually a ball and not another bobbing head would go sailing down the pool, the floating heads below turning slowly in the water to watch it go by. "Lake Superior, it is said, never gives up her dead," Martone thought as he watched. It was days later in the cafeteria at lunch that Jack Donahue sought out Martone to tell him how impressed his professor had been with the way Martone had played the game. This surprised Martone, since from his perspective he had captained his country to a devastating end. But an interesting thing had happened that night, Donahue told him. Several rounds of the game, perhaps as many as five or six turns of hands being dealt and negotiations conducted, had been played before anyone noticed Martone's absence. Then the scattered pile of cards he had left behind was discovered, and the narrative of his country's decay and doom was archaeologically reconstructed from its relics. This, then, had been the lesson all along, this dwindling and disappearance. No one had even noticed as a whole nation vanished. That's what happens in the real world, the professor had said. It hadn't been a simulation at all. This appearance of invisibility had been the whole point, and Martone hadn't been there to see it.

FROM NIETZSCHE'S KISSES

BY LANCE OLSEN (2006)

EDITOR'S NOTE: While publisher of FC2 from 1999 to 2007 I had two good ideas. The first was to hire Brenda Mills as Managing Editor in 2000, and the second was in 2002 to ask Lance Olsen to become chair of FC2's Board of Directors. Today the Fiction Collective is still alive because of these decisions. Part of what made Lance's leadership so crucial was his passionate commitment to non-mainstream writing. Although Lance and I disagreed on occasion about what the words "formal innovation" or "experimental fiction" meant, we never disagreed that FC2's mission, both political and aesthetic, was to support radically ambitious writing. Lance's own fiction has embodied this mission. *Nietzsche's Kisses*, about the philosopher's last mad night alive, sets out to locate the source of narrative, historical as well as literary, in the experience of self-alienation. Represented most concretely in the novel's shifting pronouns, Nietzsche's abstraction materializes as the uninhabitability of his present, a condition in which he loses and recollects himself, making his effort to tell what's happening a frantic effort to catch up. In my reader's report I praised the way "Nietzsche's titanic ego..., all but unknown to his acquaintances, creates a raging giant within his own skull." This suffocating isolation, familiar to us as narcissism, becomes in Lance's handling a problem of time. As in the classics of high modernism, *Nietzsche's Kisses* interprets the end of recounting, not as an achievement of knowledge, but as an achievement of life, of being at last where past and future kiss.

—RMB

"'Our satisfaction with the completeness of plot,' Fredric Jameson once noted, is 'a kind of satisfaction with society as well,' and I would add much the same is the case with our satisfaction with undemanding style, character, subject matter, and so forth. My orientation, then, rhymes fairly closely with those posed by Viktor Shklovsky for art and Martin Heidegger for philosophy: the return through complication and challenge (not predictability and ease) to perception and thought. Such a process is by nature a political one."

—Lance Olsen

5 P.M.

Every sentence is a kiss.

Yes, that's it: I searched and searched for them through the tenement inside my head and presto—they suddenly rejoin the conversation.

All the voices of history.

All the voices of history speaking to me.

Prince Bismarck being a good student—never a prodigy, mind you, never a sensation, but a solid worker nonetheless.

Every sentence is a kiss and every paragraph an embrace.

The skin sensing it.

Unless, of course, history's chatter happens to be mistaken.

There's always that possibility.

There's always that possibility among others.

In any case, this flawless morning will unfold into a flawless day. I am sure of it. If it is morning, that is, and not, say, twilight. Twilight being another possibility for what it is.

Right, here I go: the extravagance.

Let us call it the opening of the eyes.

Give it a second.

Give it a second.

More light.

It seems I can no longer feel my fingers.

I can smell time, but I can no longer feel my fingers and I can no longer feel my feet. Insignificant concerns on a day rich with such promise as this, yet it appears as if…what? It appears as if my limbs simply evanesce into air as they extend away from me.

Only yesterday the prince was capering, and now, lying beneath these hot sheets on this flawless morning, sweating, sweating and thinking, sweating and endeavoring to think, he is about to undertake the opening of his eyes.

In order to have a look around me.

There occurs movement involving the lower portion of my face, mollusk plumped on the floor of my mouth.

When my bowels last roused themselves in an attempt to stage a modest display is anyone's guess.

It could, for all I know, come to think of it, still be the middle of the night.

There is nothing to prevent it.

Unless, obviously, my eyes are already open.

There is always that.

Unless my eyes are already open and have been for let us say hours or days, in which case I have finally gone blind.

Such an event would arrive as no real surprise.

Listen closely: you can hear my clothing.

My hospital gown breathing.

I should perhaps take this opportunity to point out I would

much rather be a Basel professor than God and yet, alas, one is who one is—until one isn't who one is, naturally, at which heart thump one is someone else.

The general impression I want to say being that of drifting in a fog on Lake Lucerne.

On holiday once, on holiday in Tribschen, I launched from Wagner's dock at the edge of the yellow splash of wildflowers: the city's spires, the fountains, the church bells reaching me from the far side of the water, the spring sun rushing over my shoulders.

I rowed east toward the rocky horizon, bagful of chocolates on the seat beside me, until my arms ached, then pulled in the oars and lay back in the belly of my boat to lose myself in sugar and reflection.

I must have dozed because when I opened my eyes again everything was slate cloud, and, sitting up, I discovered the universe had disappeared.

I could barely even make out the lakewater lapping my craft's side.

I raised my oars and began to row. Pushing through the gray veils, I had the intimation it would take me all night to reach land. I therefore altered my course, only to find myself worrying I had altered it for the worse, that prior to this alteration I had been rowing in more or less the correct direction.

Imagine: the abrupt moment of contact with shore never coming.

It felt as if I would row on and on through emptiness forever.

I want to say now, here, lying beneath these hot sheets, sweating, sweating and endeavoring to think, it is precisely the same sensation, only in time.

I can no longer seem to remember whether I'm remembering or believing I'm remembering when I'm not remembering at all.

I want to say I holidayed in Tribschen.

I want to say I did not.

Every day people tell me the most remarkable things about my life.

They recount, by way of illustration, the quiet evenings I shared with this friend or that.

Did I by any chance enjoy myself? I ask.

It matters to me, you see.

And so what I shall do next is this: I shall undertake the opening of my eyes…like this…yes…like this…there they go…the great extravagance…and there is a dark shape fluttering back and forth in front of me, a huge black insect against the bright white window.

A woman, I am fairly sure.

A diminutive woman moving.

She steps out of the glare, draws alongside my bed, and the damp sheets are off me, her hands between my legs.

She works diligently, although my sense of touch isn't what it used to be.

Massaging, conceivably, or, conceivably, scrubbing.

Yes, that's it: she hums to herself, something sodden and German by Schubert, looking familiar, looking very familiar, her long gray hair piled into a frizzy bun, purple cobwebs spun across her raw cheeks, scrubbing.

Are you perhaps my mother? I ask, breaking the silence, mouth all slurry.

She doesn't look up.

Then, *voilà*, this crookshelled apparition withdraws a bedpan from what appears to be a sizeable hole in the mattress between my legs and divines its liquid contents before releasing a small winged smile into the humidity.

It's Alwine, Fritz, she says, smiling. Do you know me?

Of course I know you, I respond, slow and slurry, studying her features. You've been with us… You've been with the family… since I was Vittorio.

Vittorio?

Vittorio Emanuele. Yes, obviously.

She lowers the bedpan.

They're back, then? she asks.

A little.

And what did they tell you?

Oh…well. You know. This and that.

She consults the harsh window, the harsh door.

I know, I say. I'm sorry.

Listen to me, she says, turning back. You're Fritz this afternoon, Fritz. You were Fritz yesterday afternoon. And tomorrow afternoon? Tomorrow afternoon you will be Fritz again. Are you hungry? Your sister is coming by. She's bringing visitors. You need to eat. A bowl of cabbage soup? A bowl of cabbage soup and slice of bread? I've baked some fresh.

While contemplating the question, it occurs to me there is a woman standing in the room.

I beg your pardon, I say, but your name is…

Alwine, Fritz. Alwine.

Do you want to know a secret, Alwine-Fritz-Alwine?

If you don't eat, do you know what your sister will do?

I look up at the ceiling.

She will accuse Alwine of not feeding her Fritz. Do you want to get Alwine into trouble?

I look up at the ceiling, then lower my gaze to this person who, for some reason, strikes me as someone you can trust.

I whisper to her:

Every sentence is a kiss.

What?

Every sentence is a kiss, I repeat, louder, *and every paragraph an embrace.*

She stands there watching the show called Friedrich, then raises the bedpan like a Sunday roast on a serving tray, turns, and, careful not to spill a drop of me, makes her way toward the door.

Fritz, she says over her shoulder. Fritz. What are we going to do with you?

A good question.

The door opens. The universe pauses. The door clicks shut.

Everywhere wind surging into cognition.

Everywhere noise without end.

TAIL

And next you are overboard thrashing to stay afloat. You were standing in your rowboat balancing charily in an attempt to get your bearings your oar a cane then your legs kicked out from under you and now your rowboat is dissolving into the fog and evening contaminating the dampness and your oar must have hit you because there is lightning at the bridge of your nose. Frost is gathering on the tissues of your heart and there is lightning at the bridge of your nose and you stretch your left shoe down to poke for bottom and there is nothing below you nothing in any direction and the idea sends you beneath the waves in a scattered flux of panic and up again like a human balloon buoying choking snot and blood streaming through your mustache. You reach down to untie your shoes kick off their weight but realize with alarm you can't feel your hands your feet are bars of peacockblue pain dangling. What might be your fingers graze against what might be your laces only your joints don't bend there is live water in your mouth and up your runny nose and you are thinking *what doesn't kill me makes me stranger*. You swam as a child at the Pforta school and there were many better students than you and you read until your vision bleared in the evening trying to make up for your shortfalls and you swam and skated with the other boys and loved how swimming made you into a penguin bulleting across the pond. They woke you at four o'clock every morning save Sunday and you had to be ready for class by six and then you had a break at four then dinner then more classes and bedtime was nine and if you were lucky you had perhaps an hour to yourself all day. When you were twelve or thirteen your head caught fire for the first time and the pondwater made the flames more intense and you are losing sensation your muscles hardening everything very quick. You would push for the boat if you knew which way to push but the oar knocked off your glasses and the fog is consolidating and you slide beneath the waves a second time. It surprises you so much you instinctively shoot up breach choking thrashing bleeding snotting thinking *happiness is a complicated phenomenon* because there is nowhere to go nothing to do except what you are doing. There is nowhere to go nothing to do and it occurs to you you have probably been here before will probably be here again because in infinity there is just so much matter so many worlds then they begin repeating themselves and in all likelihood you have visited this one before and in some variations you have drowned and in some you have survived and in some you never rented the rowboat in the first place but sat under a shade tree on a bench on the dock at Tribschen and ate your bag of chocolates stuffed with marzipan paste and this is why Darwin is a thinking monkey. Evolution takes us nowhere because progress is a ring we have had tails we have tails we will have tails once more and all we can do is swallow them. If you had to undergo the present formulation three thousand times four thousand ten would you have the courage and what sort of courage would this be an example of if you only had to go under once and in the midst of that thought you become aware of your rowboat gliding unhurriedly out of a fog bank into the open and you squint unable to believe your good fortune because the thing is no more than two meters away from you it hasn't gone anywhere all you have to do is swim reach out hoist yourself in and this is how the present formulation of the story will write itself these are the contours it will take except. Except. Except this isn't how the present formulation will write itself because when you try to lift your arms to swim they don't lift and when you try to will yourself forward you slip beneath the waves struck by how shockingly cold the first inhalation is a mallet against your lungs you feel as if you are floating above yourself your body convulsing then you are smiling yes as you begin floating down trying to smile trying to smile and of course failing.

MUSIC WITHOUT A FUTURE

My head is filled with Friedrich, Friedrich announces to no one, stepping out of his mother's house at number 18 Weingarten and pausing at the threshold.

She told him to wait for her to accompany him to the market.

It is Naumburg. It is 1890. Bismarck is gone, Zanzibar is going, and the Kaiser's new direction is no direction at all. Still, it is May and it will be a flawless day. There is no doubt about it.

Friedrich narrates these facts and the morning's fineness aloud for his own benefit. It helps him arrange the convolution of things.

How, above the cream and mustard houses, above their terracotta fishscale roofs, the sky's early whiteblue is tinged with an ambient gold scintillation. How the chill promises cool sunshine the second he moves from the shadows and how everything in the lives of these people undertaking their morning ceremonies in the street before him feels as if it has been revived.

Friedrich inhales deeply.

Green air. Horse hide. The last coal fires of the season.

This is what time smells like.

Across the narrow lane, a young woman with dark pulled-back hair reaches through her second-story window to tend a box of newly planted geraniums on the sill and she reminds Friedrich of someone he once knew and he knows everything will come easily today.

Everything will succeed.

What uncomplicated astonishment to stand here at the brink of a day like this.

He pronounces the words under his breath, telling, the most important thing surely being to get the present formulation right.

The wonderful cleanliness of his task nearly overwhelms him.

His head is filled with Friedrich, overfilled, and the point of living is the discovery of how to express that fullness in surprising ways. He loves his own company because he has never met better. Obviously, he would on no account admit such a notion to anyone else (except, needless to say, in his writing, which no one reads) for fear of hurting their feelings, but the truth is that other people make him intensely lonely. They make him awkward in the face of their intellectual awkwardness. Their minds don't dance. They lumber. Their public opinions are their private laziness.

No: he prefers talking to his equal.

He cherishes the thrill of strolling along the streets of a complex town or, better, across the grassy grayblue countryside, silhouettes of trees hazing hilltops, arguing with himself, contradicting himself, trying to catch himself out and laughing at the insights his mind gives rise to without warning.

What will he think next?

He can hardly wait to find out.

Once, he lost his way hiking in the mountains surrounding Sils-Maria because he was so deeply engaged in an elegant conversation with himself he forgot to pay attention to the landmarks. His sister, visiting at the time, called the local authorities when he didn't return home by nightfall. The police came around promptly and asked her for a description of the man for whom they were to mount a search.

If he's conscious, Lisbeth had told them, he's talking.

What a splendid line for such a splendid day.

He reaches into the inside breast pocket of his charcoal suit and withdraws the small notebook and stubby pencil he always carries with him.

Hesitates.

Looks up.

Adjusts his glasses with his thumb.

He is wearing his most powerful pair, the pair with the distorting lenses, and still existence arrives through a steam bath.

The ambient gold scintillation suffusing the whiteblue sky above the houses, above their terra-cotta fishscale roofs, is waxing into an ambient silver scintillation, every minute becoming something else.

This past autumn, he writes in a tight, vertical, almost Arabic scrawl, *I was blinded as little as possible when I twice witnessed my own funeral.*

He contemplates the line and, satisfied, closes the notebook and slips it back into place, with the pencil.

Sometimes Friedrich is embarrassed by how happy Friedrich can be, Friedrich announces to no one, and, forgetting exactly why he is waiting here when such a glorious morning beckons, he gently clicks the heavy front door shut behind him, glances at the medieval wall his mother's house looks out upon, confirms the tilt of his charcoal topper, and launches into the shimmering possibility called the future.

Stepping into the lane, his hands rise up around his head like delicate white birds that will help explain to him what it is he is thinking now, what he is thinking now, what now.

It is the kind of happiness, the kind of uncomplicated astonishment, he felt almost exactly eight years ago one afternoon in Rome.

It was late April. It was 1882. Friedrich was visiting Malwida von Meysenbug, the feisty, squat, universal aunt to nomadic German-speaking freethinkers everywhere. He strolled into her sitting room after a long constitutional through the filthy city and happened upon a beautiful young woman with dark pulled-back hair reading one of his books on the sofa.

Friedrich could make out the cover from where he fetched up: *Human, All Too Human.*

He had sketched and written a good part of it while wintering at Malwida's villa on the coast near Sorrento several years before. He occupied a big high room there with a terrace outside and nothing to distract him from his work aside from the rampant gardens, the luxurious afternoon teas with the other guests, and a nearly overpowering view across the open sea to Naples and Vesuvius, a sloped molar hanging in the distance.

Upon its publication, he had given a copy to Malwida by way of thanks. Apparently, it had followed her north. Friedrich always experienced a jolt seeing someone reading something he had written. His books existed for him deep inside his organs. A swish of trespass accompanied the flush of enchantment he felt whenever someone held a piece of him in her hands. She could just as well have been holding his lungs. Even so, his spirit lifted and the woman on the sofa looked up and her eyes glinted in recognition.

She inserted a silk tassel (just past his book's center), closed the covers and, without rising, said in a diaphanous Russian accent:

Herr Nietzsche. It is a great pleasure to make your and your will to power's acquaintance.

He was thirty-eight and she was twenty-one and yet language left him, leaving him disarmed and scratching the side of his face.

He wasn't good at matters of action.

Thinking on his feet terrified him.

Is it true, then, she continued, that even our deeds and sentiments not obviously connected with a desire for control are nonetheless prompted by it? I had never contemplated Christ's tolerance and meekness in quite those terms. I am certain clergy the world over would stand enlightened.

Friedrich took pleasure in the way she had made a conscious decision not to rise from the sofa upon his entrance. He took pleasure in her wasp-waisted black dress with the exquisite white lace extending from its wrists and high collar. And, most of all, he took pleasure in the way her dark pulled-back hair and pale skin and sharp intelligence spread through the room like a crackling charge of electricity.

Scratching, enjoying, Friedrich became aware of himself being aware again.

He couldn't help it. His mind was a mouse in a maze. Language resettled his head syllable by syllable. He let his hand fall to his side and tried to straighten his back into something like poise.

That, I suspect, is why I wrote the thing in the first place, he replied.

As he did so, fairly pleased with his response, a much older woman, who reminded him of nothing so much as a blackboard eraser topped with a feathered hat, appeared in the doorway leading from the hall and embarked on calibrating this neighborhood's significance and the significance of the two people inhabiting it.

She narrowed her eyes in a manner that gave Friedrich the inkling she found everything except perhaps the small jade statue of Shiva on the hectic fireplace mantel lacking.

Ah, said the young woman on the sofa, half-turning and presenting her palm in the older woman's general direction without actually meeting her eyes…my mother, Frau Salomé.

Her voice sounded a little fatigued, as if she had pronounced those words in the recent past more times than she might have strictly relished.

…And, said the eraser with no accent whatsoever, my daughter, whom I suspect hasn't quite had the opportunity to break away from sharing her opinions long enough to introduce herself. Fräulein Salomé. Louise.

I… Friedrich began, but the eraser wasn't done.

…Although everyone, it seems, despite the fact I am honestly at a loss to understand why, takes the liberty of calling her Lou. Herr Professor Nietzsche, it is a very great honor meeting you. Malwida has spoken libraries of praise about you. Louise, please come along. We are late for our meeting with some ruins. Good lord, I have never in my life seen more fallen rocks than on our current journey. This, I take it, is what the Italians refer to as "culture"? Fine, then. Fine. Bring on the quarries…

It was childish, Friedrich announces, hands fluttering up by his ears.

It was childish and it was naïve and it lacked edge and yet the reality remains he loved Lou instantly and loved her completely.

He rounds a corner onto a cobblestone lane lined with colorful shops. Ahead, St. Wenzel's gothic dunce cap lifts into view. Pedestrians veer out of his path. They pretend they don't hear him, can't see him, but he can tell in his presence they shy closer to the shop fronts.

Friedrich is pleased.

It is time people began noticing him.

For years, the surprise has been how few have. It is a continual blow to his well-being how virtually no one in Germany, let alone the rest of Europe, is thinking about him at any given moment on any given day. How could such a thing have come to pass?

Granted: a handful of friends used to read his books with passion and admiration. They used to write to tell him so. They used to argue through the post and in the newspapers and the arguments were delicious. But then, one by one, they commenced falling away. Their letters became insignificant, respectable, benevolent, remote—less than shopping lists of tedious activities and superficial emotions embodied in thoughtless prose—and then they ceased altogether. For more than a decade now, he has brought out on average one book a year, recently at his own expense. Only sixty or seventy copies of each of the first three parts of *Zarathustra* sold. He could only afford to print forty copies of the fourth. He ended up giving away seven simply to make sure someone would look at it, and even then there was no evidence anyone did.

Presently there is almost no one out there unless it is some idiot reviewer readying to launch some idiot assault, or some one-time friend badmouthing his brain to various Wagnerites behind his back.

Or, worse, no reviewer and no one-time friend and no assault at all, just stillness and calm in the wake of a new work's appearance… and there is nothing worse than stillness and calm in the wake of a new work's appearance.

He is positive, or very nearly so, he remembers Lisbeth, or perhaps it was Overbeck or Burckhardt—someone close to him, at any rate, yes, he is confident of that—writing to inform him that a critic delivered a series of lectures outlining his philosophy somewhere up north two or three years ago.

Give it a second.

Give it a second.

Georg Brandes, yes: that Great Dane with the large intellect at the University of Copenhagen.

Which is to say…what?

The superb sky leaves no question about it at all.

When he walks down the street, pedestrians pay attention. When he enters one of these shops, every face changes. Women gaze after him as he tests vegetables for firmness and in the market he is sure the sexy young things hold back the sweetest grapes for him.

On occasion, they have been known to lower the price of fish in his honor.

There is too much din in the world already. He closes his eyes and feels the solar system corkscrewing around him.

When he opens them again, Friedrich finds himself standing in front of the ornate Rathaus. Across the square to his left is the statue of Saint Wenzel overseeing the fountain in his hat shaped like a shell. Behind him, on the eastern end, the town portal from 1680.

How, in the course of his life, did he arrive here?

At one time, there seemed to have been so many other places to go.

A handful of people drift across the square or sit at outdoor tables under red and white umbrellas reading newspapers, sipping morning coffee, nibbling pastries. Blinking, Friedrich tries to force them into focus, and slowly becomes aware of a headache glowing somewhere behind his eyes. It looks to him like a bluely burning coal.

He realizes his tie is too tight. He loosens it and pulls it through his collar. Friedrich tugs off his jacket, lets it fall to his feet and, blinking, loves, helplessly, the swaybacked horse harnessed to the old wooden cart near the statue, how the sunshine gleams off its mangy flanks. He loves the pigeons flurrying around the stooped woman in a black shawl, her arms outstretched like a scarecrow, bread crumbs in her upraised palms. He loves the fragrance of cinnamon tarts and cigarettes and horseshit in the air, the resonance of the church bells beginning to toll above these buildings, how the day's warmth speeds back and forth across this flesh.

He unbuttons his vest and removes it. He unbuttons his shirt and removes it. Reaching for his belt buckle, he appreciates Naumburg's tranquility. Its sense of understated purpose. How Germany comes to its conclusion in locations like this.

So much for him depends on the sky.

He removes his trousers and removes his socks and removes his undergarments and loves the two men in uniform making their way toward him from the café across the square, coffee cups still in their hands.

Behind them, he believes he can make out his mother waving.

Yes, Franziska: she is trotting to join him.

Where did she come from?

He looks forward to learning the answer.

Meanwhile, he smiles at her familiarly and stretches his bare arms out to his sides, mimicking the pigeon woman.

He shuts his eyes again and tilts his face to receive the incoming rays.

He concentrates deeply on distributing his love to every living thing that has forgotten him in this very special space.

FROM THE BOOK OF PORTRAITURE

BY STEVE TOMASULA (2006)

EDITOR'S NOTE: One of my enduring disappointments as publisher of FC2 was our failure to publish Steve Tomasula's novel *VAS*. It was one of the first MSS I read after taking over the press in 1999, and I recognized at once its engagement with Mallarmé's conception of the book. Unfortunately, its exploration of the page as relational space, what Mallarmé called a book's "spirituality," required a considerable act of faith, one that few MSS can justify. Our editors were thoughtful in their deliberations, but their decision went against it. So, when almost five years later I received the MS for Steve's new novel, *Book of Portraiture*, I was delighted to have a second chance. *Book of Portraiture* is a "novel" in which every page acknowledges being looked at. To say the work is *about* the relation between visual representation and linguistic representation isn't just wrong, but it trivializes Steve's accomplishment. *Book of Portraiture* continues a tradition of avant-garde practice in which the task is to bring out every word's dependence on something describable in words but not describable in the words being written *at present*. This task—what Gertrude Stein called "continuous presentness"—seeks both to disclose a violence implicit in representation and to recover from it, requiring a discipline that can be as liberating as it is demanding. For me, Steve's diagnosis of our modern alienation realizes the social mission of radical art generally and instances the larger stakes of an enterprise like FC2.

—RMB

"Language kills. Doubters need only look at the bodies piling up under the banner of 'Shock & Awe.' But politics also resides in reading, and the more a work of language moves us to read as poets and politicians write, to consider word by word what is really said / also said / left unsaid, the more political, the less passive, reading—and we—can be."

—Steve Tomasula

LONG

before the heroes

of martyrdom began to fade

from living memory, before monks (†430) discovered faith through the malleability of words, long before the heroes of psychiatry (1900) construed dreams as language, and almost four millennia before cows began to carry the genes of fish; before mile-high buildings collapsed into dust, or men and women everywhere proclaimed their bodies to be, after all, their most potent weapons, their poems, their canvas, something powerful had been straining to come into the world. Its silent efforts were there in the bloodstains aborigines made on boulders—perfect prints of human hands—first portraits that were repeated and repeated and repeated as if out of the sheer awe that they *could* be repeated, and wonder at what that might mean. This something was there in cave paintings—stick figures wielding stick spears as if to shout *I! I was! I did!* Its silent efforts grew stronger in the ciphers that ancient Chinese scratched on tortoise shells, in the tally marks of Minoan merchants, in the runes destroyed by Assyrian armies, and in the clay tablets listing animals sacrificed by Sumerian priests. But not until these efforts began to gain a voice, emerging as it did from the symbols for fish and shields and owls in Egyptian hieroglyphics could this force—

He was a trader, a teller of amazing stories who would attach himself to whatever caravan would have him. That is, he was a poet or liar, a sometime prophet, a chameleon who years ago had the audacity to merely walk out of his bondage in Egypt and yet still was the first to throw himself prostrate to proclaim the glory of whatever desert chieftain he came in contact with as he wandered the Sinai, more often lost than found....

One day's camel ride from the turquoise mines of Serabit el-Khadim, an ox lowed just as he began to fall asleep, and the image that flashed before his mind's eye was so startling that it made him sit up. Earlier in the day, while the caravan rested in the shade of a *gebel*, he had run his hands over its creamy stone and the wind-worn symbols carved into it: symbols for oxen along with other markings that reminded him of the papyrus marshes he had waded through to escape the halls of Egypt: wavy lines that to Egyptians meant "river," but also symbols of fishes and plants he did not recognize, and so assumed had been carved long ago, back when the desert must have been a lush garden, before Gilgamesh's flood carved this wadi, then receded, leaving only outcroppings and a few parched watering holes. It was the symbol of the ox head that came to him as he drifted into sleep, though, its horns pricking his slumber at the very moment he thought the Semite word for the animal, *aleph*.

Propping an elbow on the camel saddle that served as his pillow, he raised a fist, extending his thumb and small finger to give his fist horns, using moonlight to cast a shadow on the sand—a shadow puppet of an aleph—only elongated, ripples in the sand distorting his aleph no matter how he turned his hand, giving his shadow-ox an ambiguity, an aspect of a skinny, milkless goat. Or a *djinn*. Soothsayers could read a future in the sands' shifting shapes, it was said, and as he gazed into these he couldn't tell if they foretold fortuitous or evil ends—or both?—for he suddenly saw how the marks carved into the outcroppings could be used not only to represent oxen, fish, hides, or reeds—the objects themselves—but also sounds, winds of the mouth that had become his trade. And what were the words he sold if not sounds in a certain order?—a tapestry of verse and half-truths he had woven to exaggerate the plagues of locusts he had seen in Egypt or the sea turning red at the port of Sidon in order to make an omen and thus paint an Egyptian general's drowning, one worth feeding the teller to hear....

Each telling of a history, speech, situation, proclamation, translation, or revelation had to be altered, at least a little, to fit its times or the customs of its hearer. And so convincingly did he have to sell his words, throwing himself into them with the passion of a true believer, that it became increasingly worrisome for him to remember for whom he had invented which chronicle, revealed what secrets, claimed which kinship, or inserted which omissions....

With a finger, he cautiously drew in the sand the symbol for ox that he'd seen carved in stone, , saying as he did so not the animal's whole name, aleph, but only its first sound: "Aa."

"Aaaa," he said, reading it back. Then he tried "Hhh," scratching into the sand , the symbol for *het*, that is, "fence." The sight of it caused him to get fully out of his carpet, and while others snored about him, while the camels shifted against the tongs that hobbled their forelegs for the night, while the son who'd been posted to keep watch watched, he picked up a charred palm frond and wrote, 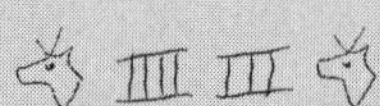, then , writing over and over and faster and faster, 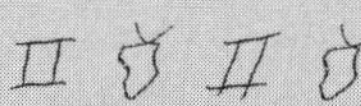 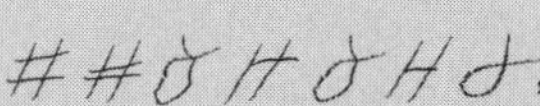, unable to believe the simplicity of his boon. It was as if the sky opened to reveal a heaven where he could represent not just things but whatever came into his mind. Not just numbers and animals as in stone carvings, but all the knots he had to remember—which camel driver could be bribed, which gatekeeper couldn't. It was a power, he saw, a power to record any version of stories, words of men, even gods unseen, demons—whatever fantasies he had ever imagined or dreamed—anything he could say.

Then he stopped. Once, in the market of Akkad, he had witnessed a hand being cut from each of two farmers who had tried to forge a clay tablet that bore their debt, and the hairs on the back of his neck tingled. That is, if he could set his speech in stone, could not that stone carry him to the bottom of the sea? Was this what the vision meant?

Resolving to tell no one of his discovery until he had worked it out more fully, he bade the night watch peace, and got back into his carpet. But his shadows of the aleph were even stronger by morning sunlight. As the caravan plodded on, his thoughts raced with the realization that the ancient myths he repeated for others were true: that *Ad-ham*—a name that meant both "first man" and "mud"—that Ad-ham did call plants and beasts and language into existence, bringing them forth from a formless garden by giving them and tigers and gazelles and lilies and scorpions each its name. But this mad creation didn't end with Ad-ham; barred from both the garden and God's grace, Ad-ham's sons—the first murderer and the first victim—and their sons, and yea, the unclean daughters of their sons and sons continued to create and corrupt and destroy with their words, unawares, even unto this day. And he trembled to find himself among their number, for he could see this curse for the power it held, a spell or a power he could multiply over those as blind to it as—

He had to be careful, though, lest it consume him as well.

Over the next journeys, he added to his device as an alchemist adds to his pharmacy, selecting those elements that are strongest, culling from his collection those not as well suited as he had first thought, replacing them with others, noting carefully how other traders recorded their transactions, finding in their symbols signs of the same genie though they did not hear its voice as clearly as he: from Egyptian messengers he learned to make a reminder of foreign names by using symbols such as , that is, *mu*, the mark for an owl, or the wavy line 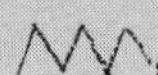, their mark for *net* or "river," not as owl or river but as the first sound of the foreign name, an *m* or *n*. Hebrew slaves in the mines of Serabit el-Khadim taught him how the outline of a camel's hump—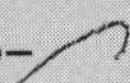—or *gamal*, as they said it, could be used for the guttural *g* that began the name of the Girgashites among them.

His invention became less and less original to him as other slaves showed him how they used symbols for other sounds: a  or *bayit*—the outline of a house—for the sound of *b*; a *d* sound indicated by the outline of a tent door , a *delth*—a set of symbols he also found in use by the Hebrews in the Wadi el Hol, a communion of signs between them. Teaching his *aleph*, *bayit*, *gamals* to a Phoenician sea merchant as a code by which the two of them might conduct business, he found his symbols come back to him by way of the Phoenician's Greek slave as *alpha*, *beta*, *gamma*....

Working out a complete stable of symbols, he also worked out how if there were an exaggeration, shortage, or abundance to be discovered, it would be in the merchandise, not the merchant, and one day, understanding how narrowly he, the messengers, traders, and slaves had been thinking of this device, he realized that the time had come for him to test its true strength. On a papyrus light enough to hide in his robes, he used black dye, a *qualam* or reed, and his invention to write out not ciphers, not recording angels nor hieroglyphs but symbols for the sounds that would portray—nay, transform—a life, and which when read back would say for him: *I—*

No sooner had he begun to write then he was given pause. The person he was transmuting himself into deserved a new name, he saw, but what? *Ra-Moses* came to mind, the Egyptian word for "Ra—the son of god is born." Likewise, he thought of *Thut-Mose*, that is, "Thoth—is born" and the more he pondered this Egyptian custom of forging a name out of words for actions, the more it appealed to him and he wrote, *I, -Moses*, that is, born of?—born of what?—writing?—*from the land of....* Again he paused. He didn't know where he was from. Or even where his parents were born, or who they were, but he knew he didn't want his new person to be a slave to his old, lost kinship, or even the body this kinship had given him, while something from the story that Mesopotamians told about Sargon always appealed to him, especially how Sargon was found as an infant floating in a qualam basket on the Tigris river.... Why not? *I, Moses, born of the Nile, swear by my son's head*, he always wanted progeny, *to the truth of the tale that follows, a tale of terrible plagues, of great migrations, and also God's voice, a tale told by many mouths....*

FROM THE JIRÍ CHRONICLES

AND OTHER FICTIONS

BY DEBRA DI BLASI (2007)

EDITOR'S NOTE: Debra Di Blasi is one of those expansive talents who'll try anything and can do everything. Shortly after becoming publisher of FC2, I read a MS of hers and was deeply impressed by its high-modernist finish. I submitted it to our editorial board for review, but the board rejected it. I was disappointed but let the author know I admired her work. Then in 2002 Debra sent us a new MS, *Ugly Town*, wholly unlike the previous, written in the idiom of hip-hop and incorporating images in the text. I wrote an ecstatic reader's report which I sent with the MS to our editorial board. The board rejected it. I was even more disappointed than before, and although I reassured Debra of my support, I knew she was frustrated. I wasn't sure we'd have another chance, but in 2005 she submitted a MS comprised of three projects, the most ambitious of which I'd already heard about. *The Jirí Chronicles and Other Fictions* demonstrates Debra's commitment to the visual interpretation of literary texts, to polymorphous idioms and styles, and to creating new concepts of fiction, not just further examples of it. But her creation, Jirí Cêch, isn't exactly literature. More material than an image, less corporeal than a cyborg, as real as a corporation but as insubstantial as a hoax, his being only crosses Debra's page. By the time FC2 encountered him, Jirí had already acquired a website, CDs, publication credits, threatened lawsuits, charges of misogyny, and a widespread reputation for fraud. Along with his continually morphing creator, Jirí embodies the puzzle of identity in our age of endless mediation.

—RMB

"The ability of the fictional character Jirí Cêch to exist as 'real' addresses the burgeoning problem of The Lie in contemporary society, where politicians, media monsters, and corporate and religious leaders are able to spin webs of deceit by means of the very technology that allows Jirí to exist as 'flesh-and-blood.'"

—Debra Di Blasi

GLAUKE'S GOWN:
THE FUNCTION OF MYTH

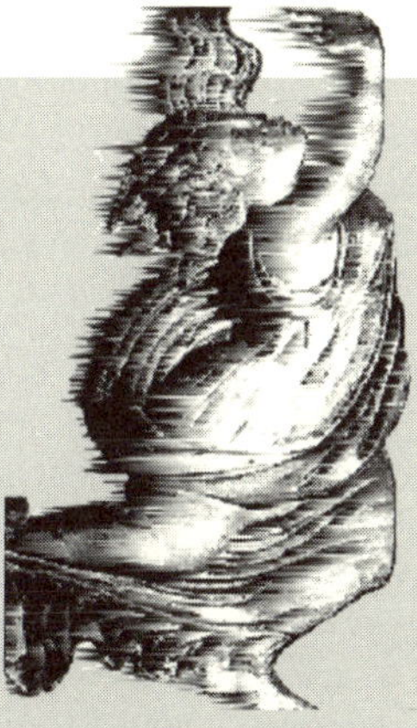

MEDEA

a synopsis

After taking the throne at Corinth, Jason the Argonaut, husband of Medea, fell head over heels for the pretty princess Glauke.[21] Medea, who had saved his ass on more than one occasion, became enraged with jealousy and sought revenge. But instead of "exacting revenge" on Jason, Medea aimed her sights on Glauke. She soaked a beautiful gown in a secret potion that "stored up the powers of fire" and sent it to Glauke. When Glauke tried on the gown[22] it burst into flames so hot they melted the flesh right off her bones. She threw herself into a fountain, but the water only made the flames burn hotter.

CHORUS: Medea, Medea, you bitch! No wonder it's your name on our lips.[23]

THE WOMAN turns to HER VERY BEST FRIEND seated next to her on her living room couch in front of a TV that's playing a video of *Lover*

---

[21] Yes, there are lots of names here, and if you know nothing of Greek mythology then it will be Greek to you. For the sake of clarity, say the role of Jason is played by Donald Trump, Glauke by Marla Maples, and Medea by Ivana Trump.

[22] What the hell was Glauke thinking!?! A gift from Medea, a woman who had dismembered her own brother in order to be with Jason?!? And what was Marla thinking!?! Signing a prenuptial agreement with The Donald that declared if the marriage didn't last five years she would get only $1-5 million of The Donald's $2 billion. How long did the marriage last? Almost five years. Big surprise. What were they all thinking, these women who love their men?!? Beautiful, yes. Wise…? Can't we blame it on environment, the inexorable way environment (i.e., the omnipotent media) molds young women into creatures who would do and say anything to get and keep their man. As a woman myself, I would like to blame it on environment, oh yes, for I am too ashamed to accept it as my "nature."

[23] This line appeared in Euripedes' original version of his play, *Medea*. His editor forced him to delete it for fear of offending the mainstream reading public.

LOVER COME BACK
a synopsis

Doris is a scrupulous virginal advertising exec who wears silly hats, and Rock is an unscrupulous womanizing advertising exec pretending to be a shy rocket scientist who's never been laid so he can (1) get in Doris's pants and (2) distract her from pursuing a new ad account for a product that doesn't exist. Basically, Doris gets to wear a lot of white—and, of course, those silly hats—and Rock gets to wear a beard and tweeds when he's not barechested and perpetually tan. The sexual tension is palpable in their love scenes. What talented actors! Considering that in real life Rock was gay and Doris was married 4 times.

Come Back, starring Doris Day and Rock Hudson.[24] THE WOMAN and HER VERY BEST FRIEND are drinking Diet Cokes and eating salad and watching the scene where Doris realizes she's been duped by Rock and therefore gets mad, real mad, as mad as Doris can get.

"By the by," THE WOMAN says to HER VERY BEST FRIEND, "you will never ever believe what I did last night!"

HER VERY BEST FRIEND leans eagerly forward, salivating almost, almost twitching with un-Doris-Day-like anticipation. "What what what did you do?"

"Well," says THE WOMAN, cautiously glancing over each shoulder, first her right, then her left, though she's sitting in her own apartment where she lives alone, while on the TV screen Doris convinces Rock to strip down naked on a beach and then leaves him stranded there, taking his clothes with her, while THE WOMAN's mouth expands in a grin tinged with evil: green sky predicting hail, "I called Jirí every hour on the hour and hung up without saying a word."

"And then what?" asks HER VERY BEST FRIEND, drool gathering in her cleft chin.

"Then what *what*?" THE WOMAN asks.

---

24 BY THE BY: Doris Day would never ever harm another living soul. I am not the only one who knows this. When I was a child my mother resembled a brunette Doris Day and everyone therefore believed my mother incapable of malevolent behavior. Even my mother believed this when she looked in the mirror and smiled at herself like Doris Day smiling at Doris Day. My mother's thought of spanking the piss out of me for drawing on the living room wall with broken crayons in shades of red melted to the mantra, "I am Doris Day, benevolent humanitarian, a phrase which may in fact be redundant, I don't know, whatever, anyway, I would never ever harm another living soul, not even my spoiled brat of a daughter." Yes, it's true: Doris made my mother a better human being and she saved my ass.

"What else did you do?"

"Why, nothing else!" Normally, THE WOMAN would never ever begin a sentence with "Why,...!" but she has been watching Doris Day for approximately 57 minutes, and Doris Day has gotten under her skin, transformed THE WOMAN into a woman whose language resembles Doris Day's language, not only in its vocabulary but its timbre: that sexy-but-celibate breathiness that is Doris, all Doris, why yes, Doris!

"Like I said," THE WOMAN continues, "I called him on the phone about a hundred times and then hung up!"

HER VERY BEST FRIEND recoils—not from horror but from an exquisite boredom, tangible and pungent and weighted as if Death himself [*Why is Death always a man, Nature always a woman?*] had just settled a wet mink coat around her shoulders.

PLEASE NOTE:

Days later at a cafe, a tomato seed[25] clings to HER VERY BEST FRIEND's napkin. She picks at it until it comes off under her fingernail. She must dig it out with another fingernail. She brings it to her face and studies it, thinking it resembles some object from inside the body: vile, best kept hidden. She shudders. Wipes the tomato seed under the table's edge.[26]

25 ***SHAMELESS SELF-PROMOTION *** See sections 9 and 11 of "Say What You Like" in my first book *Drought & Say What You Like*, winner of the Thorpe Menn Book Award.

26 Days later a child will run her little fingers under this very same table's edge and discover the tomato seed and pick it off with her tiny fingernail and stare at it long and hard. Then she will hold the seed toward her divorced-and-now-a-weekend-father father and exclaim, "Look, Daddy! A booger!" Daddy will glance around the cafe to see if anyone has heard his daughter's vulgar cry of delight, then brusquely clean the "booger" from her tiny finger with his paper napkin, then slap her hand hard and hiss, "Don't pick your nose, do you hear me?" And she will somberly nod her little head—though she will not be able to make the connection between the table's booger and her nose—and will rub her stinging little hand and start to cry until she remembers she is also not supposed to cry. When she grows up, she will become the Chief Financial Officer of a Fortune 500 company and date far younger men and be disparagingly referred to as "Big Bad Ball Buster" by males of equal or lesser corporate rank.

"Wasn't that just awful of me?" asks...no, *pleads* THE WOMAN. Awkward demanding plea couched in Doris Day vernacular. Doubtful and hopeful all at once.

"Yeah," HER VERY BEST FRIEND mumbles unconvincingly. "Awful."

Desperate to be bad, very bad, bad to the bone, THE WOMAN says: "It's probably a crime. A misdemeanor, at the very least. Harassment. I'm sure I could get arrested for it."

"Right," says HER VERY BEST FRIEND. Her eyes roll to the ceiling then stare at Doris Day singing on the TV screen, waist impossibly skinny below her impossibly pointy breasts below her impossibly golden hair, and quite suddenly she turns to THE WOMAN and asks, "Are you gonna eat the rest of your salad, or what?"

THE ART OF GETTING BUMPED

In ancient legends the combustible cloak[27]
was a weapon for exacting revenge.
—*Archaeology Magazine,* March/April 1997

There is nothing "exact" about revenge. As a science, it's not. As an art, it's possible. After all, it's the creativity of revenge that makes it worthwhile. Originality of the act. Brilliance: Medea also murdered her children so that Jason would have no heirs.

FIRST SON: Oh, what can I do? How can I escape my mother's hand? Where can I hide?

SECOND SON: I don't know. Dear brother, we are lost!

Lost like the screams of children disappearing into water or smoke.

27 Also known as *tunica molesta.*

SUSAN SMITH.[28] DEBORA GREEN.[29]

I had never felt so lonely and so sad in my entire life. I was in love with someone very much, but he didn't love me and never would. I had a very difficult time accepting that...I dropped to the lowest point when I allowed my children to go down that ramp into the water without me.... My children, Michael and Alex, are with our Heavenly Father now, and I know that they will never be hurt again. As a mom, that means more than words could ever say.... My children deserve to have the best, and now they will.

—from the confession of Susan Smith

I'm sorry my children are dead... Maybe God wanted me to be here to teach or tell me something. I cannot believe this is His plan for the rest of my life.

—from a letter written by Debora Green in the Topeka, Kansas Correctional Facility

GAZING AT THE WORLD'S NAVEL...

we discover lint.

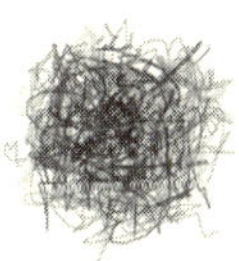

The human genome is a pigsty, bulging with non-genes, ex-genes, freeloader genes, viral detritus, pocket lint and chewing gum. All but a few percent of it appears to be doing nothing at all.[30]

```
Date: Mon, 25 Mar 2002  3:04:02-0500
To: prettygrl@bohemia.cz
From: jiricech@earthlink.net
Subject: Ontological concerns

Dear You:
God created heaven and earth, and somewhere in
between a Man and a Woman rose up out of the dust
```

---

[28] Depressed over her bad marriage and bad love affair, Smith drove to a lake, put her car into neutral, stepped out, released the parking brake, and let the car roll into water with her two sons strapped inside.

[29] Depressed after her husband had an affair, Dr. Green set her big house on fire. Two of her three children did not escape the flames.

[30] *Source:* Natalie Angier, for *The New York Times* online, June 26, 2000.

and recognized in the other not so much the means by which desire could be met but the end of loneliness. They must have connected in that first encounter, Man and Woman, must have seen in the other the image of who they were inside their own mind--Narcissus and his reflection, perhaps?--otherwise it would have ended there: no more dancing toward each other, dancing around each other, dancing inside each other, trying to get a scent on the shape of "companionship."

I tell you it smelled like the shape of a piano about to fall on my head.

love,
Jirí Cêch

PICTURING THE PAST

Quiz

(1) Do you keep the promises you make to yourself?
No.
(2) Then how can you keep your promises to me?
Because I value you more than myself.

THE WOMAN cannot get the image of HER VERY BEST FRIEND's bored face out of her mind—though the TV is on and there's a war in Eastern Europe and people she has never met, now will never meet, *never ever,* are dying, will be dead in a matter of weeks days hours minutes seconds, are already dead, rotting even, mere flashes in the history of humankind (unkind humans!)—though she picks up the remote and turns up the volume and hears nothing—though somewhere, *out there,* indeed in a million neglected places, lives are coming to a horrible and tragic end—though all this and so much more, the face of HER VERY BEST FRIEND nevertheless stares back at her—*O how exquisitely bored!*—and she can think of absolutely nothing worse in the whole wide world.

(I gotta tell ya: I am *annoyed* by THE WOMAN, her shallowness, her self-absorption, her smallness. I've been her more times than I care to confess. Therefore I would like to eradicate her—well, maybe not *her* as *entity* (after all she's just invention, necessary configuration in a work of fiction that is about more and less than what it appears to be about), but rather her as *personality trait* (i.e., seriously flawed).)

(And isn't even this process of writing fiction[31] the ultimate act of conceit: *I think I know something important.* Tell me: What is more important than those distant deaths occurring now now now now now now now now now now now now now...?)

> **Then again if I don't say it,** thought Euripides, poised over parchment that was already taking on the distinctive scent of mold, **who in hell will?**

The gears in THE WOMAN's brain turn and grind and chew on the past, over the unhappy face of boredom, into the calm blank-slate-of-a-future where possibilities for revenge are bountiful and sweet! She turns off the TV and sits for a moment in the silent dark. She begins singing, quietly: "Euripides doo-dah, Euripides day! My oh my what a wonderful day!"

THE THRILL OF DISCOVERY

```
Date: Thu, 28 Mar 2002  17:01:24 -0500
To: prettygrl@bohemia.cz
From: jiricech@earthlink.net
Subject: Mythology
```

```
Dear You:
Everyone thinks the dragon is a mythical beast,
but I have proof of its existence. This particular
dragon claims she's in love with me but what a
strange way she has of proving it. Every morning
there's dog shit on my doorstep. Fresh dog shit! I
```

---

[31] Substitute: poetry, drama, personal essay, screenplay, etc.

```
don't know where she gets all of it; she doesn't even
have a dog. But there it is, practically steaming
it's so fresh.
Sorry you had to hear this. :-(
Still, I thought you should know. :-)

love,
Jirí
```

Revenge is wicked and unchristian and in every way unbecoming...(But it is powerful sweet, anyway.)
—Mark Twain

Dear Mr. Twain:
Why is revenge sweet? I think it is bitter bitter bitter. The dried-blood taste it leaves in your mouth between your teeth remains far too long. Like Limburger cheese. Like literally kissing someone's ass.[32]

MEDEA: Let no one think of me as weak, the object of their simpering pity or contempt...

But, Medea! *Sweetheart!* Don't you get it? Don't you understand that the mere act of revenge is a confession to having been somehow wounded: betrayed, insulted, humiliated, shamed. And not only have you been wounded, you've stooped to advertise your wounds, for revenge lets THE *[black]* ~~W~~HOLE *[in the]* ~~WIDE~~ WORLD know your pain, therefore confirming what you already suspect: *You're not worth your salt, baby.*

So the asshole left you for a younger more beautiful woman, so what? It's not about you, it's about him: His need for power and acceptance, more hair, bigger pecs, a thicker longer harder dick.

Take my advice: The best revenge is to lick your wounds in private—or find another lover and lick him. In public always pretend that it's not blood you're trailing behind you but an extraordinarily passionate and somehow corporeal...*aura!* That,

32 Okay, I've never literally kissed anyone's ass, though I have pressed my lips to a lot of other things, including Limburger cheese. My ability to relate Limburger cheese with someone's anus is the result of **IMAGINATION!** The point being, I suppose: The best revenge takes imagination.

or learn to write fiction wherein you can exact your revenge sweetly while simultaneously claiming to improve humanity.

5. Please read the following passage for comprehension:

> A certain Czech director whom I met at a certain film festival said he once asked his wife (a certain Czech actress whose name begins with the letter D) what she would do if he ever had an affair. D replied, "I'd kill her." The director cried, "Why her? Why not me?" And D pinched his scruffy cheek and cooed, "I could never kill you, darling, you're my husband!"

HOW FAST ARE YOU GOING?

```
Date: Mon, 01 Apr 2002  10:41:55 -0600
To: prettygrl@bohemia.cz
From: jiricech@earthlink.net
Subject: Here and There
```

Dear You:
Now you can go from lost to found at the speed of light. The way we find each other here in virtual space, our virtual love for one another. Let's never meet. Let's never learn each other's gestures, the way you might push your red (blonde? black?) hair behind your ears over and over again and again until I want to scream, break your wrist, wait until you have fallen asleep some fog-ridden night and take the blue-handled scissors and cut off your beautiful but unruly red/blonde/black hair. Trust me now: I don't want to know the smell of your morning breath, unwashed crotch, stale farts & belches. From this remarkably clean distance even your anus smells like fresh-bloomed lilacs, or cinnamon sticks in coffee, or the breezes of my youth in Bohemia forever vanished beneath the smoke and dirt of culture, or lack of culture.

(Yes, it's true: more dog shit on my doorstep.)

Oh, You! There you are! There! at the speed of light and I love You. Please don't betray me by insisting we meet. Don't prove your infidelity by wanting too much.

Please,
jc

THE COLOR OF REVENGE

She believes everything must have a color. Therefore:

What is the color of revenge? Not red, an impulsive hue of quick anger and undeterred lust. No, revenge is slow burning, cool and calculated, blue and clean like propane. She dresses in pale blue silk, naked beneath the cool slip of a dress, nails stripped of polish, hair still wet from a good scrubbing and no cream rinse or conditioner to weight it down.

PICTURING THE PAST: PART TWO

Quiz

(1) Leave me the hell alone, will you?
But why don't you love me anymore?
(2) I just don't, that's all.
Tell me the truth.
(3) All right. I've met someone else. Satisfied?
She's younger than me—and a lot taller.
(4) How did you know that?
You're parting your hair differently.

WHEN PEOPLE SEEK EXCELLENCE THEY LOOK FOR A SIGN

Date: Fri, 05 Apr 2002 16:11:45 -0500
To: prettygrl@bohemia.cz
From: jiricech@earthlink.net
Subject: I Want You

Dear You:
Here the day begins when the sun comes up. No more lingering in bed where it is warm and smelling of sweat and cum! Yes, I masturbate. What did you expect? I'm a man with sexual energy not easily quashed. If you were here that energy would go into you--literally and figuratively. The thought of my cock in your cunt excites me even now.

But let me repeat: I don't ever want to meet you. The probability of our mutual disappointment depresses me so much I want to weep, claw at my eyes, tear at my hair, and I've wept and clawed and torn so much already.

argh!
Jirí

HOW FAST ARE YOU GOING?

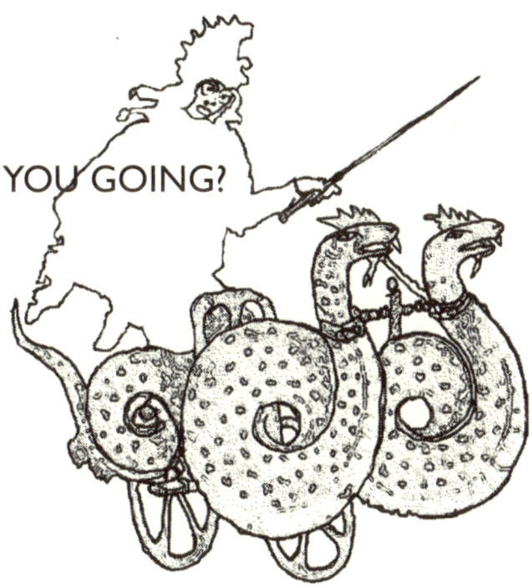

(Medea appears above us in a chariot drawn by dragons.)

THE WOMAN and HER VERY BEST FRIEND are eating enormous salads at the Cheep Salad Bar[33] and talking about work and new shoes as if the war in Eastern Europe were a commercial for ***New and Improved!*** tampons. Though THE WOMAN now dislikes HER VERY BEST FRIEND to an irreversible depth, she pretends affinity. Nevertheless HER VERY BEST FRIEND senses something amiss in THE WOMAN's behavior but attributes it to PMS or gas.

Why the pretense? Because THE WOMAN has a secret that she shall soon reveal, a gleam of victory and pride in her eyes (victory in right eye, pride in left) to HER VERY BEST FRIEND who will stare in awe, she is certain, awed by her wit and intelligence, stare in awe at least up until the moment THE WOMAN says:

THE WOMAN: **Moses removed his sandals before the Burning Bush, afraid to desecrate the ground from which God arose as living flame. He knew his place in the scheme of things, humbled himself before a power so incomprehensible that its only route of manifestation was a shrub whose fire would not go out. Moses recognized omnipotence and was thusly rewarded with the power to part waters.**

---

33 Salads again, as if eating healthy, when in fact each salad contains over 1,000 calories and 34 grams of fat, and the lettuce and other fresh vegetables have been heavily sprayed with preservatives to extend their shelf life, and the cottage and cheddar and blue cheeses were made from cows fed hormones and antibiotics in order to produce more milk. As I write this cancer cells have begun multiplying in the left breast of **HER VERY BEST FRIEND** while here it has just begun to rain outside my window. I can hear the trembling of leaves, whisper of grass. All birds have gone silent, and the breeze is sweet and cool and clean. Such moments make one reconsider the weight of things—not the body's weight for it will lighten to dust or ash soon enough, but the weight of what's on **THE WOMAN's** mind as she waits for **HER VERY BEST FRIEND** to finish yet another story about her loathsome boss. Outside it rains and there is nothing I'd rather do at this moment than stand barefoot in the wet grass, lift my face to the sky, recall the first time I stood in a summer storm, and for a tender moment believe I am once again a child weighted only by rain. Incredibly, it is this very same yearning that flashes through **THE WOMAN's** mind as she bites into a tainted snow pea, therefore missing part of **HER VERY BEST FRIEND's** I-loathe-my-boss story. Which, in hindsight, she knows was a blessing.

But I'm getting ahead of myself. A half-hour before the Moses bit—which has absolutely no relevance to this story, not even to me (who wrote it), I just like the image of Moses going barefoot, thinking the soles of his feet would somehow be cleaner than the soles of his sandals—THE WOMAN speaks:

THE WOMAN: I placed an ad in "Personals" under Men Seeking Men. I received 72 responses and replied to all of them with unbridled enthusiasm, signing Jirí's name and listing all of his phone numbers—home, office, and cell—plus his pager number and his e-mail address. I enclosed a photograph of him, the one I took at the beach last summer where he looks kind of like Rock Hudson in *Lover Come Back.*

CURIOUS MINDED Very attractive PWM, 42, over 6', 180, muscled, hung, seeks HWP SGM to explore long repressed sexual desires. Please be gentle! Respond to Ad#1022A

[34]

HER VERY BEST FRIEND is dumbfounded. She says, "I'm dumbfounded." Later that day she makes the long walk from her parking space to her office. She is preoccupied and moody. By the time she sits in her ergonomically correct chair and brushes a strand of hair from her knitted brow and picks an aphid from the Wandering Jew on her desk, she has decided that (1) THE WOMAN is insane, (2) she no longer wishes to be THE WOMAN's VERY BEST FRIEND, (3) Doris Day's acting talent was grossly underrated, and (4) she no longer wishes to be associated with THE WOMAN in any way, shape or form. Her wish will come to pass. THE WOMAN will not give a shit.

[34] PWM = Professional White Male. HWP = Height/Weight Proportionate. SGM = Single Gay Male.

AND A MOUNTAIN OF EVIDENCE TO PROVE IT

Date: Wed, 17 Apr 2002 10:50:08 -0800
To: prettygrl@bohemia.cz
From: jiricech@earthlink.net
Subject: Scatological concerns

Dear You:
Well, it's not dog shit, it's pig shit. Don't misconstrue: I'm not a shit expert. I'm not even into scatological humor. But I took quite a large pile to the local vet and had it analyzed. She, the vet, wasn't eager to accommodate my query and was for some reason upset with the *amount* I'd brought as evidence, but I paid her as much as it would have cost to surgically remove shit from a pig's anus, so she agreed to do the analysis. Pig shit! I asked her, the vet, where someone would have gotten pig shit in this city? She told me, "Well, it's not shit from a pot-bellied pig, that's for sure. The turds are too thick." (I don't think she actually used the word "turds.") "Then where?" I demanded, for I was by this time extremely vexed. The vet said, "There's a corporate pig farm up north, about two to three hours away. They have plenty of pig shit. Maybe she got the shit there." And I said, "She? She? What makes you think it's a *she* who's leaving pig shit on my doorstep?" And the vet gave a smug little snort of a laugh and said, "Who else would exact such clever revenge but A WOMAN!" Then she handed me all the pig shit in a plastic bag, which I took, though I'm not sure why.

Oh, You You You!

The whole world has gone to shit, hasn't it? For You are there (where I wish You to remain) and I love You and am lonely for the woman You are there not here where You'd be ~~ordinary~~ ~~pathetic~~ ~~redundant~~ somehow less than You are there.

love,
jirí

CHORUS: O this cannot have a happy ending!

Date: Sun, 21 Apr 2002 08:19:15 -0500
To: prettygrl@bohemia.cz
From: jiricech@earthlink.net
Subject: The Power of Myth

Dear You:
Replicating a moment from the prehistoric past, a dragon stands defiantly outside my window. If I were a coward, I'd be scared shitless. No pun intended.

jc

CHORUS: O this story will end ~~sadly~~!
" " " " " ~~madly~~!
" " " " " badly!

CRIME—BOTH ORGANIZED AND PETTY—CAN BE DIFFICULT

All right, maybe this isn't about Glauke at all. Maybe it's about Medea. But why, I ask, why not Glauke? Why do victims not pique our interest? Why only the victimizers? When we think of Susan Smith, why don't we first remember her children, wonder about them in their last moments of living, the utter disbelief in their fluttering little souls, pounding on the rear window of the car sinking into the dark dark death-water, screaming, "Mommy! Mommy! MOM-MEEEEEEE!!!" Utter disbelief as only children can disbelieve, utterly: believing the opposite more palatable story must be must be oh has to be true, doesn't it, Mommy? Mommy!?! MOM–

Worse perhaps than their deaths is the victims fading in our collective memory while their perpetrators grow to mythological proportions. And so do we love more deeply, admire more particularly, the killer in our souls?

Quiz
circle your preference:
(select only one)
prey **predator**

Date: Wed, 01 May 2002 19:50:38 -0600
To: prettygrl@bohemia.cz
From: jiricech@earthlink.net
Subject: Watch Out!

Dear You:
It must be a coincidence, some glitch in the space/ time continuum, incontestable proof that we are destined for one another (as long as we keep our distance) for it can't be otherwise.

But how could you possibly think I'm the culprit? I don't even know where to get pig shit, having no idea what the hell a "corporate pig farm" is. All I can say is, if there's pig shit on your doorstep then there must be a dragon nearby. Watch your step, darling--figuratively and literally! And think of me and my own hellish sidestepping here while You are there. And tonight why don't You dream of me hovering like some future saint over You, virtually real, real enough for love, the way we love here in this clean world of emptiness.

always, always,
Jirí

THE WOMAN: Moses removed his sandals before the Burning Bush, afraid to desecrate the ground from which God arose as living flame. He knew his place in the scheme of things, humbled himself before a power so incomprehensible that its only route of manifestation was a shrub whose fire would not go out. Moses recognized omnipotence and was thusly rewarded with the power to part waters.

Maybe Moses does have something to do with this story after all. Moses kneeling before the burning bush, a bush aflame, flame as the voice of God: vengeful God who could and believe me would kick some major ass when it came to exacting revenge. Frogs and locusts and disease and fiery (again fire!) hailstorms?

We don't need a psychopath to teach vengeance. We have God.

HOW FAST ARE YOU GOING?

(Medea appears above us in a chariot drawn by dragons.)

THINGS CERTAINLY AREN'T WHAT THEY USED TO BE

No. Certainly not.

When a jet-lagged body thinks it's morning not even a hearty dinner will help. Not even the chiming of church bells in the piazza nor a slap in the face nor ice water on the genitals. Will help.

Yes, after a long night of killing on the other side of the world, THE WOMAN is tired but can neither sleep nor stay awake. She hovers somewhere in between, caught in a bardo state wherein reality and dreams overlap so precisely that there is no distinguishing fact from fiction/fiction from fact. Much as in the case of a reader who suspects that the author's inventions/intentions are more deeply seated in truth than imagination.

Thus THE WOMAN wonders if, in a small third-floor apartment in Prague, crumpled in a corner like a rag doll carelessly tossed aside, a pretty young Bohemian woman by the name of You is really burning to death inside a *tunica molesta* or if in fact it was all just a fantasy to mollify the desperation rising inside her like a wet wasp from a cracked mud-heart.

CHORUS: No Woman could resist that gown.

Not even You who thinks herself above crass materialism. And so You put on the lovely dress, the surprise gift, and stand before the long oval mirror admiring Your beauty. And You think it must be love—an astonishing and welcome form of self-love—that makes Your skin burn beneath the gown. Until the burning/the loving intensifies, grows unbearable beneath the fine fabric that smells faintly of petroleum. And it is then the world converges—scraps of stories loosed in time folding into one another, gaping seams stitched tight and catching fire. Fire of Your love, God's voice afire, You are on fire and not even a cold shower will put it out.

No. No.

> "[P]etroleum, sulphur, and lime... ignite and burn in ways similar to the descriptions of Medea's...cloak. Petroleum products are notorious for flowing, clinging, unquenchable flames.... Sprinkled with water, quicklime becomes slaked lime, which can generate enough heat to cause spontaneous combustion, and water would feed these flames."
> —*Archaeology Magazine*, March/April 1997

CHORUS: Ah, revenge! Sweet revenge. Sticky revenge! Humanity's favorite pastime. Exxon never had it so good.

Jesus-God-and-Mary-too THE WOMAN is tired! She collapses onto the bed and thinks of Doris Day in *Lover Come Back,* there at the movie's end where Doris is pregnant on a gurney, being wheeled into the hospital delivery room just as Rock arrives to rescue her from solitude and single motherhood and silly hats. *Rescue her not necessarily because he loves her,* thinks THE WOMAN, *but because he knocked her up.* She lays her hands on her flat belly and thinks, *If only I'd gotten pregnant. Oh, well. Too late now. Too late.*

She stares at a water stain on the ceiling of this foreign hotel room—in Vienna? Budapest? Sofia?—and thinks how its shape reminds her of him, the man for whom she feels such passion that to call it "love" seems a denigration, a bastardization of the soul. Water stain resembling his face with chin scar and lazy eyelid and one crooked tooth on the bottom like a weary young soldier no longer able to stand at attention.

"Ten-hut!" she hears: rasping of knife on whetstone.

"Ten-hut!" fading now.

Fading: "Ten-hut!"

"Ten-hut!"

"Ten-hut!"

FROM WAS: ANNALES NOMADIQUE

BY MICHAEL JOYCE (2007)

EDITOR'S NOTE: The hypertext writing of Michael Joyce was already known to many of us when, through Lance Olsen's intervention, Michael submitted *Was*. In my reader's report I remarked on its ambition "to encompass some sort of whole—literally all cultures, societies, classes—in a form of fragmentation," while others noted its exuberance, as though a non-narrated world, where anything could follow from anything, were arousing, not just scary. In one sense, the discontinuities of *Was* should feel familiar, for they mimic the 21st century conditions of everyday experience. Conceptual boundaries, by which we organize sensations into stories, now receive only sporadic institutional and material support, making the divisions between high and low culture, sincerity and hype, moral action and profit, or national cuisines, styles, and languages continually permeable. A collage looks to us like nature, placing Michael's work in an inverse relation to our daily lives. What we ordinarily do without reflection—scanning radio stations while driving past billboards trying to locate ourselves on the GPS—we must do deliberately reading *Was*. Each passage is composed of qualities, events, objects, and relations, while the narrative subject, the noun who bears these qualities and intends these relations, emerges belatedly as their connection. The result is that our point of identification resembles an epiphenomenon, an effect of the story it shapes. It's as though we were experiencing ourselves being produced. I find this dynamism of self and other highly erotic.

—RMB

"Increasingly I see all serious writing as having political significance to the extent that it insists upon the precision and person of the human voice in the face of fundamentalisms and neo-fascisms, including—perhaps especially—our own, which treat words as mere tokens: ductile, expendable, bloodless, corrupt."

—Michael Joyce

was thought not were the yellow the irrepressible ever who said who said ends Ashtoreth one Wednesday, one Wednesday in June the damp the dampness in everything (light, profusionist, no I mean heat)

forty times now, bowing, clogs along foggy bottom news from the front, wooden boxes neatly in rows

the last the lost wandering *allées* (lips pressed to the neonate's skull, powder scent) willows all now gone from their ripeness

and what of the stipple, the limp, the lost what-was, despite the damp odor of canvas, the salt-cracked lips, inordinate corridors? who can say who can say distant machines growl through *die Nähe* (*durch*)

she goes out

she goes out again

bereft, put-upon the dogs circle, their bloodied knees glistening damply

along thought now, begins with if, not begs as he misread, and if, so considered, say sawdust sausages and diesel fumes or the faded parasols and flutes of Prosecco, silver bucket of sardines *sur le quai Branly*, too tardy to set off, redolent of interiority, thinking, thinking a seizure, a pleasure, a string purse, the death of a tiny thing, a beetle without a common name, bloodless, foxing the endpapers of the calf-bound 12mo of Terence's *Comoediae* she brought back from Caracas, if then? how to live, I mean.

I mean I mean

again she goes out, *la charrada (charros y musica)*, amusing herself—etymologically so, things

neighborhoof, once misspoke, *l'amuse-bouche*, cherry lipped

global creolization = URL

olé olé, under skirt's goat beard, almond scent, headcheese

benign complication, dramatis personae: *due*, viz., the dantesque: "*volentier parlerei a quei due*"

hears a good story

set forth a skiff doomed to barratry, fouled in her scuppers, sea-cocks seized with velvet rust, tulipwood planks damply aromatic, porpoises abeam land locked look at her thighs, the seas the seasons by the lee, I, no, nothing, pink drinks on ice, tumblers sweating feathers, elliptical palm leaf shadow, the Tamil princess's teeth shredding sugar cane (*Gramineae Saccharum officinarum*), those days glorious, glint of the chalice held aloft in pink manicured fingers, sentimental gangster (hums)

Milonguita,

los hombres te han hecho mal

y hoy darias toda tu alma

por vestirte de percal.

saxophone portico and lurid petticoats, echoes languidly intrude, relentlessly not making sense, what else is music, Davide amigo?

dead plastic telephone, curiously cocoa stained basalt

head inland

katabatic gusts rising up into the lowering overcast, winds through the pass, winds pass, winds past, whistling

hangs in, spake the man at the bar, eruption unregistered, barrista's overlapping swirls yawning, tamps a mahogany *kafé*, MTV on the telly

Jó napot kívánok. Egyetemista vagyok. Everything means something to someone: waterfall pinball music, the Gigue Fugue of Bach on a mobile phone

suckling creature tucked under her blouse, vaguely marsupial, mounts the steps of the trekker's Toyota jitney, backpack squarely situated last night's knifing bloodless, gibbous moon, potato and ramp frittata bubbling in lard, yet no one moves

bakelite (corrects him) no matter, the fat bloom whitish upon a block of ghosted Oaxacan chocolate, say, *La Soledad* or *Guelaguetza*, now a miraculous photograph *de la La Virgen de Juquila*, three euro, mister

my seester

the dog's abrading tongue, the nun like a dirigible, this way and that

pyramids of Calabicita, black radish, *Thymus praecox*, slumbering peaches, melon gash crawling with dark winged raisins

let's get out of here, let's

yes

refugee consciousness, a radio lozenge, certain unforeseen cul-de-sacs, multicolored phone cards and the right festive hat, motor vehicles bureau, sultry white presidio

I want to waltz once

more.

slow descent of the mothership over the dry lake bed, a miraculous pouring forth, distant murmur, an empty stadium, all we have lived for lost, or who can tell (so irritable, she says), the hovering shade offers a welcoming respite, for once almost making sense, sweet shoots stir themselves, labial: cumulus

under the shadow their shadows lost, one two three, one, two three, one two the same train arrives seven times running *am Bahnhof*, each time the same cast and crew disembarking, east time he thought, as if a film loop, *La Ciotat* et alia, nervous conductor tapping the crystal of his wristwatch, endless recurrence no excuse, Togolese redcap's soprano sax aria, *Agapornis pullarius*, 1964 definitive, listed at 200 francs, the coolness of the glass arcade after the compartment

prandial shuffle of cards, *sept de cuillères*, watches her sway across the plaza, shadow oblique, unveering

hesitation about trusting casement, compass, snapline, pencil (rayograph salamander their logo; slogan unknown), physics of a pawn shop diffraction grating, small town diadem, blue chalk measure of an afternoon

the precision of ennui, this moment, this (sways unveering), x7

SMS = telegram

postcard of a *parcheggio* in Rifredi (*Line Firenze-Pistoia-Bologna*) 4.5 km from the Uffizi, asphalt inscribed with graphically crisp hatching, Egyptian temple facing the *laghetto*, Hellenistic temple beyond the lemon trees and the stables, off-duty gypsy woman napping on the lawn, Hogarth's Curve, loss of innocence perpendicular to the descent of narrative *dans le rêve lucide*, lacks patience with this and who can blame

will you love me?

when?

and again the day begins without summoning, sun wandering purposelessly, is of course its purpose, such cleverness at breakfast, laughter like ice cubes on the hotel terrace, tarry cigarettes, corporate countess with a harlot's lips, pert breasts neatly packaged as twin gabardine parcels, belted waist, Blackberry tracking satellites from a clutch purse, toast crust detritus, neatly ringed crimson cork tip filter deftly swept away, smoothes skirt abaft, aright, moves off

no nightingales in the new world, the Polish poet said, this is a problem (rueful smile, dark-haired wife midway in the auditorium), nor do your blackbirds sing

harbour seals venture far up the river

it is no matter

though you would think it otherwise it is impossible to see oneself in the mirrored surface of a CD, she said, incorrectly it turned out

it has been good

then what, the fog riven into drifting forelocks, dusty stones *come pane casareccio* in the morning sun. (then and what) two and a half hours before noon and, acedia, a name for every thing, waft of cloacal salt scent *il Palazzo Contarini del Bovolo*, faraway Veneto, distant Ophir, *dopo* an hour before coffee again makes sense, until then (here is the origin of art), driftwood twigs twirl languidly in opalescent oil skim, beard of yellow pollen clinging to them

(then what | when that), i.e., global reversibility of cellular automata, viz., unidentified middle-age man of uncertain nationality wearing yoked gingham cowboy shirt plus Teju lizard boots with hand-tooled and painted uppers, duty-free at Schiphol shopping for salt licorice

16 min

the longing for event weighing on his shoulders like a field piece, *crus ansata, fissura coronalis*, good shepherd, a lace of bloody sweat on his forehead, it is a long story, a lonely motorcycle along a nearby stone *passaggio* soon lost, the transit of venus accomplished nightly via nickel-chrome alloy cylinder tumbling slowly through arid darkness, graphite composite and epoxy skin pinging @ thirty cycles per second, Dasabimbaras approaching the threshold of the universe (it is all very exciting but his companion, imagining the smell of straw, longs to breathe the air outside the dark theater)

baptized Eve, awkward embarrassed rictus one finds charming (rehearses the possible replies: atom, atman, admin, ad man, *al-atwah*, haha), smiles

(Advert: Reinforcement works from 8mm Ø to 42 mm Ø any size or shape, subcontract ok.)

greeting grasps his hand longer than one might, softly softly

Christian, spoken as if giving her a small coin

do you like to coffee? is not how it is said (as if in a sea or a game)

has a story begun then?

Once a time was and a met strange near the far in land, windshield wiper flaying, failing, clay smears splay across semi-clear orbital segments, grouse tail, cloud abyss, bus engine knocking, dozing in the scent of cloves and perspiration, soft breast against the *Brachioradialis*, ear pillowed against the *Serratus Anterior*, a/k/a boxer's muscle, the world will always welcome, time, goes on a spherical plane a vast molecular crowd, garnet muscovite olivine suspension, a loose particulate upon an excited surface, sand spew, awaiting the sun's returning, sharply dancing crystal soldiers, commoners, defrocked geomancer spitting tobacco (viz., *Scytodes thoracica*) to whom it's all a game

he detests children, spat likewise

unruffled awaits, she tranquil (at the bottom of the nubbed espresso cup a beach of chocolate sand, feeds it to herself on narrow spoon, *corpus corporum, amen*

amen

unblinking

recapitulates, inside this mote (so pronounced) a scream and, of course, the head; but then, thus far that is, love isn't in question, for naught all the goings and coming soon what next (it's annoying, meaning boring the way one announces it), a heaviness at her center as if suddenly putting on weight, leaden swallowing, cramps perhaps or dawn, a limp worm, snoring, sickening wafts of fermenting honey or sperm, a sliver moon, sets, while she

sleeps

no referents, *sans Giovanni* or the muse of Calais (a blind stab), we are left unturned, no twins on opposite shores, hithering, apophatic yawn, yet you are well educated, one day quotidian bibliographers will explore the disappearance of the cross-country bus ticket as a cultural form (spondee giving way to dactylic), but what of the sinew? the sense of the

calligraphic nonsense on boxcars, ptyalizing boys, ratio of perfection, and in the tunnel nothing but the dull gaze, face to face ("believe," fr. 138) outside the coach the rail clack, *cara Doricha*, in the window of the future someone will remember, believe, belief, shot forth to light and her face erased, a smear of pallid green replacing its features, iron colored lake's dark and ragged edge where the eye was

finally, disguised by dreams, they arrive, a hundred years old now, carrying their house rolled up upon their back, rotting sail, boots coming apart at the seams, sunken eyes, his limp useless smile, the dormitory in the hostel smelling of chlorine bleach, men on cots crying out for wives, a smokestack at some distance spells out its black litany against a yellow sky and through the walls someone, in the shower a woman, siren, sings, "the oak's deep heart and the fisherman's oar," Mandelstam's song of wood

that's the story of, *la gloire de*, rendezvous aborted, e.g., Sasikiran v. Harikrishna, Qb2+, one night paid but left (1) cot untouched (2) half-uncial note at front desk (= blue's traveler tune, avs.): *xtian no hope no rescue eve*, (3) plum lipstick kiss infra sig., wax faintly bergamot (disinterested clerk watching Canal+ reality teevee, deposed, gestures toward the only door apropos), all night through the darkened quarter spiraling toward the terminal, teenage hookers in glitter-dusted Diesel knockoffs and open-toed sandals sipping soft drinks through colored straws, sickly colored dawn striated sherbet parfait, skipped westbound train and waited for the east, retracing last night's, missed, last, -30-

she saw him off from a distance

FF: a city like London but not (cf. Lubjana, Lexington, Lahore, Lisbon), still a river, "picturesque" brick towers, pomo mews, Bauhaus quays, disneyfied Futurist ferris wheel, nightly fireworks, shops *avec panini*, flavored soaps, hand rolled/hand tied jasmine balls in green glass replica apothecary jars, *Kanom Krok* smoking over coals, Pig Snout on the tap

the inevitable turn toward narrative: c.v., blogspot MISPER report, vacuous profile cum dubious photo, nostalgic burnt ammonia smell, Marconi Wireless cablegram, urgent uppercase, carbon-stained finger whorl, clerkly diction: anent which else such *oder sonst noch so gibt, u.s.w.*

symmetries of pavement or work for hire, dispatches from a series of cybercafés, *neti-neti* returned-replied to, pinging the aether, bcc litany: St. Jude patron of lost causes, St. Anthony patron of the lost, St. Margaret of Antioch, *ora pro nobis*

full six months in a shared flat with an office girl named Devi, each other's refugees, not barring the occasional brush up against, frying cauliflower, green cardamom seed, assiduously lotioned, scrawny flanks, wept in sleep, awoke lucid to the touch, savory nubbed disks of sable soft upon her chest, rising, dark eyes as the story goes, fond of Blandy's Rainwater Madeira, apt to claw thereafter

seldom herself entertaining friends behind closed doors, mobilely upward once insisted earnestly

left one day and didn't come home, both of them

12 pp handwritten life story—austerely looping inked peacock-blue cursive courtesy Little Flower Convent Girls High School, Guruvayoor, Kerala—in his Invicta backpack

packet of lavender pastilles on the sideboard wrapped in pink ribbon for her part Eve disappeared staying where she was, a serpentine stratagem, looping back on one self, cf. "genuine Christine," bifid, i.e., licking once own ouns with (width?) doubled tongue, sleeps lightly moaning; amoan, the worm turns, viz., Voltairine De Cleyre (1900), the bird of omen

panhandle, shovel, whiskbroom, fraying denim over ankle length khaki, hitech breathable hiking boots, constellation Andromeda ikat indigo bandana

bitch, puta, kutu, Hure, *Durga Tripura Rahasya*

bedding down in matted grass beyond a cane fringed swale, pale straw swirl where deer lay down, river smell and musk and tiny violets, precise hopping of winged creatures branch to branch, moonlight frottage and vacant dreams: scow sighs and rising, moans against the hawser, ghosts pass along the trail in single file, dimly phosphorescent, lowly crooning, the breath of them like smoke, silent owls devour steaming mice

in the black glass of the acrid pool Hecate's sunken eyes, mask of oxblood clay where the lover has sealed them

I left you to love

awoke to dog's tongue and vagrant frond of hot sun across her face, the hound nuzzled into complicity shushed, ranged sniffing still back toward the master's orbiting call, a herd of dull tin bells baahing at some distance, limbs aching, hiss of melodious piss at the trunk of a beech tree, its accompanying perfume, ankles itch, dried smears of grey mud at hip and shoulder brush easily off, morning toilet (a girl's dream of coloring the lips with berries)

she resolves to find a path to the city and become a private secretary or to find

something beyond the damp stiffness of sleep will not ease in her hip, left, arthritic she supposes, aching rotational sense of the socket itself, a wiry spike of pain with each footfall: *Dzién dobry, prababka*, made a salve of comfrey cooked in butter and rubbed it on the hip, tissue thin hands caressing the girl's flank over and over again, *cicha woda, cicha woda, serduszka*, in English: darling, darling, *chrzesniaczka*, dear godchild, what has happened to us

years pass implacable as flowers, the architecture of Babcia's bony shoulders familiar beneath the washcloth imbued with pungent Czech soap, yet not nursing but nursed, in retreat from, not love, but the constancy of emotion, learning (*via negativa*) non-ness and *patientia*, the imagined rustic cottage a flat in a dreary brick and glass socialist tower, hallway smelling of *chrzan* (sharp root) and *kapusta*, the inevitable cabbage—and yet

and yet Babcia kept a bony milkgoat (*koza*) in a shed toward the back of a friend's weedy lot, zealously wished the girl could find a *polski chlopak*, Polish boyfriend, and for hours on evenings after Angelus passed her time before the television whispering the names of things, filling the child's ear with the honey, *miod*, of the mother tongue

iPods, she had read in the newspaper, scientific proof, sapped the brainwaves of the young, siphoning memories to the stratosphere, downloading (speaking the word in English: down low) *Polski Rap—Zakazane Piosenki*

forbidden songs

spits: *Dzién Szaka-l'a-Bafangoo*, as if the name of Satan, crossing herself (saner than some, no crazier than most) life in a suburb, *tesknota*, viz., *saudade*, "a sorrowful longing," a series of digital cellphone self-portraits, no one calling, email as pointless as Babcia's rosary beads, a shelf of canned soup above the stove

lingering once—the young priest making a surprise visit in his blue cassock and retro biretta—she list from the steaming bath as his soft tone and Babcia's singsong wove, the flesh along her thighs pink with scald, her breasts buoyant

that night resolved to dream this, without result

months later, once upon a time, finding a gauze packet under her pillowcase, a charm of rose hips, lavender buds, and bay leaves tied with a pink ribbon, in the morning made a tea of it, Babcia silent over dry toast

smiling once upon

perhaps imagined you would outlive her, as if in a fairy tale or a bus schedule, 22:13; 22:21; 22:30; 22:47, driver having a smoke in the night, the cloud above him blank panel of a comic book, glaciers afloat on themselves

or follow reindeer into Lapland

she answered the phone and he was not there, clutched a fist between her thighs, Babcia's clear glass rosary wrapped around her fingers, cold

borrowing a cardboard suitcase smelling of death and camphor, vicinity by definition where one has stayed too long

for his part skated, nearly four hours daily, northward also along interconnected rivers, wife slung on his back like a parcel, sharp heels checking against his waist, warm circle of her breath on the back of his neck freezing into a silver medallion, twin babies crosswise seal pups at her breasts

Hans Brinker along the Rideau Canal, it is all made up, still the weight of it, the push of lost love, real, limestone turrets rising into view

message in a dream, empty dial tone

on a bus among pilgrims (Santiago-Mendoza) harrowing Los Caracoles switchbacks Cristo Redentor tunnel, *salve regina, vita dulcedo*, Germans snoring unperturbed, among *gli altri* one lost cause, blind drunk moaning, turns out to be an American mercenary, whispering with the border guards, machine guns swaying at their hips, laughing aloud as he boards the next bus back

thinks to join him but the guards are suspicious and will not hold the bus

Los Penitantes, San Martin de los Andes, Las Islas del Sol y de la Luna

Nordic skis sold in Mendoza to a befuddled Huarpe vendor in the Mercado, taking the next bus back, the same yawning teenage *protector de la frontera* as the day before, finger on the trigger, staring and then, *vaya vaya*, sullenly tossing the passport back across the formica

daytripper, *mula quizás*

four successive days arising before dawn in the hostel dormitory, thimble of *agüita* or peppery chocolate in the maze of streets near the *término*, diesel aroma of the idling autobuses, and every morning the American soldier already there, feigning drunken slumber before stumbling onto the Mendoza bus, twice looking back on the fifth day taken in for questioning

(*en español*) what's the story, *chacotero*? you some *copuchento*, eh *fleto*? some things you cannot know

(protesting) *soy un payado* (in English) busker, you know, mate

the strumming gesture in air

¿Verdad, huaso? where's your guitar (laughing), in Mendoza with your skis?

no drugs in his pockets or backpack, no payback in planting it, day wearing on

face slap hard enough the marks last an hour

vaya, asshole, stay away from the bus station, *¿Entiende?*

¡Y compre una guitarra!, shouts the pimply fucking *milico*

cabros, boys, laughing together, sun already high

days later on the plaza the same American soldier in a clean white shirt

1500 km National Road, No. 3, cab of a Word of God truck driven by a local *taquillero* playing Christian hiphop, i.e., Gospel Gangstaz and KJ-52, jumping out along the Patagonia coast, at the bottom of the world seabirds, cellphone useless

hello hallo echo

a constant roaring, lace lapsing over stones, rumors of dolphins

stock up on Montecol bars and bottled water, thereafter (*oficina municipal Puerto San Julián*) calquing: *Perdóneme por favor, yo desean caer en amor*, pardon me, I wishes to fall in love

to fall, *tu falle*

je ne sais past

bus sliding off the road margin on a high pass, tumbling end on end, *et in saecula saeculorum* (no longer operant)

amen (a boy's fantasy, we proceed more slowly to our death)

one sole story (sensei): "the hitchhiker or the wormhole in the universe" (The Shipman's Tale a variant)

a virgin whisper proffers comfort beneath her skirt but no room within her, soft descant (not descent) of angels sotto voce

the third glorious mystery our lady's retro-evolution, closed lotus bud of undeveloped vulva per deci-bead interval

sealing up her opening with damp mud, desiccate vespid queen (a/k/a nest mother) awaits the end of winter (December, tierra del fuego)

a longing for

him, for her

cut to: the chase (Saint Castin and other stories, viz., "waiting woods, sensitive in every leafless twig in silence and dim around a lodge"), a new world

what are the conversations besides bed? (beside her low bed a waterglass, full, citronella candle, unlit, a yellowing notepad, pencil mamilla, balm of Gilead, devout comix) where are you from what was how long have you were you

FROM IT WAS LIKE MY TRYING TO HAVE A TENDER-HEARTED NATURE

BY DIANE WILLIAMS (2007)

EDITOR'S NOTE: Diane Williams's fiction shares with the work of late sixties visual artists called Minimalists a wish to escape figuration. Their goal was to finish the project of modernist painting by producing shapes that stood for nothing, objects without distinction of surface and depth. This quality of objecthood has its prose parallel in literality. To write while constantly dispelling context, forestalling the amassed situation of drama, is a discipline that, when followed exactingly, produces the same enigmatic thereness as Tony Smith's *Black Box*. It's this quality I find fascinating in Diane's fiction. Her highly energized flatness, which can sound as varied as myopic obssession or manic chatter, is in my reading the result of words adhering tenaciously to their surface. One feels as though stories are everywhere, comprising this dense atmosphere of the unsaid, but there's just no telling what they amount to. Every utterance remains in abeyance, waiting on the voice's recollection. The result, at least for me, is an intense interest not based on any prospect of eventual disclosure. This interest—I call it presentness—is what the promise of restored order, in politics or art, always tries to repress. If my fascination with narrative doesn't result from sequence, from one word following another, if nothing seems a consequence of what came before, then why do I read? Diane's work is so significant because this isn't a question just about Diane's work.

—RMB

"My preferred opinion is that all of our behavior and speech has political significance. I am often in despair about how crude my behavior and my speech are and note that my private politics are too frequently anathema to me."

—Diane Williams

SWEET

It was sweet of you to come. I am glad you are here because otherwise I'd be so lonely.

To get me here they had to pick me up off the sidewalk and put me into the limousine and I tried to stop them from doing that.

One assumes there is an end to this initial phase.

I saw Lesley and asked to talk to her because she is usually nice. She just wants to be finished with this and to become a doctor. For some time now she's been considering that employment.

The man remember I told you about?—who calls me?—called me and he wanted to come over and I told him that now really wasn't a good time for me to have sexual relations, but he came over and what we did was peculiar, not very good, very odd, not right.

He said, "I always tell them hot! hot! hot! Otherwise it's cold. What is the matter with you?"

(I can't believe I told you that.)

There is in his face a dingy hopefulness. As the afternoon increases itself, of course, he is hopeful.

At Bloomingdale's, he put tinsel down the neck of my jacket in the back so that he wouldn't lose me.

He is tall. He has red hair and a goatee. That's what he looks like. I met with him this morning and at length we discussed that things have not been going swimmingly.

He is standing right here. In level flight he is faster. He is probably flying out of here on Friday. He's a pilot.

I have much more of the story of my life and not much of his. He barely does a thing, and then he goes ahead and does it.

He is plenty sore when weather keeps him from traveling with the wind. He hit the ground to avoid hitting another biplane. He burnt his hands. He had a fracture of the skull—I mean scalp wounds—and then what adds to the confusion is the dreamlike crack that developed on his head which some call a gash, others say it is the invisible damage.

I think it will be hard to give you and accurate report—a gross report, yes.

I sleep for a few hours, turn around and drive all the way to Baltimore without stopping and run into Chester. We are sitting at a front table and I feel comfortable that my attention is on incredibly important matters. Equally important to me is my deepening and developing interest in national and global politics.

This is the next day and I go buy expensive silk pajamas and two very heavy books.

Even though I'm broke I take several people with me to a restaurant. Across the street at the bank I take three hundred dollars from my account.

I get into bed when I become displeased. My brother and his wife stop by and I tell them we will eat a late dinner. I have had a bad case of food poisoning. All in all it is a fine Christmas. It's efficient and polite. Although, in the same manner a bowel movement is held back—a feeling dawns in me—which is not hiding, and which seems quite separate from my other feelings: I feel good that circumstances are well in hand, that I have returned from being alive.

THESE BLENCHES GAVE MY HEART

Life is fair I must confess. I am indebted to Erika Amor for the years 1946 and 1947 which were marked by the full flowering of the fairness. It can be expressed thus—that she did not imagine me a shy person, determined not to disobey. I had an idea she liked me and I chose her.

Her father said, "Stay with my daughter."

I agreed to, not impolitely. Lots of times it was a pleasure to be with her and I was frightened. (Some days they tell you what you said and that makes the blood flow out of your face so that all of the color goes out of your face.)

She accepted a glass of liquid and I took her to the window where she talked.

"Bring me the towel," I said. "You can lie down here instead of there."

Arms folded up over her torso—being thoroughly stretched through the torso—her hips are stuck. Her hips roll finally. From the excitement I rub her underlip. I spank the girl flat. She is near now.

The green chair under the phone?—that was hers and the dark wood chair under the window?—that was hers—untouched by the sex, the ax.

Across the way is a cozy Hungarian restaurant with its Kugelhopfs and sausages and The Roving Finger Barber Shop which has been there since 1950. Much of the shop is going to be demolished to make way for Malaysian Crafts.

I feel that my only big problem over the past year has been to trim myself with enough devils, beautiful women, owls, and hooded figures that will be of more interest than anything else I can make clear. Blank.

FLOWER

"He is the only one you will sleep with and you two will consult with each other about everything!" her father said. "Go live with him. He will welcome you. I am certain. Do you want to be rich?" her father said.

"Yes," she said, "I am sure."

"Susan," said the father.

"Yes?"

He said, "To get that nipple to stand up, squeeze it."

INSPIRING ONE

I am living in a lively way with slight slobs now and then. My face squeaked under the pressure. I came to as many conclusions as possible, which puffed out loudly along with sobs. In this I was much helped by Fred. I took a look at what looked eerie—Fred. I am excited. He appears to have just had very good news. He can be receiving it every day.

If I don't refer to anything sexual, I'll be a much more likeable person, for lack of a better idea.

I am a weak woman of thirty-two in a metropolitan area. Life might be gaily spoken of.

What Fred said: "I only hope and pray. I should so much like to help you. I hope you are keeping well. I hope you will have peace of mind. Do not bother to answer me. Of course, don't reply. Please accept my sympathy. Sorry for this intrusion. I would love to see you again some day. Please never think of answering. I am horrified."

Some moths later I was about to go on a dangerous expedition to see Tiny. I can tell you about Tiny. She gave me her stationary. She's the messiest writer of bills. She used to have crinkling paper, but this time it had Tiny Boynton written on it in big letters. And she's been together with Marcel all these years and it's a very poor relationship, but then he had an affair, of course. They must have seen one another enough to have twins. I don't know how she does it. I used to chat with her. She spends all day long and she takes all the dogs on this big loop. I was wondering, not knowing what her schedule was. She walks around in jodhpurs and a riding crop and totes the dogs along, and so I was desperate and I was running after her and I introduced myself and I am at the end of the world!

FROM KISSED BY

BY ALEXANDRA CHASIN (2007)

EDITOR'S NOTE: Alexandra Chasin's *Kissed By* was recommended to me in 2005 by David Jauss, with whom I'd been friends at the Iowa Writers' Workshop. When I read it I was struck both by David's critical acumen and by Alexandra's inventiveness with her medium. Each of her texts develops from a concept that connects its story with its means of expression, its language, form, print, page. In most cases you can ask either what Alexandra's fiction signifies or why it's made as it is and still come out with the same answer. For me, that answer has to do with relinquishing control over experience. *Kissed By* validates otherness, not merely as a metaphysical condition or epistemological limit, but as temporality, as the historical precondition for meeting strangers, not just grasping them. In a work like "Two Alphabets" the seeming arbitrariness of alphabetical ordering is linked to consequences of a serious kind, a car wreck, which itself seems linked to arbitrary orderings, those of heterosexual couples and national languages. What Lance Olsen, in his reader's report, called "deferred desire" at the level of theme and structure describes for me this juxtaposition of the significant with the accidental. It's as though nothing of consequence has to be as it is, a fact as true of social systems as of alphabets. I find Alexandra's exploitation of this contingency exhilarating.

—RMB

"The author's role is to write whatever she wants to write however she wants to write it. If authors have strong political opinions, and if they wish to persuade other people of the righteousness of their opinions or even galvanize people into action, in that way they are no different from other people with strong political opinions.... I like to think my writing, as well as that of other leftists, could have revolutionary impact, but could it—does it?"

—Alexandra Chasin

TWO ALPHABETS

Authorize. Barbary. Carburize. Daedalus. Elegy. Fenderbend. Generate. Housearrest. Ironize. Jerryrig. Kilowatt. Licorice. Marrakesh. Numerate. Ordinal. Patronym. Quietus. Retrospect. Sonorous. Tenterhooks. Ululate. Vespertine. Westerner. Expletive. Yesterday. Zeroing.

A foreign language text

A is for alcohol, not accidentally.

Abdelhadi
Abrupt beginning, no?
Aïd el Kebir

All the light bulbs in the house burned out just now. Not all at once, but one by one, over the course of this excruciatingly long evening. It was almost a total coincidence.

Antidisestablishmentarianism. The hippies appropriated this historical handle for opposition to the withdrawal of state support (originally from the Church of England) to mean its opposite—to mean, keep the state off of our bodies, out of our minds, and out of Indochina—even while the next generation sitting at school desks elected to save it its pride of place as the longest word in the language, English. It held its own against the contemporary coinage of *supercalifragilisticexpialidocious* because the latter is, while longer, made up.

There appear to be only these possibilities:

> He, she. I. (More formally or generically) One. (Very occasionally) You. (Theoretically) We, they.

There appear to be only these possibilities:

> Eddie Frank Gus Hank
> Linda Mary Nick Norm
> Ray Rex Rick Roy Russ
> Shelley Susie Tom.

Awed is what I was, by the power of language (or was it sex?) to bring things into being. Over-awed perhaps, as I had yet to learn how frighteningly simple it is to invent people—two girls and a guy standing on the roadside, shook up, the worse for wear, the varsity jackets that betray them as foreigners hanging open, red haze, pretty faces, her lips, his clean-shaven chin, the other one's green eyes—for the purpose of their destruction. You would wish to be acquainted with these young and pretty people, to have them travel unharmed a while longer. I would too; there is nothing I want more. They don't even appear to know enough to be scared, as at the side of the road they wait to understand the consequences of what just happened. Red haze. Each of the three avoids looking at the other two. The guy walks around to the other side of the car.

There was a car crash. A driver lost control. Those words bear with them an image and the automatic question of people involved. Are they our young friends? Bent, burned, and smoking. Shattered. The echo of a squeal to a halt. That's the automobile, probably. But had there been a fourth figure—wouldn't you expect so—another guy? Now you have a bad accident in mind. Yours could not possibly be the same as mine, but each one dramatizes the sudden and radical disfigurement of our most everyday expectations. Neither of our imagined crash scenes could render accurately the postures of the three, their expressions, what they know or don't know, but there they are.

> Drizzle hovers over the new landscape. The accident sizzles into the coal gray evening.

Because there are 26 letters in the English alphabet, the possibilities of the English language do not exceed the following—or do they:

> 26 one-letter words plus 26-squared two-letter words, plus 26-cubed three-letter words, plus 26-to-the-fourth four-

letter words, plus 26-to-the-fifth five-letter words. Etc. Up to the 28th power. See above.

Bicycle, blue, on which my neighbor, Abdelhadi, accidentally rode through the scene and saw the car that had been parked up the hill all week, surrounded by three small fires and two dazed young women, but when he stopped to try talking to these last two, he found that they spoke only English. Wait, he tried to tell them, wait here. He thinks maybe he saw another figure on the other side of the car, echo of a familiar jacket, as he jumped back on his bike and flew for bi- or trilingual help. A minute later, he heard a big boom, he says. But he was already around two bends, couldn't see back, and kept rolling forward, figuring that he should just keep going, not lose any time. Blue bicycle with empty baskets going home.

when in the iron cage
seize the cage bars
bend them bend them

the spongiform bars of the cage
bend them

It was not in order to create a carbon copy of myself that I had a kid. I had a kid because that was what one did in the old days; one married the prettiest girl at college who wasn't already engaged to someone else, and one had a kid. Before that, one, or two, really, had sex, of course. In those days.

Carcass, or should I say corpse

In this case, local color is not a device. It happens to designate my neighbors, my friends. Foreigners trekking around Morocco typically notice the black and blond deserts, the red mountains, the green oases snaking alongside the few riverbeds, and in spring, the pink blossoms of the almond trees, under the famously azure sky. The famously sheltering azure sky. These features of the landscape are *unique au monde*. But if those travelers see Abdelhadi and his compatriots at all, they see someone exotic, strange, and even greedy and/or stupid, judging by the way they avert their eyes from the racks of pottery and geodes by the roadside, and haltingly address him and the other men who sit at the outdoor tables at the village café. He is anything but. He is perceptive, inventive, and as kind as the day is long to his wife and children, to his parents, and to his friends, who, he says, include me. I am the strange one, whom he and Hicham and Jallah and Karim condescend to address in French because my Arabic remains rudimentary.

Common: there is nobody that something like this hasn't happened to; there is nobody that exactly this *has* happened to.
Compound prepositions, among others: according to, apart from, as to, aside from, because of, instead of, on account of, out of, up in.

Conjunctions
Dark house

Defamiliarization

The dream is always the same. The dream is always the same, always different versions of infinitely expanding architecture, lots of apartment hunting with the historic wings unfolding as my ex-wife and I take the guided tour through and among the treasures; visiting other people's precocious houses poised farther and farther over the water, or merging magically with the forest or the hill—nooks and crannies and hidden staircases forever; institutional numbers with all the trappings—the doors and corridors and correctional officers, and the labyrinth of functional buildings. Random House.

Eight years old. That's the age he was when I left. Eight, nine, ten, etc. Up to 23. See below.

Either, neither.

Evening. Meaning *what?*—so many things, not nearly enough. Less and more than night.
Faith, or lack thereof.

Fête du Sacrifice
Flesh of my flesh, out of my flesh, because of my flesh, finally apart from, forever apart from, my flesh.

Funny. *What* is so funny.

Sniffing gasoline.... Why do so many people get high? So many different ways?

You'll think I was, but I wasn't exactly, a hippie; I was both too young and too old. Or too straight and too smart. I did marry. I did work a job. But I guess it must have been a fairly strong countercultural impulse that drove me out of my old life in the States. The will to cliché got me coming and going.

His name is not Roy or Ray or Ed or Hank or Tom. Or Nick. His girlfriend's name is not Linda or Shelley. That's obvious, right?

Houses, and more houses. Mud-walled and built by hand. Cool to the touch.

Huts with thatched roofs. About fifteen years ago now, I left the big city, the big country; I left the apartment blocks and the gridiron and moved abroad. I went native, as they say. Fifteen years later, I was hosting a small gathering in the particular house I call my own, with four young people, not seven kilometers from where they crashed and not half an hour before. Before of. Before from. One of them is mine. It couldn't be worse. Is it too late for *before* again, or at least *instead*?

I don't have a car. My rusty bike, so long unused it seems ready to grow roots, is a laughing matter in the village. I am to wait here, Abdelhadi says. I trust him.

I have a very close relationship with language. It and I are intimate.

Inconceivable: I may never see the face of my child again.
Indelible, inedible, in-fucking-credible

Interior monologue
Interjections
In the belly of the beast, and then again, out of it

when in the iron cage
seize the cage bars
        bend them bend them

It is not from Italian, the language of love, but from mathematics, the language of physics, that we draw our rule. Numbers, permutations, factorials. Glory be to mathematics which reminds us of certain truths: dismal, inescapable, with bars. I moved away but I have not managed to lose my math.

I've read a lot of shit by people like me back home. If there are any other possibilities, I need to know now, not later. NOW.

Just when I thought I could breathe easy. He had become an adult, *like* an adult, and he drove himself here from the airport on the other side of the mountains in a rented car, and his girlfriend with him. I was so pleased that he wanted me to meet this grenadine-eyed girl. She was warm, and she got in several good puns, and although they stayed for days, she didn't wear one outfit that didn't leave her belly winking out from between her shirt and her shorts. I mean, she was cute. And they seemed happy. In the final hours, another young couple, friends from school who'd been backpacking around the area, came over for drinks, after which they all took off together. Literally into the sunset. Or rather onto it, as they trudged up the hill toward the road where anyone with a car has to leave it parked because the only way into my place is to walk. The last time I saw him, he was superimposed on the setting sun.

Kidding myself
King Mohammad VI. Like his father before him, King Hassan II, he holds the post for which there are no nominees.

Lessons in a foreign language

Red Light Green Light:
    Make meaning
    Make meaning
    Make meaning
    Stop making sense

Lift off
Left off
Left of center

Mansions: maybe somebody's father's house has many, but not me, not mine, not in my house, goddamn it.

Maybe something like this has happened to you.

The meter is the basic measure of distance, the unit from which all other measures of distance, whether longer or shorter, are derived: centimeter and millimeter no less than kilometer. Here in the metric system.
Midriff

Mother tongue

My biggest mistake: not to say to him: Don't let him drive, the other guy. I didn't say it because I thought it was obvious the guy was drunk, and obvious that someone who couldn't meet my hand to shake it without concentrating on the gesture should not drive. At least one of these things may not have been obvious to the four young adults who left my hut after a pleasant cocktail hour of sorts just before the mosquitoes kicked in. I clasped my own little guy in a big square hug, and he let me, for the first time in years, which confirmed what I suspected as he came down the hill at the beginning of the visit: he was finally taller than me.

My hut is a very very very nice hut. I must have brought with me a brain full of songs I'd heard on the radio.

Next and last… forever
Next to last

Ninety percent of conversations in English are composed of the same 200 words, sociolinguists have proven, by way of mathematics. Math persuades me. And it's easy to imagine which 200 words they are: the substanceless kind we can't live without, the dust mites and pillars of our speech: pronouns, and conjunctions, and half the prepositions. The article. Imagine a part of speech so important to the ecology of English that even though it has only three members, it deserves a category unto itself. Such are the articles. And how do they function? They introduce the nomials, the nominals—no no, that's not right—the noun or nouns. The difference between *the* and *a* is the difference between one and many. There is no article for none, for zero, for used to exist, but there should be.

Obviously, his name is not Nick.

Offal. This is the most awful night I could ever imagine, the worst delivery of news, impossible now and tomorrow, too, to swallow. Don't let Abdelhadi come again, bringing any more of that shit around here.

On dreams in narrative prose, consider:

– type of language
– length
– placement (when)
– how many characters do it
– function

On viscera and evisceration, consider the following and the foregoing.

The order of things: younger becomes older, shit is passed down, flows downhill, floats downstream, older dies before younger. Ring out the old, ring in the new. From up to down is the order of things. It doesn't matter that this is untrue, or rather that it is arbitrary. It doesn't matter that you could argue that down to up is the order of things, or that what goes down must come up, or that what comes around goes around, or is it vice versa? You'd be right. So what. Many orders work; this happens to be my elected one. If I must add this order to my list of wrong choices, I will never understand anything again. I will cry until morning which will be night.

The ordinary, the occasional, the extraordinary. Imitation of the one real, negation of the idea of a one-and-only real, any realistic unreal. These seem to be the possibilities.

Or so you'd think. And so I've thought, lo these many years of words and dissatisfaction.
out from under inside between see above metal reworked in any new inferno please

How to Outwit Yourself
Parsing sentences

Personal pronouns, also of which there are very few, soldiers in the war between the sexes, the agonizing rucksack of history on their camouflaged backs. Prepositions, of which there are more than articles to with from, form another part of speech. Proper nouns: Kiddo, Buddy, Pal.

Pomegranate-wine drunkard
Possessives. My son, not yours, not *yours*, and not *his* either to drive off the side of the goddamned road.

These seem to be the possibilities:
    I You He She. One. We You They.
These seem to be the possibilities:
    Ray, Roy, Norm. Nick.

These seem to be the possibilities.

The potholes, the goddamned potholes. But no, it couldn't have been the potholes. The potholes would blow out a tire, unalign an axle at worst. They wouldn't send a car off the side of the road.

Prison through *prism*

Perhaps I should qualify. You get a few infinite categories, after all: nouns, verbs, and their qualifications. There—oh joy—is the range, the expressivity associated with language, and the invention and naming of the new.

How different the sense if I had written: There was a *cat* crash. It would not have been quite so serious.

Radio range, getting out of it

Rainbow, which broke out like an irony. There had been no rain beforehand. I know that spot of road and I can imagine the rainbow over their heads as they crawled out of, up from, onto the embankment, if you could call it an embankment. Red light green light blue light for a moment suspended over my head, barely visible in the evening sky that would in another moment swallow even the indigo, and I smiled at the joke at the time, because Abdelhadi had not yet reached the village on his bike.

The end of Ramadan is marked with a sheep-sacrificing festival—*Aïd el Kebir*, *Fête du Sacrifice*—that commemorates what Abraham did not have to do to Isaac. In the story, the deed was ultimately displaced onto a member of a lower order caught in the brambles nearby. On the first day of the festival, which falls next week this year, Moroccans ritually slaughter sheep and cook and eat only the hearts and brains. On the second day, they move on to other parts, the intestines; on the third, they smoke the meat. Shofar sho good—until this year.

Reading, writing, and arithmetic. I brought these with me, along with a duffel bag of clothes, which have faded and frayed.

Really, the festival is a party. No harm done. On the contrary, everyone is happy cooking and feeding themselves and their families and friends. One year, this party fell during spring break and the kid came over and we brought home a length of the intestines that Abdelhadi's wife, Leila, had given us, and laid it out like the tracks of a train set. You could say we played with our food, but, or because, we were unaccustomed to the taste. You could say I'm no bloody Abraham.

Rebel

Reference works, of which I brought two: a dictionary and *Words Into Type*, the latter being the kind of book you used to see on the shelves of editors and copy-editors, with everything you could ever want to know about grammar, preparation of manuscripts, typography, and illustrations. And proofing. And use of words. Almost. Everything you need to bring Shit Into Being. The kind I used to see. And need. After a couple of years here, I could not look at this book anymore without its acronym jumping out at me: *WIT*. But I could not see the humor. *WIT* makes an excellent doorstop, for propping open the door on the many blue days when the only visitor will be a butterfly. If that. I might as well throw the dictionary on top of it now.

Reject
Round-house

Same numerical situation in French, for example, only the particular 200 words are different. For instance, instead of *glue-sniffing*, the French use the word *wine-drinking*.

Shit. Shit shit shit. Oh shit. *Oh shit*, they said, those guys in that movie, as they jumped, and the scenery mounted behind them as they plunged down. I haven't been to a movie in fifteen years, but I used to see one every week. I think I took that *shit* too seriously. I didn't realize how young they were, those guys.

Sometimes life's not easy; other times, it's hard.
Spill ink. As with oil, blood, and, famously, milk, it's no use crying.

Sometimes it's charred.
Tense doesn't begin to describe it; nor tenses them.
Tents

That's the difference between conversation and literature, my friends—74,000 minus 200 odd words *and*...

The guy was out of it, my son's friend. It was obvious to me.

These are the possibilities.

The tide comes up and goes out in the toilet.... That is the order of things. Do I really have running water and electricity in my mud house? Yes, and that's just one of the hypocrisies I still practice.

To be, to do, to get, to have, to want. Some say those are all the verbs you need. With verbs, you always get four for the price of one, because each one has these possible constructions: affirmative, negative, interrogative, negative interrogative. I say, not *to go? to need, to write?* Not *to need to go write?*

La transcription de l'arabe dans l'alphabet latin n'obéit pas à des règles rigoureuses.
Travel
Trip

Under certain conditions, the dream of a house can hurt like real life.

...*and* a couple of advanced degrees. Which I had under my belt, and used to append to my name in initials before I realized I could do my work anywhere. It was theoretically possible.

You-niversal

Unreliable utilities. That's what we have here. So when I read, late into the night, and the light suddenly goes out, I don't know if it's the bulb or the electricity. I always assume it's the electricity. I'm not always right.

Varsity athletics explains my son's friend's jacket. The dude said he was on the soccer team, when I asked. He pointed to the little soccer ball on the sleeve. Although he was just a fan, my son has had has an almost identical jacket, except for the soccer ball, like the girls'. Two guys in similar jackets, one of whom may still be standing in or near a ditch by the side of the road. It is a possibility.

Prepositions that are an inseparable part of a verb should be capped:

> Getting Down to Cases;
> How to Lay Off a Line Through a Given Point That Shall Be Parallel to a Given Line;
> Things to Do With and Find Out About a Book... A Pomegranate. A Rental Car.
>
> > A Parental Figure. A Soccer Ball. A Wool Blanket. Electricity. The History of a People. The Iron Cage. A Ticket Stub. A Handprint. Mud. But I regress.

One way out of your wits is to have a child.

We'll see.
How will I—what we used to call—cope? How?
What

What can I say? If I have outlived my child, I will never understand anything again. If I left him when he was young, it was not because I did not need to be in the presence of his growing body. It was not because I was not fascinated by the rate of expansion of his vocabulary. It was not because his handprint in clay was not the most precious piece of art I owned. It was not because his cocked head and his questions were only casually beautiful. They were not. His curiosity was acutely, hugely, bone-warmingly sweet. And it was not because I could tolerate his cries. I could not. Nevertheless.

What's *next*? Or rather, *where's* next? Because it's absent from the list of prepositions in the book. And what about *next to*? Isn't that a compound preposition? What am I missing?

When I left, he was eight years old. It was because I could not tolerate his mother, my mother, the city, the hypocrisy in which the higher professions are saturated. When I thought that the stub of an airplane ticket was proof that I had in fact left, I was still naïve. When I left, he asked me, "Daddy, can I come to your new house with you?" even though he had stopped calling me "Daddy" the year before. And he *had* come to my new house, several times over the years. When I thought that his visits, filled with arguments but also camping and lessons in packing and laying a mud brick with hair and straw knit up in it, and, more recently, Scrabble, which he brought two trips ago—when I thought that those visits were proof that you can never lose a child even if you abandon him, I was as yet totally untutored in loss.

When? In the iron cage.

Wool blankets brown and white like sheep. These we stretched and hung from sticks we stuck in the sand at the corners of our camp, brown and concave shelter sagging between us and the aforementioned sky. They colored our differing dreams different darks while we slept.

Why did I not encourage or even coerce him into learning the local language? I felt I didn't have the right. He went and studied classics, dead languages, more irony than I can take.

Words for this? *You* tell *me.*

Words Into Type, page 381: about, above, across, after, against, along, amid, among, around, at, athwart, before, behind, below, beneath, beside, between, beyond, by, concerning, during, except, excepting, for, from, in, inside, into, of, off, on, onto, out, outside, over, past, pending, regarding, respecting, round, since, through, throughout, till, to, toward, under, underneath, until, unto, up, upon, with, within, without.

Examples precede and follow.
Expatriate. Ugly word.

Exterior monologue

Youth

You. Yes you.

Zzz. Into and out of the dark night, at around and ever after midnight, on and off the lights. Who shuts his eyes sees houses going on and on and on.

FROM THE BRUISE

BY MAGDALENA ZURAWSKI (2008)

EDITOR'S NOTE: Magdalena Zurawski's *The Bruise* won the 2006 Ronald Sukenick Innovative Fiction Prize, awarded by FC2 and *American Book Review*. In selecting her MS from the nearly 200 entries, Lance Olsen noted its "surreal erotic visions," Brian Evenson praised its "almost blank style," and Susan Steinberg called it "brilliant." What attracted me was its unusual, highly concrete disclosure of narrative's origin. When a creative writing professor in *The Bruise* chides his students for writing about writing, he conflates a warning against self-indulgence with an unthinking defensiveness of his own. What such criticism represses is the way fiction like *The Bruise* is about itself, not as a specialized literary activity, but as an everyday experience. That is, Magdalena's work represents our commonplace feeling of out-of-placeness, of not fitting with our surroundings, as both the source of her narrator's literariness and a result of it. I found wholly absorbing this way that M—'s incessant narration gradually displaces her body and life. It's as though I'm watching myself undergo the loss of my world, an experience uncannily like reading. The suggestion is that, once anyone becomes her own angel or ghost, there's simply no telling how to be herself again. This investigation of representation's complicity in the problems it seeks to overcome is, for me, the mark of any serious writing—or politics.

—RMB

"In *The Bruise*...I wanted to examine at very close range the ways in which a person struggles to inhabit her own body when 'God and Country' deem such an inhabitation inappropriate. Most importantly, I was curious to see what resources within a person rise against such oppressive social forces."

—Magdalena Zurawski

THE TRANSLATION

I lived in an attic room of one of the older dormitories on the side of campus that used to house the women's college before the university turned coed. My room was small but had a large closet in which I was able to fit the dresser that came with the room without blocking my access to the hanging rod. The day that I moved into the room I placed the dresser flush against the back wall of the closet so that if I opened the closet door I stood directly in front of it with its drawers opening directly towards me and its left side flush against the left wall of the closet.

The closet was deep enough that I could still take one step into it and turn right. And it was wide enough for me to still walk three paces to the right of the dresser before getting to the hanging rod that hung perpendicular to the face of the dresser. On top of the dresser I kept my soap shampoo toothpaste toothbrush and washrag in a small plastic bucket unless I had just come out of the shower and then I would not keep the soap in the bucket but rather on top of a lid from an old margarine container until it dried. I kept the margarine lid on top of the dresser as well exactly next to the bucket so that the front edge of the lid and the front edge of the bucket were equidistant from the front edge of the dresser and when the washrag was wet after a shower I draped it neatly around the perimeter of the bucket so that it hung parallel to the bottom edge of the bucket until it dried too.

The bucket was white so I was careful to purchase only white cakes of soap white washrags a white toothbrush white tubes of toothpaste and shampoo that came in white bottles. Occasionally though my scalp would begin to itch and its skin would flake and for this reason I was forced to purchase a tar shampoo that had an amber color and came in a clear plastic bottle. In order not to disturb the arrangement of white that I kept neatly on top of the dresser which was oak I kept the tar shampoo in my sock drawer the top drawer of my dresser which was a fine decision since most of my socks were dark colored browns or blacks or grays. It was a better choice than for instance keeping the shampoo in the middle drawer with my underwear and bras which were white or in the bottom drawer with my T-shirts which were all white and my pajamas which were all blue. Besides I held the belief that things needn't be too orderly once in a drawer. In any case the difference in tone between the oak dresser itself and the objects on top of it made a subtle but pleasant contrast and the brightness of both kept the arrangement from appearing heavy and depressing and so I could be sure that its appearance would not affect my mood negatively when I woke in the mornings and was forced to open the closet door in order to prepare for my shower.

When I had finished arranging the closet I was pleased by the results and I only regretted that the closet was not big enough to hold my bed so that all items related to the care of my body could be neatly hidden from sight there behind the closed door since they were only needed late at night or early in the morning and it seemed strange for them to take up such a large portion of my living space. Had the closet been larger I could have slept in there keeping the closet door open at night so that fresh air or heat could enter depending on the season of course. Then in the mornings I could wake and wash and close the door on everything to do with my body and use the entirety of the room for those things that related to my studies specifically my bookshelves my books and my desk.

I had become very interested in the first stanza of the first poem of Rilke's *Duino Elegies* the entirety of which I was supposed to read for my German literature course but since my German was fairly poor I could only plod my way through the text by rendering a tedious translation for myself which required much dictionary work. Only then could I begin to grasp fully the poem whose first line had so absorbed me.

By about 1:00 a.m. on the first night that I began working on the poem I had sketched the first stanza for myself in English. I had printed a clean version of it by hand onto a piece of looseleaf paper so that it would be easier to read than the working version in my notebook. Because I was tired from leaning over the dictionary for most of the evening I took the piece of paper and instead of sitting in my reading chair I lay down on my back on the bed. Since I am not in the habit of doing so I can only think now that I must have been extremely tired. And there I began to read the lines I had written:

Who if I cried out would hear me among the order of angels?
And even if one of them pressed me suddenly to his heart
Would I not die in his stronger being? For beauty is nothing
But the beginning of terror which we just barely endure.

Yet we admire it as it calmly refrains from destroying us.
Every Angel is terrifying.

It is clear to me now that it was the cry in the first line that appealed to me—that sound that would break the sealed capsule of a day as if there were something in me that could move beyond me. I thought about the sound for quite a while and concluded that it could not be a name. It could never be a word of any sort but only a sound. An unplanned unknown sound. Something the body could make independent of the mind's idea of it. A bellow. A marker of one's space loud and certain of its own uncertainty outside itself. There was nothing in me strong enough to make a sound like that.

But I knew where it would come from if it could come. I unbuttoned my pants and I pulled my shirt out and lifted it up so I could see myself. And I took my finger and made circles on my stomach dipping just under my navel and staying just inside the ribs. I made these circles slowly. That was the loudest call I could bear to make.

And when I began to feel the angel pressing on top of me—when I knew she had come I kept calling not with my fingers but only through my breath moving in and out of my mouth beneath her ear. She pulled me closer into her and for a moment I thought she was beautiful and I did not open my eyes but I imagined a face for her and the face I imagined wasn't unusual. It was the face of any girl and to make it angelic I gave her long curls and these fell upon me and I felt calm beneath her and I let her touch me and I let us be lost in one another. I didn't want to open my eyes to see her so I clasped her face with my hands and felt its form soft in my palms. It felt just as I had wanted it to feel and I pulled it close against my own. I could feel the heat from the streak of red across her cheek. It became too hot against my face so I pushed away. I felt cool again for a moment but then her body grew warm around me and she began to move faster against me and her heat gradually took me over and except for my face and thoughts I could not tell the feeling of myself from the feeling of her.

But soon I had the urge to open my eyes and I did but I couldn't see her face only her hair and I felt suddenly where my body ended and where hers began and so I felt nervous. I couldn't move my neck because she was so close on top of me but I strained my eyes downwards and when I did I saw her swollen breasts crushing my own and I could see the small hairs on them and I thought of hog flesh as the tops of them grazed my neck and the underside of my chin as I struggled to break free. She had grown so heavy that it was impossible to pull away from her. I could only feel her hairy swine breasts pricking my skin and her body pushing the breath out of me. Her wings flapped rapidly up and down thrusting her hips hard against mine. I felt the springs of the mattress pressing painfully into me from underneath.

Her wings were white but filthy like a pigeon's and longer than the length of me. They closed upon us making a cave for me beneath her. And their smell surrounded me: an unwashed dog. She grunted in pain each time they came down because her left wing had no room to fall along the right side of me but would bend and scrape against the wall and sound like a branch swiping across the side of a house in a storm but here it was incessant like a heartbeat and since the wings came so quickly the grunts were rapid too. They became louder and louder as if they were coming from deeper inside of her and she didn't stop but pushed her wings with greater force as if she were testing her own strength. It became more difficult to rise with her since she was pushing me with every round deeper down into the mattress. I was sweating now and had no more breath in me and then with the strength of terror that the helplessness gathered I rose again and gasped and heaved and quickly shook my head. I had wished her away.

When I entered the women's shower room the light was turned off as it usually was when I entered to shower but this time I was entering to shower at night which I never did and because I never turned the light on when I entered to shower I had to consider carefully what I was going to do now. I only had to think for a moment about whether to turn the lights on and then I saw that the streetlights surrounding the parking lot out back were sending an orange glow into the bathroom that reflected off the white tiles and the chrome and the mirrors that lined the walls across from the showers. Mornings I always opened the window twelve inches before showering so I thought that if I did this now more light would flood the room and there would be no reason for me to break my habit now and turn the light switch on despite the hour. I walked to the shower stall as I always did and opened the curtain. I placed my bucket in the right-hand corner furthest from the showerhead and then hung my towel on the hook outside the stall.

At the window I could see the wind was blowing hard and the streetlights made a shadow of a tree branch dance across the frosted glass in front of me. When I opened it the light and shadow fell flat off the glass onto my body and the light and shadow that didn't fit onto my body fell off my hips and stretched out onto the floor. Limbs moved on my stomach and if I looked down on myself to see where they fell I could feel a slight pressure through my robe—a warmth as if I were being touched but of course I wasn't being touched but seeing the shadows of the branches there made me feel as though I were being touched. As long as I looked it was as though I were being touched and so I felt touched.

In the shower I could hear the branches etching against the glass behind the sound of water. If it weren't for the sound of them there was nothing I could have seen that would have made me think that there was anyone outside the curtain and I would have just showered in the dark. But the scratching on the glass made me think I wasn't alone and sometimes I would stick my head out of the curtain to see if I were alone and I would see myself alone in the mirror looking at the light and shadows. It's difficult to say why I felt I wouldn't be alone but there was something about the way the branch moved that made me think of a girl dancing outside the curtain and when I opened the curtain and stepped out to dry myself the light and shadows were there again and in the mirror I could see I was in the shadows and I knew when I saw her there that she wouldn't ever leave me and I was scared though I wasn't in the dark anymore. I was standing in the light now too.

It's difficult to say how I brought her here or how she had fallen into the mirror because when I turned around to look in the stall she wasn't standing behind me but was just there in front of me in the mirror. She was trapped in the glass though in my bed she had been able to fall on me in sleep. Poems make it easy to dream of angels but the girl she had no wings so she couldn't have been the angel. I thought that I knew that I didn't know her so I thought it best not to move. And even though she was someone very much like me still she was strange and I was scared and I couldn't have been just looking at myself and been so scared. And then I moved closer to the mirror because I wanted to make sure she wasn't me. And she followed me to the mirror so I thought for a second I was right. She was me and I didn't have to be scared and I moved my eyes to the right and then to the left and she did the same but then I thought I saw her lip curl about to smile but I was too nervous to smile so I knew that she wasn't me. She was some stranger come to trick me and in the second that I thought she wasn't me she felt too close. She was too close to me and I was scared she would creep inside me and before I even thought what to do I swung. I swung and I wanted to hit her but I hadn't hit her. I didn't hit her and I fell. I had fallen. I fell against the mirror and she was gone. And then my head began to pulse where it had hit the glass so I put my nose to the mirror and watched the blood push there to make the skin swell. The skin above my eye rose and stretched. A darkening bruise swallowed it.

Something shone in the light and where it shone I felt a sharp pain and when I pushed it it was hard and it cut into my finger. I pushed the bruise from the side to squeeze the glass out like the puss of a pimple and when it came out my head bled a little.

When I saw the blood I hoped that I wouldn't vomit but whenever I see my own blood I vomit and I was sure now that it was my own blood and it was because I touched it. And I was sure that it was my own body getting sick because I saw myself buckle over in the mirror. I couldn't see myself get ill because my head was down but I could see the floor and I could see what came out of me onto the floor and I could feel what came out of me and when I was done having everything come out of me I looked in the mirror and saw that my lip was still dirty so I knew it was me who was ill. And then Amanda came into the bathroom by chance and turned the lights on just after I finished being ill and suddenly the shadows and the branches were gone and I was just standing there under the fluorescent lights in my plastic shoes next to my own vomit with my head bleeding and a piece of the mirror missing. I couldn't tell her what happened because it was hard for me to explain my imagination especially on a night when my head was bleeding and there was a piece of the mirror missing.

I told her I had gotten dizzy because I ate something bad and then the heat of the shower made me feel worse so I got out and was going to go to my room to lie down but before I could leave the shower room I fell and vomited there right outside the shower in front of the mirror because I was so weak and I asked her if she thought the bruise was bad and she said *No M—. It doesn't look too bad. It will probably go away in a few days.* But it didn't.

AT THE TABLE

The hanging lamp above the table shone out against the darkness outside the kitchen so that if someone had come up to the window my mother and father and I would not have seen her face but she could have stared at us furtively from the dew-covered grass of the dark yard as we sat there lit under the hanging lamp that hung above the kitchen table. At the table once the dishes were cleared my father began to tell us a story that night and even though I was very small—small enough to feel protected while sitting at the table between my mother and father—as my father told the story I couldn't help both to listen to the story and as I was listening to the story also to think that there was someone at the window in the darkness watching me listen to the story and thinking that there was someone at the window watching me listen to the story had the strange effect of making me imagine myself listening to the story as I sat there and listened to the story. And maybe my father sensed her at the window too because for some reason on this particular night he told us a story that he hadn't ever told us before. He told us the story of something that happened to him when he was not much bigger than I was on this night that I was both listening to him tell the story and watching myself listen to him tell the story at the kitchen table.

What my father said that night was that when he was a small boy big enough to know how to swim but not big enough to swim in the river by himself he was sent to the river with an aunt who was to watch him swim. But when my father was swimming in the river his aunt who was sent to watch him swim began to read and didn't notice when he was pulled under water by the current of the river that came whirling around him. While the aunt who was sent by my father's parents to protect him from drowning lay in the grass along the river lost in the sentences of her book his small body was sucked under water so quickly that in a matter of a few seconds he lay at the bottom of the river exactly as if his small body had been put to sleep in a real bed. And as he lay there almost sleeping at the bottom of the river that never should have been like a real bed his ghost rose out of him like a ghost rises out of any person when he is a small boy about to drown at the bottom of the river and there is no one there to save him. But instead of leaving his body at the bottom of the river and taking his spirit somewhere else his ghost floated out of him and hovered above him and watched his body struggle not to sleep at the bottom of the river and because his ghost rose out of him but did not leave him and instead floated above him and watched him his ghost could see what the boy needed to do to save his body. The ghost could see exactly what rock the boy's legs needed to push off from so that he could propel his body head first through the surface of the water and rise into air and breathe again. Because the spirit no longer was inside the body of the boy the spirit could help the body of the boy save itself because the spirit could watch the body when no one else did and it was the spirit that told the body to push off that rock with the last of its strength and break through the surface of the river and it did break through with its mouth wide open sucking in air at last though no one else except the ghost had been able to watch the body and save it from drowning. And when he came out of the water where he had almost drowned he didn't say a word to his aunt when she turned to smile at him. He just sat down next to her and let the sun dry the mud off his back.

And even though his ghost had been able to save him from not drowning the story made me think from the moment that I heard it that my father by fathering me had made me a person in his own likeness and though my father had only lived a few seconds with his ghost outside of his body my body seemed to move in the world watched by its own ghost always as if its ghost had never yet come inside it and was always waiting to one day be a part of me so that I could finally become myself. And though I believed that the way I was forced to live with my ghost outside of my body was the result of being my father's daughter the more I thought about it the more I could not deny that my father's ghost had left him only for a few seconds to save him from death but my ghost hovered next to me for years with the hope of one day coming inside my body so that I could finally be born into life. And I could tell that my ghost was eager to come inside my body because unlike my father's ghost my ghost didn't ever rise above me but floated just close enough alongside me so that I couldn't help but think of it as my own shadow hoping to slip inside me—the object that cast it.

My ghost followed me so closely that if for instance I moved my arm to grab an apple I had not only the feeling of the apple in my hand but also the feeling of watching someone's arm grab an apple so that I felt both that it was my arm grabbing the apple and not my arm grabbing the apple. Something that so clearly should have felt like my own experience seemed both to be my own experience and the experience of another person who I never was able to reach but always seemed able to watch. Even when I would see this strange hand press the apple into my mouth I could barely feel the mealy flesh on my tongue though I could very clearly see myself chewing the very apple I just saw a strange arm lift and push into my mouth and this made it seem as though the experience of eating the apple was not my own at all even though I had a piece of its skin stuck between my teeth.

And because I wandered around empty of my own spirit there was a way that my body needed to fill itself with something until it was ready to take in its own ghost and permit me to begin my life and become a real person. So my body filled itself up with all the words I read in books so that the passages that I read dwelled inside me as if they themselves had been my own acute memories of actual lived experiences and although at the time it wasn't clear to me why it was the words I read in books that something inside me chose as a substitute for its own ghost it seems to me now that maybe just as my father's ghost had seen a rock at the bottom of the river for his dying body to push off from and save itself my ghost had sensed that each little passage of literature I read for school had its own spirit and that each time my body was able to swallow the body of a book it also ingested with it a complete spirit that was not separate from its letters. And so for this reason I believe that in some strange way my own ghost was trying to save me by forcing me to ingest these books that it hoped could show me how to live finally through example. The problem my ghost did not foresee was that even though each passage I memorized showed me how something that had a body could also have a spirit inside it in order for the words to teach me this lesson I had to let them fill up the empty space where my own spirit should have lived so that the books and parts of books that lived inside me both taught me what it would be like to live with my spirit inside me and left no room for my spirit itself. But it was difficult even for me to notice sometimes that my ghost didn't dwell inside me because despite the fact that I often felt like the quietest person at our table so many of the words that lived inside me would come out of my mouth that even though in hindsight I can't help but think that it was very apparent that these words I spoke were not my own words the passages that I had memorized were so spirited that both my friends and I were charmed by them enough to assume that the spirit of these words was also a part of my own spirit. So that while I was reciting some passage so fervently that the words themselves felt a part of my body and the whole table couldn't help but stop to listen to me both my friends and I were too intoxicated to notice that I was also standing alone outside the refectory with my nose pressed against the window watching both my friends and me forget I wasn't even there with them.

Because of this problem of not being ever truly inside myself I was attracted to things that seemed to be just themselves and nothing more and though there was almost nothing in the universe that didn't in its being refer to a world beyond itself I found that the sparrows around campus were nothing but themselves all day long and never seemed to question the fact that they really were sparrows and I could tell this by the look in their eyes as they were eating or searching for something to eat. Their look was so intent upon scouring the ground for a possible meal that I could not help but think that the sparrows believed fiercely in the fact that the ground they walked on existed and most importantly that they too existed because they walked intently upon the ground and thought little of it.

And ever since L— in writing class found it so difficult to imagine a possibility for her story that wasn't part of her own true story even though the professor had yelled at her for lacking imagination I couldn't help but become intrigued with her for refusing to write a story that didn't contain anything but what she knew to be her own true experience because I could not imagine ever being able to know if my own experience were a true one but she seemed intent upon the fact of herself as if it contained no trace of fiction. So from the day she handed in her story about the dream of the child born with the wooden leg I in the refectory began to watch her instead of watching myself whenever I found myself reciting passages at the table and although she couldn't help but watch me while I was reciting the words that had come to live inside me I couldn't imagine that she watched me because of the words I spoke but for some other reason because a person who lived as true to herself as L— did would know that the words I spoke were a substitute for a part of me that was still missing and so even though she looked at me while I spoke I knew it wasn't the words I spoke that made her look at me but rather the bruise because the bruise was the only part of me that I knew was real and a person like L— could only bear to look at what was real. And even though her intolerance for anything imaginary did not make her a great writer it did make her a real person and there was something so beautiful about how she was able to be a real person that it was difficult for me to stop watching her and so as the words I memorized spoke through me and compelled me to look at L— it became difficult for me to stop wanting to become a real person too.

So once I noticed that L— would look at my bruise while I spoke at the table I could not stop looking at her because I wanted always to see if she really was looking at me and so once

I started looking at her often I could sometimes not tell if she was looking at me because she wanted to see the bruise on my forehead or because now that I had begun looking at her every time I spoke at the table she could feel me looking at her first and when she looked at me she could only see the bruise clearly. But even though after a while I couldn't tell if when I began to speak I looked at L— first or if she started to look at my bruise first it still was clear to me that she was always looking at my bruise when she looked at me because I was sure that the bruise was the only real part of me and I was sure that L— would only look at the part of me that was real. And I was so excited that somebody in the world finally noticed a part of me that was real that now when I would begin to speak at the lunch table and look at L— I would also imagine her walking over to me and sweeping the hair out of my eyes and kissing the bruise on my forehead and that made me think that it was really the bruise that made me look at L— because I knew that the bruise came to me because I was lonely and L— was someone who could help stop me from being lonely. And though there was nothing that I hated more than my friends looking at me during lunch to see how my bruise was doing when I looked at L— I hoped she would look at me and really see the bruise and the way that she looked at me made me hope that she could really see me and see the bruise and the story of my imagination and this would help me finally become a real person.

FC2 1999–2009: BIBLIOGRAPHY

FALL 1999

Sex for the Millennium	Harold Jaffe	collection
In the Box Called Pleasure	Kim Addonizio	collection
Re.La.Vir	Jan Ramjerdi	novel

SPRING 2000

Sewing Shut My Eyes	Lance Olsen	collection
Dictionary of Modern Anguish	R.M. Berry	collection
Liberty's Excess	Lidia Yuknavitch	collection

FALL 2000

Not a Chance	Jessica Treat	collection
The Fast Red Road: A Plainsong	Stephen Graham Jones	novel
The Wilderness	D. N. Stuefloten	collection

SPRING 2001

Aunt Rachel's Fur	Raymond Federman	novel
High Drama in Fabulous Toledo	Lily James	novel
Girl Beside Him	Cris Mazza	novel

FALL 2001

The Blue Guide to Indiana	Michael Martone	collection
The Complete Tales of Ketzia Gold	Kate Bernheimer	novel
The Noctambulists	Peter Spielberg	collection

SPRING 2002

False Positive	Harold Jaffe	collection
Soul Resin	C. W. Cannon	novel
Shootout with Father	Marianne Hauser	novel
Why I Don't Write Like Franz Kafka	William S. Wilson	collection (reprint)

FALL 2002

1998.6	Matthew Roberson	novel
Girl Imagined by Chance	Lance Olsen	novel
Wakenight Emporium	A. B. West	novel

SPRING 2003

The End of Free Love	Susan Steinberg	collection
Real to Reel	Lidia Yuknavitch	collection
Gone	Elisabeth Sheffield	novel
The Death of the Novel & Other Stories	Ronald Sukenick	collection (reprint)

FALL 2003

The Bird Is Gone: A Manifesto	Stephen Graham Jones	novel
The Blond Box	Toby Olson	novel
Dahlia's Iris: Secret Autobiography and Fiction	Leslie Scalapino	novel
Reruns	Jonathan Baumbach	novel (reprint)

SPRING 2004

Everyday Psychokillers: A History for Girls	Lucy Corin	novel
The Wavering Knife	Brian Evenson	collection
Borges' Travel, Hemingway's Garage	Mark Axelrod	collection
Hogg	Samuel Delany	novel (reprint)

FALL 2004

A History of the Imagination	Norman Lock	novel
The Garden in Which I Walk	Karen Brennan	collection
Dirtmouth	Alan Singer	novel
The Collected Short Fiction of Marianne Hauser	Marianne Hauser	collection

SPRING 2005

The Body Parts Shop	Lynda Schor	collection
Disability	Cris Mazza	novella
Forgetfulness	Michael Mejia	novel
Last Fall	Ronald Sukenick	novel

FALL 2005

Public Works	Christopher Grimes	collection
What Begins with Bird	Noy Holland	collection
Michael Martone	Michael Martone	collection

SPRING 2006

Nietzsche's Kisses	Lance Olsen	novel
The Book of Portraiture	Steve Tomasula	novel
Hydroplane	Susan Steinberg	collection

FALL 2006

Return to Manure	Raymond Federman	novel
The Complete Tales of Merry Gold	Kate Bernheimer	novel
The Bitter Half	Toby Olson	novel

SPRING 2007

The Possibility of Music	Stephen-Paul Martin	collection
Like Blood in Water	Yuriy Tarnawsky	mininovels
The Jirí Chronicles and Other Fictions	Debra Di Blasi	collection
Was: annales nomadique	Michael Joyce	novel

FALL 2007

Kissssss	Steve Katz	collection
It Was Like My Trying to Have a Tender-Hearted Nature	Diane Williams	novella and short fiction
Kissed By	Alexandra Chasin	collection

SPRING 2008

The Trouble with Being Born	Jeffrey DeShell	novel
Correction of Drift	Pamela Ryder	novel in stories
My Amputations	Clarence Major	novel (reprint)

FALL 2008

The Bruise	Magdalena Zurawski	novel
La Medusa	Vanessa Place	novel
Ledfeather	Stephen Graham Jones	novel

SPRING 2009

Impotent	Matthew Roberson	novel
The Illustrated Version of Things	Affinity Konar	novel
Forms at War: FC2 1999–2009	R.M. Berry	anthology